# Norman Mailer

The
Man
and
His
Work

# NORMAN MAILER
# The Man and His Work

by Robert F. Lucid

LITTLE, BROWN AND
COMPANY
BOSTON
TORONTO

LIBRARY OF CONGRESS CATALOG CARD NO. 78–161853

FIRST EDITION

T10/71

*Published simultaneously in Canada
by Little, Brown & Company (Canada) Limited*

PRINTED IN THE UNITED STATES OF AMERICA

# Contents

# Acknowledgments

I should like to acknowledge the assistance of the American Philosophical Society, without whose subvention it would have been more difficult to assemble the materials in this volume, and the assistance of Louise Hamlin, without whose help it might have been impossible.

R.F.L.

**Norman Mailer**
The
Man
and
His
Work

# Introduction

In one's culture, as in one's life, the truth often dawns slowly, and frequently it is long after a fact has been solidly established that we come to perceive its existence. I think it has been only recently that we have begun to perceive the truth about Norman Mailer: among the generation of writers who emerged from the war and devoted their lives to the creation of a body of literature, he is one of the very few who have grown into a permanent, irreversibly realized presence. One may recognize it with surprise. Mailer? But it is of course a fact. His is a presence, furthermore, particularly rich in complexity — so rich, indeed, that like a burdensomely complex perception about oneself, gnawing urgently at the edge of consciousness, we have persisted in pushing it aside, content to account for it as an odd and passing aberration. Only after we have tried ignoring it, scorning it, minimizing it, making clever jokes about it, are we forced to admit the fact of its seriousness and its importance.

*3*

That Mailer is a serious and important American writer is probably the buried thesis of all of the essays in this anthology, even those which set out to pillory him for his endless and famous failures to behave as a serious and important artist should. But for all of the treatment of his strengths and weaknesses, as an artist and as a man, there is remarkably little overt analysis of what are perhaps the most common questions one hears posed about Mailer. Why, the questions go, is Mailer's life so saturated with publicity? Why doesn't he just write his novels and let them stand, or fall, on their intrinsic merits? Why does he have to be a public writer? These are proper questions, and these introductory pages — in the absence of an essay on the subject in the anthology itself — may be the proper place to try to work through to some answers.

Perhaps one should recall at the start that the role of public writer is not a Mailer invention. To speak only of American letters, there has been a tradition of such figures since our earliest literary generation. Washington Irving may have been the first, a man whose accomplishments as a literary artist made him an instantly recognizable figure in circles much wider than the literary, and which won him appointment as our ambassador to Spain. His recognition and acclaim came from far more people than the readers of his books, and this — along with institutional recognition and reward — may have been the initial hallmark of the public writer. The institutional rewards continued into the next generation, where Emerson was everywhere saluted as the sage of the nation and Longfellow, on visiting the gallery of the Senate, saw that body rise and adjourn as a gesure of respect. After the Civil War — an experience not designed to support the notion that individuality and creativity would automatically win through — the public writer was still to be found, but in the person of Mark Twain and, later, Stephen Crane, he was less easily identifiable with national institutions. Twain's white suit and cigar and public posture of satiric defiance helped dramatize the division which had formed between the individual in the culture and those political and economic centers of power which Twain so frequently attacked. During the Spanish-American War, Stephen Crane's swashbuckling white trench coat became what was to be an enduring symbol of the artist turned foreign correspondent, the popular uniform of a man who could, presumably because of his creative power, not only create but observe and survive in the midst of destruction and chaos. In their separate ways, Hemingway and Fitzgerald moved the tradition on. Hemingway shaped a legend that he could, precisely because he was an artist, outshoot, outsoldier, outlove, and generally outperform any institutional man he met in competition. And if Hemingway's was a success myth, Fitzgerald's was a failure myth, one that implied that for all of his personal reversals and evident tendencies toward self-destruction, his was still the life of the artist — richer, more exciting than the life of the institutional man. This may be the key to defining the public writer: whatever his disguise or the peculiarity of his personal style, he asserts that the cultivation of the imagination, and the individuality which is a part of it, does not separate the artist out into a different world from that occupied by the individual in society (this is the stuff of a different artist myth). Rather, the public artist asserts through a public representation of his own life that he and the individual in the culture have common cause against that institutional sphere which had, in an earlier time, given such promise of respect and reward to them both. In all cases, the public writer first asserts his credentials through the acknowledged excellence of his art, and then, while not abandoning that art, he produces the popular, public legend about himself as well. How consciously this is done, and what the complex of private motives might be on the artist's part, of course varies from person to person, but it is a fact that he is involved in a cultural tradition, and a distinguished one at that.

Mailer's part in this tradition follows the established pattern. Though he became famous overnight with the publication of *The Naked and the Dead* in 1948, his fame was specifically literary, and the quality of his personality, the tone and style of his life, got no more than the ordinary attention awarded to a best-selling first novelist. Mailer didn't enter the public arena in any serious way until after the publication in 1955 of his third novel, *The Deer Park*. Then he began writing a personal column in *The Village Voice*, published the apocalyptic essay, "The White Negro," in *Dissent* magazine, and began work both on a long new novel and on the assembling of *Advertisements for Myself*.

*Advertisements*, published in 1959, is more than a skillfully arranged survey of Mailer's work to that date, it is a manifesto. In it Mailer enunciates, more clearly and consciously than had any of the public writers in the tradition before him, what the real relationship is between the public writer and his audience. Telling, in the introduction, of the tribulations of his career as a novelist, he suddenly shifts his point of view — which up to then had been simply fixed upon the "I" — and says:

> I write this not solely out of self-pity (although self-pity is one of my vices) but also to tell the simple truth: I have not gotten nicer as I have grown older, and I suspect that what has been true for me may be true for a great many of you.

He is not, of course, assuming that most of his readers are novelists, but rather that the experience of the novelist can, if properly considered, stand as a clear illustration of the experience of the individual in the culture. He cements the alliance as he continues:

> If I put down words so final as these, it is not in any sense that I alone have been mistreated — on the contrary I have had more good luck and conceivably more bad luck than most writers (which tends to give one the hard satisfaction

of knowing a little more of what the swindle is about). No, these ill-mannered bleedings and gripes are to record a clear record: I had the luck to have a large talent and to use some of it, and if I know how very much more I could have done if new luck had come my way, well — that is not my story, but everyone's story, every last one of us could have done more, a creation or two more than we have done, and while it is our own fault, it is not all our own fault, and so I still feel rage at the cowardice of our time which has ground down all of us into the mediocre compromises of what had been once our light-filled passion to stand erect and be original.

Shifting his rhetoric from "I" to "you," and concluding with "we" and "us," Mailer identifies with his reader, and by implication with the individual at large. Behind the particular argument is the general assumption that most people, in their attempts to maintain personal standards, identity, and imaginative vitality, turn toward some public figure who appears to have dealt with the same problems. They identify with him. All but explicit is Mailer's suggestion that the ideal figure to identify with is the artist, whose lot it is, after all, to preserve his strength and independence without the collaboration of institution or committee. If Mailer's audience accepts his premise that the society has shown itself to be overtly hostile toward creative individuality, then he invited it to accept also the traditional figure of the artist as a paradigm to help illuminate the problem large and clear. Quite simply, he offers himself.

Mailer's treatment of himself as a public figure develops through five books, after *Advertisements,* and before getting into the question of why he should have chosen the role, and what the consequences have been, we should perhaps examine the details of his evolution as a public writer.

As originally presented in *Advertisements* the Mailer figure is a product of a recent, and to him still distressing, set of initiation rites. American publishing and the critical community have turned out, contrary to his sentimental expectations, to be hostile toward his kind of vision, and he feels that there have been efforts to destroy both his work and his faith in that work. The Mailer we see here is the angry opposite of the well-mannered, self-effacing youngster who began a career eleven years earlier, and the thing he is most involved in doing is presenting his credentials — actually arguing to establish the case that he is, critical response to the contrary, an American writer entitled to the respect which attends the production of excellence in art. Now if Mailer fails for the reader in this attempt, then what follows will be an argument without a foundation. Many of the essays in this anthology will address the question of the overall quality of Mailer's work, but for the purposes of the present discussion it is necessary to assume — as indeed I do believe — that Mailer's credentials as an artist were, by 1959, very much in order.

Certainly the next emergence of the Mailer figure assumes, rather than argues for, his identity as an established writer. In another compilation of his own work, *The Presidential Papers* (1963), he is no fledgling product of professional initiation, but a writer altogether confirmed. In *Advertisements* the hero stormed the walls of the literary establishment, getting into a place where he had been denied, but the walls breached by the more impish gadfly of the second book are, with some interesting exceptions, not literary at all. His field of expertise has widened dramatically, as he addresses himself directly to the President of the United States on the condition of the country as a whole. Juvenile delinquency, radical federal legislation, the Cuba crisis, the ambiance of political conventions, the cultural implications of championship sport, even an experimental foray into the form of the Platonic dialogue — all of these Mailer breaks into, seeking to establish authority there. It is clear that the artist, in his incarnation in *Papers*, has left off asserting his credentials as an artist and taken up asserting the authority that they granted him. Crucial, too, is Mailer's use of John F. Kennedy as a foil, since it enables him to cast his artist-hero into the same arena with a figure who, after all, was a nearly perfect type of political hero.

In format, *Cannibals and Christians* (1966) resembles the two earlier volumes, and we have, once again, the spectacle of the accredited artist acting overtly as cultural critic, but the tone of the book is subtly different. The Mailer we see here is neither the angry young man of the first book nor the irreverent gadfly of the second. The new tone is quieter, less arrogantly certain of what every immediate action ought always to be, more prophetic in a longer historical range. The variety of topics covered in the book is wide enough — the need for a new architecture to respond to urban sprawl, the Goldwater nominating convention of 1964, mass media, popular culture, Vietnam — but there are also no less than five kinds of interviews with the author, and there is the concluding story, "The Last Night." In the story, which depicts the destruction of the planet in terms that are regenerative as much as apocalyptic, and the longer interviews, Mailer all but puts aside rhetorical contentiousness and drives toward analysis of basic problems which underlie topical issues. He is nearly the pundit, sure at last of his audience, engaging in a serious and measured speculation concerning the relationship which might fuse the poles of radical and conservative thought in the culture.

To a degree not possible to analyze here, the Norman Mailers of these three volumes of collected pieces are, of course, personae, created versions of a public artistic personality. But while each of the books has its unity and its own version of the hero, as compilations of pieces written over varying periods of time and in different genres they are necessarily fragmented. It would be possible to read through all three, judiciously skipping Mailer's running commentary on the assorted items, and miss almost completely the evolving design with respect to the public artist figure. But in the three nonfiction books which follow them, there is a Mailer persona at the center of each narrative, its hero and object of dramatic attention. From *Advertisements* through *Cannibals* one could see a development in Mailer's "I" toward the abstract, and at this juncture the break is made complete — Mailer produces an effaced narrator who, standing apart with the reader, focuses his attention on "Norman Mailer," a quite separate being.

In *The Armies of the Night* (1968), the first of the three nonfictional narratives, reader and narrator stand back from and survey a Mailer whose heroism is quite attractively open to question. A reluctant warrior in the cause for peace, broodingly suspicious of the psychological motives of professional movement people, he is steeped — under the narrator's ironic gaze — in the vanities and minor vices of the man who was so mad as to take the plunge which was *Advertisements,* and who has now been torn between private creation and public performance. His sense of history is so riddled by his sense of himself that his most serious problem is rising to any historical perspective at all. His hangover, for example, takes on a thematic significance which, for a time, rivals the combined importance of the military-industrial alliance, the peace movement, and, of course, the role of the artist in the public arena. He is thus a comic figure, a target of unrelenting irony — in fact he is altogether reminiscent of the hero of *The Education of Henry Adams.* Different though these two Harvard graduates may seem to be, both are presented to the reader by their "narrators" with a double edge. In earlier books, Mailer's "I" presented himself directly and addressed the audience in terms of take-me-or-leave-me. But now the possibility of rejection is richer. Both Adams and Mailer, to some degree, reject their self-personifications. But both put the reader in the position of pressure — could the reader do better? Has he? Accepting the narrator's invitation to condescend to the hero, the reader must face the danger of asking if he would have prepared himself for the twentieth century better than Adams or if he would have responded to the explosions of his time, momentarily culminating in the Pentagon March, better than Mailer. Since these questions are hardly rhetorical, Mailer — like Adams before him — has come upon a way of establishing a denser relationship with his reader, and it may be no coincidence that *Armies* brought him the largest reading audience of any single book since *The Naked and the Dead.*

Though *Miami and the Siege of Chicago* (1968) employs the same narrative device as *Armies,* the hero is really not the same man. Periodically he gives off a flash of the comic hero of *Armies,* but the situation is so different — two hopelessly predictable political conventions — that quite a different protagonist is required. The voluntary march of hundreds of thousands of Americans on the Pentagon was self-evidently a major historical moment, requiring nothing from Mailer to inflate it. He thus focused not on the moment's greatness but on the comparative lack of that quality in the hero trying to live up to it. In this he vastly humanizes the experience. But in *Miami,* with the exception of the Chicago protest scenes, the situation is almost reversed. Surely the simplest way of responding to those two conventions would have been to forget about them. So we meet a different Mailer, one who leads us into the evidently stagnant spirals of America's convened political party system, coaxing us to share with him the role of Diogenes. Who knows, he seems to suggest, if we don't find honesty we may at least find something worth learning. And we do. Muting the ironic tone and emphasis on personal idiosyncrasy that he used in *Armies,* Mailer focuses sharply on the experience of penetration. He sends his hero, The Reporter, through mazes, devises strategies and tactics for him, working always to dramatize the ability of the individual to worm past the censorship, the media version of what's happening, into a private vantage point. It may be that what one

*11*

comes upon is a bleak prospect, but at least one can see on one's own "what the swindle is about." If the important thing for the hero in *Armies* was not to become lost in the vastness of the moment, the importance here is for the individual not to give up in disgust at the absurd smallness of the moment. Some command of the imagination, of course, is required in both cases.

Mailer's most recent volume of nonfiction has not, at this writing, been published. *Of a Fire on the Moon*, which treats the flight of Apollo 11 to the moon, has, however, had three sections serialized in *Life* magazine (itself an interesting detail concerning Mailer's widening audience), and it is possible to infer from these a connection with the earlier books. We have once again the third-person (the device is clearly an ideal way, in Mailer's view, to suggest the ambiguity of identity involved when a writer uses "himself" in his work), this time called Aquarius, and the problem posed for the figure is similar in kind to that of the previous volumes. As before, the artist-hero stands outside of an arena, and his task is to find his way round the obstacles which prevent entry. But the arena in this new book is technology, the mystery world of the twentieth century, where expertise is less a quality than a very sacrament. So out of the collection of masks and uniforms and roles he has stored up, the public writer emerges with something new: Aquarius, it turns out, has been an engineering student in college — aeronautical engineering at that. The plan of the book, clearly, will involve bridging what is perhaps the greatest cultural gap of all — the distance between the world of the creative individual and the world of the team technological effort.

What strikes one about these personae of Mailer's, both in the compilations and the narratives, is their great variousness. At center always the artist, they have as many masks and amateur skills as there are areas in the culture where they find themselves engaged. Engaged is always the right word to describe the kind of public figure Mailer is projecting, for he moves aggressively into political, economic, educational, religious, military, technological arenas as he chooses, almost as if to teach us something. There is indeed something distinctly pedagogical about the way he invades so many areas for us, displaying a hundred different moods and attitudes when he is in them, above all trying always to evoke the essence of the moment through his endless conjuring of metaphor. His lesson may be that the culture is not a jail for the individual to serve in but a terrain to be explored, as in fact individuality is a territory too — one that invites exploration at least as much as does the culture.

Before returning to the matter of Mailer's design in having become a public writer, we should at least touch on the relevance of his fiction to this matter. Most of the fiction does of course build around the presence of an artist-hero. Absent from *The Naked and the Dead*, he first appears as Mikey Lovett in *Barbary Shore*, then as Sergius O'Shaugnessy in *The Deer Park* and "The Time of Her Time," then as Steve Rojack in *An American Dream*, and finally as D. J., the hero of *Why Are We in Vietnam?* Most of these are fledgling artists, and the central problem they face is how to preserve their talent and their imagination in the face of powerfully destructive forces — forces which have ruined McLeod in *Barbary Shore*, Eitel in *The Deer Park*, Shago Martin in *An American Dream*, and Rusty in *Why Are We in Vietnam?* The most mature of them, Rojack, poses the problem most clearly. Like Fitzgerald's Dick Diver he has a body of work to get to, a canon of creativity which, and which alone, will justify his existence. Like Dick, responding to corrosive forces without and within, he swerves from the path that leads to his work and becomes immersed in the transitory, the foul, the destructive. But unlike Fitzgerald, whose answer to Dick's ruined career would have been discipline, self-denial, devotion to the exile of the artist, Mailer seems to imply that Steve did what an artist must do. He must get to his work by going through, not around, the destructive elements that surround him. If waste, selfishness, and corruption are a part of us and part of our society, then we must live with them and experience them, and not hope to flee from them. Whether Mailer's Rojack will win through to his work is not answered in the novel, but it is clear that he at least has a chance, and it is strongly implied that he has earned that chance by immersing himself in precisely the elements that had the strongest chance of ruining him. It may be useful to keep this vision in mind when we turn to the question of Mailer's motives for adopting the public writer role.

The prescription, in the fiction as well as the nonfiction, seems to be that retreat is not a defense; the individual who hopes to remain whole must risk the dangers of going forth and meeting adversity head on. It is hard to believe that Mailer's own prolific creativity in the years since *Advertisements* is not an argument that meeting adversity head on will produce victory. Publicly leading, indeed almost documenting a private life which is in many ways clearly a series of testing confrontations with potentially destructive forces, he has produced a kind of practical argument for playing close to the line. Throughout all of his work he has posited the fact that a war is going on in our society between institutional force — "totalitarianism" he calls it — and the counterforce of individuality. At the heart of individuality, whatever its flaws and frailties, lies imagination, and thus the prime target of institutionality is imaginative creativity — the artist's definitive characteristic. The figure of the artist is the most appropriate one with which to oppose institutionality's invasion, but the difference between the artist's imagination and that of the individual at large is, in Mailer's view, only one of degree — the artist gives form and line to the vision which, in fact, he shares with or even derives from his fellowman. It is therefore inevitable that there should be a bond between artist and individual in the war. The public artist's function is to give evidence of the presence and viability of the imagination and, in the process, to suggest that an appropriate strategy for the besieged non-artist would be art itself. He rejects the mandarin assumption that art needs no spokesman, that it speaks for itself to those who can hear, and that those who can't lack essential sensibility. Recognizing that art is an optional experience, and recognizing too the tradition of antipathy toward art which is a reality in our culture — an antipathy based on the assumption that art makes you weaker, not stronger — he becomes its spokesman through the device of his public performance. Put at its very simplest, the cultural mission of the public artist is to help people see that they have more individual power than their institutions have taught them to believe.

But what of the motives of the public artist with respect to his own work? What can he say to the charge that while there may be something generous about his public role, it is at its best an unsatisfactory use of creative talent, inevitably draining off from the body of his work a quality which that work would otherwise possess? An artist's first, perhaps his only debt is to his work, goes the argument (see James Baldwin's essay in this collection), and to use his talent in any other way is to cheat that work, through a misplaced sense of loyalty at best, a crippling vanity at worst.

Critics, at least some of whom have appreciated Mailer's work and wished seriously to understand him, have directed questions concerning "wasted talent" at him for years. The questions rest on the major intellectual and critical assumption that an artist's creativity is so far understandable that one can, in the great tradition, prescribe for its care and preservation. Mailer himself half-jokingly acknowledged his doubts about his own way of working, admitting to the thought that *Cannibals and Christians,* for example, was perhaps a "meaningless endeavor — that the only way to hunt these intima-

15

tions is in the pages of a novel, that that is the only way this sort of mystery can ever be detected." Yet, faced with the Joycean formula for artistic strategy — "Silence, exile, and cunning" — he had to doubt that the ordination was mandatory. "One hopes not: the patient is too gregarious for the prescription." Still, the impolite question remains: Is all of his extranovelistic activity good for Mailer as an artist or bad?

In a *Paris Review* interview Steve Marcus put the question, politely, in specific reference to Mailer's writing of nonfiction, and Mailer answered it. The answer was somewhat circumlocutory, but it came down to the assertion that the things Mailer did outside of his novel-writing were done so that he could "keep in shape" as a novelist, but "in a peculiar way." To illustrate, he told a story about a fighter named Harry Greb, who had his own highly unconventional training methods:

> Harry Greb, for example, was a fighter who used to keep in shape. He was completely a fighter, the way one might wish to be completely a writer. He always did the things which were necessary to him as a fighter. Now some of these things were extremely irrational, that is, extremely irrational from a prize-fight manager's point of view. That is, before he had a fight he would go to a brothel, and he would have two prostitutes, not one, taking the two of them into the same bed. And this apparently left him feeling like a wild animal. Don't ask me why. Perhaps he picked the two meanest whores in the joint and so absorbed into his system all the small, nasty, concentrated evils which had accumulated from carloads of men.

If the writer is analogous to the fighter, then the critic is the fight manager, certain that he knows a set of rules which will tell the fighter how he can conserve his power and deliver his best work. But Mailer is arguing that creativity is not subject to formula, that it is a mystery — the last one we are ever likely to explain — and no critic can tell an artist how best to bring the imagination into play. Here lies the private explanation for why Mailer sought out and played the role of public artist. He put himself into the public arena, both through writing nonfiction and through engaging in a whole range of apparently nonliterary activities — the boisterously public private life, the making of movies, the running for political office — to get into shape in his peculiar way. Put in the blunt terms of the Harry Greb parable, these activities are Mailer's two whores. Less bluntly, he is saying that the creative mystery of the artist is individuated. What induces creativity in one artist stultifies it in another. If the blaze of attention that is part of the life of the public artist would wither the talent of some, it might well make his flower. Indeed, given the complexities of personal background, the million variables that combine to make up an individual, publicity might even become an absolute prerequisite for his acts of creation.

In the case of Mailer the role of public artist, whatever its benefits may be to the individual members of his public, can easily be seen as the largest and most comprehensive in the very considerable array of devices he has employed throughout his career to, as it were, trick work out of himself. He got "The Man Who Studied Yoga" and *The Deer Park* out of himself by fantasizing that he was embarked onto the Napoleonic sea of an eight-novel magnum opus. In 1959 he announced a coming great new novel, and of course it has yet to appear. What has appeared is a shelf of at least seven other books, not to speak of three movies, and it may well be that these are "compensatory" for his not having done that particular novel. He publicly and pugnaciously committed himself to serializing *An American Dream* in *Esquire*, thus tying himself to magazine deadlines. Why do that, and run the risk of a rush job on his novel? After final publication had taken place he said that if he hadn't serialized it he would still be tinkering with chapter three. All of these exercises in imagination-isometrics may be smaller parts in the large design which is Mailer's role of public writer. In the very last analysis his claim that he is essentially a novelist, and that all of his other work stands in a lower order of importance to his novels, may be the greatest trick of all, a device enabling him to produce that rich array of multigeneric art which is his canon to date.

The best explanations are often the simplest, and the simplest explanation for Mailer's resurgent burst of work since he took on the role of public artist is that the role was a help to him as a private artist. To suggest that he could have done more work, or a different kind or even better work if he had eschewed the public role is merely arrogant. And to denigrate the positive cultural contribution he has made in his public role may be premature. Mailer will be a legend, as the other public writers became, and he will be inflated and debunked and analyzed as they have been, and the time for deciding what he left us of value in that legend has not yet arrived. It is not, however, his faithfulness to the legend which should impress us at last, but his faithfulness to his art. The intricate strategy he has devised to make himself create may have confused and misled many of his critics, but it has been his greatest masterpiece. It has nothing about it of silence, it does not involve exile in any simple sense, but of cunning it has a most marvelous abundance.

R.F.L.

September 1970

# PART ONE:
# Overviews

# Norman Mailer

## by Richard Foster

When Norman Mailer's *The Naked and the Dead* was published in 1948 it was all but universally acclaimed as a major novel marking the appearance of a new American writer destined for greatness. During the next twenty years, however, though he had some warm defenders, the negative judgments among critics substantially outnumbered the positive as book after book appeared: novels, a play, collections of stories and poems, and gatherings of essays and other fugitive pieces. And yet, unlike most of his generation of novelists — the "war novelists" and the urban Jewish writers — he has pursued a course of individualistic development and change which has continued to command the attention of peers, critics, and public; if his readers have sometimes been

This essay originally appeared as *University of Minnesota Pamphlets on American Writers, No. 73*, published by the University of Minnesota Press. Copyright © 1968 by the University of Minnesota. Reprinted by permission.

baffled and frequently hostile, they have grown ever more interested. To use a Maileresque analogy, he has rather resembled an overmatched boxer who, floored in the second round, springs back and sustains the fight far beyond expectations through variety and inventiveness of footwork and temporizing punches.

The match is still not decided. But however it finally comes out, there can be no doubt that the overmatched boxer will at the very least be remembered for his remarkable performance. Mailer's adversary through the 1950's and 1960's has been the current embodiment of operative cultural and literary norms, that plodding but powerful opponent of idiosyncrasy and innovation which Eliot long ago dubbed "the tradition." Mailer had won his first round with a skillful and moving but conventional novel in the realist-naturalist vein. Everything since *The Naked and the Dead*, with the exception of a handful of stories from the late forties and early fifties, has been radically innovative in both substance and essential form — without satisfying current conceptions of what constitutes serious literary experimentation.

It has been Mailer's apparent lack of artistic "seriousness" that has troubled his serious critics most. When they were not either ridiculing or dismissing him, their main cry was the lamentation that a major talent was being wasted on trivial material or debased by sloppy craftsmanship. F. Scott Fitzgerald, whose work and career were in many ways similar to Mailer's, was criticized during his lifetime on much the same grounds. But what needs to be stressed in Mailer's case, as in Fitzgerald's, is that he is indeed a serious "experimentalist" writer, though an experimentalist of a different order than our moment in the history of "the tradition" allows us easily to recognize, accept, and understand.

James Joyce was the kind of experimentalist who applied innovative techniques to conventionally "realistic" fictional material. He sought out and found new routes to the old novelistic destinations. D. H. Lawrence, on the other hand, was the kind of writer who discovered new destinations — new materials and knowledge, and thus new obligations for fiction. His technical innovations, always less sophisticated, formal, and predominant than Joyce's, were functional consequences and by-products of what can only be called an experimentalist approach to the *subject matter* of fiction. In the course of writing *The Rainbow* and *Women in Love*, Lawrence discovered, as he told Edward Garnett, that his subject was no longer "the old stable *ego*" of human character, no longer the "diamond" but rather the "carbon" which is the diamond's elemental substance:

> There is another *ego*, according to whose action the individual is unrecognisable, and passes through, as it were, allotropic states which it needs a deeper sense than any we've been used to exercise, to discover are states of the same single radically unchanged element. . . . Again I say, don't look for the development of the novel to follow the lines of certain characters: the characters fall into the form of some other rhythmic form, as when one draws a fiddle-bow across a fine tray delicately sanded, the sand takes lines unknown.

These metaphors describing the substantive nature of Lawrence's experimentation with both matter and form after *Sons and Lovers* might as easily apply to Mailer, whose work after *The Naked and the Dead* has been similarly concerned with the "allotropy" — the changing "rhythmic form" and "lines unknown" — of the "carbon" of human character under complex stress. And like Lawrence, Mailer seems to have become aware of his new departure only after standing away from the new work in hand to see what he was doing and why he was doing it. While working on *Barbary Shore*, he has recalled in an interview, he found his Marxist intellectual convictions continually distracted by compulsive preoccupations with "murder, suicide, orgy, psychosis." "I always felt as if I were not writing the book myself." Other statements by Mailer indicate that much the same creative pathology also ruled the composition of *The Deer Park*, his third novel. The personal stresses and anxieties that underlay the writing of these two novels, and the stories that were spun off from them, found confessional expression in Mailer's fourth book, a compilation of fiction and nonfiction pieces with unifying connective additions called *Advertisements for Myself*, which is the author's intense, immediate, and unabashedly public reappraisal of himself, in 1959, as both artist and human being. Anxiety, compulsion, and hints of psychosis had been the disruptive and only half-conscious creative causes behind *Barbary Shore* and *The Deer Park*. Following the purgation and illumination represented by *Advertisements*, they become, in the later novels *An American Dream* and *Why Are We in Vietnam?* and the related pieces in *The Presidential Papers* and *Cannibals and Christians*, the consciously molded substance of Mailer's hypertrophic images of life in America at mid-century.

A detailed account of this course of change and growth must be left for later. The important fact is that after several more books, plus a string of other accomplishments — including play-producing, movie-making, a fling at architectural design, and a great deal of moral, social, and political punditing, both on paper and on the hoof — the author of *The Naked and the Dead* emerged in the mid-sixties, despite his still uncertain reputation among serious literary people, as decidedly the most active and vivid public figure on the American literary scene.

Like his first published novel and stories, Mailer's early life was at least conventional enough not to foreshadow with any definiteness the panoply of idiosyncrasy that was to come later. Born January 31, 1923, in Long Branch, New Jersey, to Isaac and Fanny Mailer, Norman Mailer was raised and schooled in Brooklyn, graduating from Boys' High School in 1939. While at Harvard, where he earned a B.S. degree in aeronautical

engineering in 1943, Mailer began writing in earnest, con-
tributing to the *Advocate*, working at his first two (and still
unpublished) novels, and winning in 1941 *Story* magazine's
annual college fiction contest. In 1944 he married his first wife
and was drafted into the Army, serving in the Pacific theater
until 1946. During the next year and a half, part of which was
spent in Europe, where he was enrolled as a student at the
Sorbonne, Mailer wrote *The Naked and the Dead*, which was
published with immediate and dramatic success. The public
purchased it in such numbers that it held at the top of the best-
seller lists for nearly three months. A movie contract was soon
in the works; Lillian Hellman was slated to adapt it for the
stage; and Sinclair Lewis was moved to dub Mailer "the greatest writer to come out of his generation."

Though Mailer himself once half dismissed his first novel as
a "conventional war novel," and though it was conceived and
composed in a manner that Mailer was not to use again in a
major work, *The Naked and the Dead* is much more than a
"war novel." The embracing action of the novel — the taking
of a Japanese-held Pacific island in World War II — is rendered with the skilled realist's commitment to the truthful
and vivid depiction of actuality. But in the year of its publication Mailer put on record his view that *The Naked and the
Dead*, though cast in the realist mold, is "symbolic," expressive
of "death and man's creative urge, fate, man's desire to conquer the elements — all kinds of things you never dream of
separating and stating so baldly." And there is no mistaking
that the island itself, and the mountain at its center which
Sergeant Croft commits himself and his platoon to conquer-
ing, acquire an almost Conradian symbolic significance in the
eyes of their chief beholders. Here is the soldiers' vision of the
setting of their destruction:

> It was a sensual isle, a Biblical land of ruby wines and golden
> sands and indigo trees. The men stared and stared. The island
> hovered before them like an Oriental monarch's conception of

heaven, and they responded to it with an acute and terrible longing. It was a vision of all the beauty for which they had ever yearned, all the ecstasy they had ever sought. For a few minutes it dissolved the long dreary passage of the mute months in the jungle, without hope, without pride. If they had been alone they might have stretched out their arms to it.

It could not last. Slowly, inevitably, the beach began to dissolve in the encompassing night. The golden sands grew faint, became gray-green, and darkened. The island sank into the water, and the tide of night washed over the rose and lavender hills. After a little while, there was only the gray-black ocean, the darkened sky, and the evil churning of the gray-white wake. Bits of phosphorescence swirled in the foam. The black dead ocean looked like a mirror of the night; it was cold, implicit with dread and death. The men felt it absorb them in a silent pervasive terror. They turned back to their cots, settled down for the night, and shuddered for a long while in their blankets.

In an interview three years later, just after completing *Barbary Shore*, Mailer made this interesting disclosure about *The Naked and the Dead*:

> I don't think of myself as a realist. That terrible word "naturalism." It was my literary heritage — the things I learned from Dos Passos and Farrell. I took naturally to it, that's the way one wrote a book. But I really was off on a mystic kick. Actually — a funny thing — the biggest influence on *Naked* was *Moby Dick*. . . . I was sure everyone would know. I had Ahab in it, and I suppose the mountain was Moby Dick. Of course, I also think the book will stand or fall as a realistic novel.

This last qualification would also apply, of course, to *Moby Dick*. For Melville saw in the actual hazard and struggle of whaling, as Mailer did in war, the revealed pattern of the grandeur and tragedy of the whole human enterprise. Combat, for Mailer, is the chief means by which the higher laws of life become incarnate in human experience. War is his external subject matter in *The Naked and the Dead*; but his internal theme is the "crisis in human values" — identity, humanity, man, and the nature of their enemies in our time.

With war as the background typification of generalized external crisis, Mailer develops his internal themes by two principal means: first, extensively, through a number of Dos Passos–like diagnostic biographical portraits of a cross section of the fighting men; and second, intensively, through the protracted psychic struggle of mind and personality that takes place between Major General Cummings, the crypto-fascist commanding officer of the invading American forces, and his aide, a questioning liberal named Hearn. Both men have been shaped, though in opposite ways, by reaction against the privileged sterility of their Midwestern bourgeois backgrounds. Cummings is the self-created prophet of a new totalitarianism who commands, in the name of his faith in order and authority, the breaking of men's spirits and the destruction of their wills. Hearn, bitter in his discontent, by nature a loner and yet tenderly humane in his half-guilty identification with the men he commands, is the uncertain voice of the liberal ideal of free man. Most of the fighting men are portrayed as already deprived, twisted, or stunted by the disintegrative and totalitarian forces and counterforces at work in their world, the forces whose contention has culminated in the war which now envelops them all. These men are the data of the dialectical contest which is taking place between Cummings and Hearn. That contest, the original of similar recurring patterns of individual contest, including sexual, in most of the rest of Mailer's work, ends in a kind of draw. Hearn and his convictions are wasted when he dies as a casual accident of war on an irrelevant mission. And though the campaign is won, Cummings is in essence defeated because the agency of victory is not his active military intelligence but rather a chain of chance accidents beyond his control.

One notices not only that a true hero is lacking from the

novel's epiclike action, but that his opposite, a forceful antagonist, is lacking too. And yet a large enveloping energy has gathered, thrust forward, and come through to significant issue. A great spasm of nature, an inevitable motion of history, has superseded the efficacies of individual men in a world that has begun to move across Yeats's threshold of apocalypse where "the best lack all conviction" and "the worst/are full of passionate intensity."

But at the core of this vast action, his presence stressing the hero's absence, is Sergeant Croft. After the death of Hearn, he leads the platoon on its doomed assault upon the mountain, dominating his men by the sheer intensity of his undefined "hunger" for the mastery of life. A rough prototype of D. J. Jethroe of *Why Are We in Vietnam?*, Croft has been sired by a tough Texas dirt farmer on a woman conventionally "weak . . . sweet and mild." His father encourages in him a predator's taste for hunting, and he is by nature "mean." Why? "Oh, there are answers. He is that way because of the corruption-of-the-society. He is that way because the devil has claimed him for one of his own. It is because he is a Texan; it is because he has renounced God." The author interprets Croft in an aside as follows: *"He hated weakness and he loved practically nothing. There was a crude unformed vision in his soul but he was rarely conscious of it."* This embryonic "vision" is different from Hearn's superannuated liberalism and Cummings's authoritarian calculus because it is an animal thing — an energy with fierce tendencies but no "form." Croft represents the kinetic life-substance upon which such alternative ideologies as those of Hearn and Cummings must depend for their unforeseeable realizations. In his irrational will and passion, he is the human microcosm of the vast upsurge of inhuman forces in history which express themselves in the ironic irresolutions of the total action of *The Naked and the Dead*.

*The Naked and the Dead*, then, even if substantially conventional in form and style, is nevertheless one with the rest of

Mailer's work in the apocalyptic energies of its vision. Those energies begin to find their requisite new form, and with that a new sort of voice, in the first of Mailer's "experimental" novels, *Barbary Shore*, published in 1951. *Barbary Shore* was the product, as Mailer has written in retrospect, "of intense political preoccupation and a voyage in political affairs which began with the Progressive Party and has ended in the *cul-de-sac* (at least so far as action is concerned) of being an anti-Stalinist Marxist who feels that war is probably inevitable." The omniscient authorial point of view of *The Naked and the Dead* is abandoned in *Barbary Shore* for first-person narrative, which is to continue as the preferred narrative form for Mailer's books thereafter. ("Memory is the seed of narrative, yeah," says D. J. Jethroe, narrator of *Why Are We in Vietnam?*) The book becomes, thus, an adaption of *Bildungsroman*; its narrative substance is the hero's education for life in our time — or reeducation, since he is suffering from amnesia somewhat inexplicitly induced by war and the breakdown of traditional political idealism. The setting is a Brooklyn rooming house operated by a sexually promiscuous and morally neuter proprietress named, with an irony appropriate to her role as life's presiding norm, Guinevere. In this setting, the case histories of three roomers are presented: an impotent, betrayed, and self-betraying idealist of the old revolutionary left; his demon, a stolid and perverted interrogator for the rightist "totalitarian" establishment; and a mad Cassandra-like girl whose derangement is a consequence and expression of history, and whom, as an exacerbated mirroring of his own distressed psyche, the hero half loves.

The heaviness and inertia of the novel — its garrulous expositions of ideological conflict and the dazed passivity and blankness of Lovett, the hero-narrator, before all he sees and hears — is only a little relived when at the end he sprints into an inchoate future with a mysterious small object entrusted to his keeping by the failed leftist before his death. The precise nature of the object, which is hotly coveted by the furies of the right, is never specified. But what it means is perfectly clear. It is a symbol or talisman of the sacred idea of man free and whole; and in the moment of the narrator's active commitment to it in the face of the terrible odds and enemies ranged against it, and now against him as well, we are meant to feel that it has taken on the existential power of life itself.

Even this early in his career — after only two novels — it is clear that Mailer's imagination, unique in his generation, is cast in the epic mold. As bard and prophet to an age in which history is at odds with nature or "destiny," he tells in a fevered voice of the permutations of the heroic imperative in a postheroic world. His theme is the struggle of life and form against death and chaos. But his subject matter is history. And as he pursues the theme of the ideal through the matter of the actual he makes a discovery: in our time the sources and resources of life have shifted, to use the shorthand of Mailer's own symbology, from "God" to "the devil." The vision of life at stalemate in *The Naked and the Dead* and *Barbary Shore* is explained by this discovery, a discovery whose fullness of realization in a changed imaginative vision comes clear in *The Deer Park*, published in 1955.

Desert D'Or, a resort of the rich and powerful modeled on Palm Springs, is the principal setting of *The Deer Park*. It is a denatured interior world of concrete and plastic, of harsh light and blinding shadow, thrown up in defiance of the encircling desert outside. This pattern of division between natural and unnatural that is established in the setting extends also to the characters, in whom desire and will, feeling and thought, the wellsprings of motive and motive's fulfillment in action, have been stricken apart. The natural current of the life-force has somehow been broken. And the inhabitants of this world of trauma and aftermath constitute a gallery of parodies of the human image ranging from the absurd to the piteous to the monstrous. They are, as Mailer wrote in a note to his adaptation of *The Deer Park* for the stage, "in hell."

*30*

Sergius O'Shaugnessy, the hero-narrator of *The Deer Park,* is both an orphan and, like Lovett of *Barbary Shore,* a symbolic waif of historical disaster. His surrogate home in the Air Force and fulfillment in the exercise of the war pilot's impersonal skills of destruction have been snatched from him in a sudden accidental revelation that he is a killer: "I realized that . . . I had been busy setting fire to a dozen people, or two dozen, or had it been a hundred?" In recoil from such horrors of the "real world" he suffers a breakdown, is discharged, and on the winnings from a prodigiously lucky gambling venture, he comes to Desert D'Or, retreat of the gods of the "imaginary world," to rest, drift, gaze, and spend. A blank slate to be written on, an empty vessel to be filled, and — his vision of the burned flesh of his victims having rendered him sexually impotent — a low flame needing fuel, Sergius O'Shaugnessy is the framing consciousness of an ample world crowded with people exhibiting versions of his own predicament. Among the most important of these are Charles Francis Eitel, a gifted and formerly powerful Hollywood director, and Marion Faye, dope pusher, impresario of call girls, and connoisseur of the moral nuances of sadism. Both of these men become friends of O'Shaugnessy and objects of his studious moral attention.

Eitel has had a golden age, a brief heroic period in the thirties when as a true artist he made courageous movies on contemporary social themes, and when as a man of intergrity he put his life on the line in behalf of the fated struggle for democracy in Spain. In reflexive response to the corruption of integrity which has overtaken his art as he has risen to power in Hollywood, Eitel rebuffs a congressional investigating commitee seeking from him incriminating political testimony against his colleagues. In consequence, the industry blackballs him; and his loss of power and identity in the "imaginary" world is measured in personal terms by his loss of potency as both artist and lover. This sequential pattern of aspiration, action, corruption, moral illumination, renunciation, exile, and impotence precisely parallels the pattern of Sergius's life.

Eitel is the distillate of the best values of the past by which Sergius has been fathered and orphaned, and for Sergius, consequently, the question of Eitel's destiny — the question of his potential for rebirth and self-renewal — has crucial moral significance.

Eitel stumbles upon a "second chance" in the form of Elena Esposito, and he muffs it. Another man's castoff, she is soiled, tawdry, and simple. She is a poor dancer and a worse actress, and her manners are absurd. And yet she has the dignity and courage, and finally the beauty, of a being wholly natural. Eitel's affair with her becomes the nourishing ground of a new life for him. His sexual potency is restored, and with it his creative potency as he begins to work on a script which he imagines will be the redemption of his integrity as artist and man. But this new access of life fills him with fear; it is the stirring in him of the heroic imperative, with its attendant commitments to solitary battle, lonely journeyings in the unknown, and the risks of failure and defeat. The doors of Hollywood begin to open again, and the thrones and dominations of the "imaginary" world solicit his return: all he must do is confess and recant before the committee, and he may pass back through those doors. Half because of fear, half because of old habit, Eitel takes the easy way of surrender, shunning the hazardous alternatives (as Elena, significantly, does not) represented by those dark angels of life and truth, Don Beda, high priest of satyrism and orgy, and Marion Faye, the hipster prophet of criminal idealism. His harvest is the life-in-death of security through compromise, the corruption of his script and his talent, and eventual marriage to a broken and exhausted Elena, which is possible now that they are no longer "wedded" in a sacramental sense.

Elena is a noble figure — defeated, but honorably so, in her fated but heroic contest with time and what Hardy calls "crass casualty." Eitel's enemies have been lesser ones — history and social circumstance — and his defeat is pitiful rather than noble, because he has "sold out." But he has at least the saving grace of his ironic intelligence, which enables him to understand, when she proudly refuses his first offer of marriage, the principle of Elena's nobility: "the essence of spirit . . . was to choose the thing which did not better one's position but made it more perilous." Later on, when she has no more resources of refusal and he nourishes upon her defeat by "sacrificing" himself in marrying her, he understands his own corresponding cowardice: "there was that law of life so cruel and so just which demanded that one must grow or else pay more for remaining the same."

Eitel is Mailer's version of the traditional hero in his last historical incarnation. Vision, passion, and courage have dwindled in Eitel to intelligence, compassion, and guilt — the "cement" of the world, as Marion Faye contemptuously labels the last two, which binds men, enfeebles them, and turns them into spiritual "slobs." Eitel's very strengths are weaknesses, his virtues are faults, in a world where the apocalyptic beasts of anxiety and dread are raging in prisons of compromise and falsehood. And as the novel draws to its close and Eitel begins to fade into the penumbra of Sergius O'Shaugnessy's memorializing imagination, we are aware that the passing of the man is also the passing of the values he represented. Flanked by comic Lulu Meyers, a movie sex goddess who on impulse marries for "love" rather than career, and by tragic Marion Faye, whose anarch's code of black moral reason leads him behind prison bars, the now enlightened Sergius is the chief chalice-bearer of new human values. He becomes a bullfighter, stud, and teacher of both arts. And he begins to write, his books presumably fired by the existential perils and ecstasies of combat and sexuality. Though the novel ends on a cheerful note of metaphysical exhilaration, Sergius, both as a character and as an archetype of new styles of human value, is vague and inchoate as well as faintly absurd. Sergius has survived all sorts of traumas and temptations and come through to freedom, but he is not very much more fully realized as an examplar of new values in action than was his predecessor, Lovett. He has come to terms with the world that has wounded him, and like the good Emersonian "fatalists" that all such Mailer heroes are, he affirms it as his destined inheritance from nature and history. But neither he nor his author has yet found the requisite life-style, the new heroic mold through which to turn understanding and affirmation into creative, perhaps redemptive action.

Life threatened in our time by the forces of death is Mailer's subject everywhere. When he writes as a realist, as in *The Naked and the Dead*, life is stalemated and defeated by the forces of death. In the next two novels the intensities of anxiety and dread underlying Mailer's subject matter begin to dominate the rational, circumjacent forms of the realist, distorting them in the direction of the expressionistic and the surreal. And with this modification of form comes a coordinate modification of the heroes in whom the issue of the life-death struggle is finally centered. The narrator-hero of *Barbary Shore*, for whom the action encompassed by his consciousness is an elaborately instructive morality play, in the end escapes paralysis and spiritual death. The similarly educated narrator-hero of *The Deer Park* not only escapes but, as he bids fond farewell to the memories of the defeated and destroyed, discerns in the very chemistry of the disease and decomposition all around him the flicker and spur of new possibilities for life. "Think of Sex as Time," says "God" in a final dialogue with Sergius, "and Time as the connection of new circuits."

*Barbary Shore* and *The Deer Park*, both of them fictional investigations of the operative laws of death and endings, are novels that end with beginnings. Mailer's next novel, *An American Dream*, published in 1965, is in every way an extension and intensification of the manner and substance of its two predecessors. It begins, significantly, with an ending: the hero saves himself from spiritual death by committing a murder that restores him to life, action, growth. Seen in relation to *An American Dream*, the two preceding novels have the look of a single imaginative action of a precursory nature: a complex psychodramatic "sloughing-off," to use Lawrence's terms in *Studies in Classic American Literature*, of the "old consciousness" of an outworn idealistic humanism in preparation for a "new consciousness" requisite for survival and significant life in a psychotic world bordering on apocalypse and yearning toward death. The experiential educations of Mikey Lovett and Sergius O'Shaugnessy in *Barbary Shore* and *The Deer Park* are preparations of this "new consciousness" for active engagement with the world. Steve Rojack and D. J. Jethroe — respectively heroes of *An American Dream* and *Why Are We in Vietnam?* — are the beneficiaries of this process. Rojack, in a moment of freeing impulse, murders his rich, preternaturally domineering, death-threatening wife Deborah, a "bitch-goddess" of American power, and the summation of the death-force of historical fate. The charge of this self-galvanizing destruction of his immediate enemy propels him into action, turning fear, fatigue, and despair into a redemptive energy of desperation. With a courage nourished on the ultimate dread, the dread of death, he runs a varied course of triumphs — besting the sexual enmity of a cold nymphomaniac, the hunting wile of the police, the competition of a Negro stud of legendary sexual prowess, and an engulfing sea of guilt and self-doubt summoned by Deborah's father, Barney Kelly. He even finds love along the way, with a tender, used, and charming cabaret singer named Cherry. A composite of American realities like Deborah, she is Deborah's opposite and complement, a plucky victim of the forces of which Deborah is the emblematic goddess and proprietress. At the end Rojack is still running — his roles and costumes of war hero, congressman, professor, television personality, and husband of a socialite left far behind — now toward the darker and simpler challenges of the jungles of Guatemala and Yucatán.

In *Why Are We in Vietnam?* (1967), D. J. Jethroe has already reached his Guatemala and Yucatán. High on pot, the
prose of the Marquis de Sade and William Burroughs, and the
cheerfully psychotic inspiration that he may be the voice of a
"Harlem spade" imprisoned in the body of the son of a white
Dallas tycoon, he tells the story of how he got that way. It is an
initiation story (new style) as *An American Dream* was a new-
style story of sacrifice and redemption. The initiation, product
of a hunting "safari" to Alaska with his father Rusty, D. J.'s
best friend Tex, and assorted guides and associates, has two
phases, both of them involving radical divestments and ultimate tests of courage. In the first phase, D. J. breaks spiritually
with his father when, out of habits of competitive vanity and
self-justification, his father claims the grizzly bear that D. J.
has mortally wounded, violating not only the father-son bond
as reinforced by the hunt (stalking their dangerous quarry
D. J. sees himself and his father as "war buddies") but also the
sacred blood bond between killer and prey. Thinks D. J.,
"Final end of love of one son for one father." The second
phase of the initiation, fruit of the alienation and frustration
sown by the first, is the twenty-four-hour northward foray of
D. J. and Tex, alone and without guns or instruments, into
the wild heart of the Brooks Range. In an ecstasy of fear and
trembling they witness a pageant of savageries — wolf, eagle,
bear, caribou, and moose, the figments of natural life locked
in struggle with death — culminating in a cosmic eruption of
the northern lights that is so magnificent and intense as to
bring them to the border of orgy and fratricide: "they were
twins, never to be as lovers again, but killer brothers, armed
by something, prince of darkness, lord of light, they did not
know." They make a bond in an exchange of blood, "the deep
beast whispering, Fulfill my will, go forth and kill." At the
end, D. J., now eighteen, looks beyond the Brooks Range of
his initiatory "Guatemala and Yucatán" toward his mature
destiny: "Hot damn, Vietnam."

D. J. is the voice of the anxieties and compulsions that have accumulated beneath the patterns of America's history and exploded at last in the manifest violence and chaos of its present. In the electric North, which is the voltaic pile of a continent's repressed, distorted, and perverted life-energies, he has faced Demogorgon, and he comes back metamorphosed, a rudely American voice of bardic ecstasy and prophecy. Completing the journey of transformation only begun by Lovett and Sergius O'Shaugnessy, D. J. and Steve Rojack have successfully tracked the power of life, thieved by a conspiracy of history with nature from its traditional home in the light, to its new home in darkness. In accomplishing this, they become exemplars of that "new consciousness" requisite to continuing life's ancient battle against death in a psychotic world bordering on apocalyptic crisis.

Richard Poirier, identifying Mailer with Eliot's vision, sees him as similarly spurred by the "de-creative" aspects of creation.* But if this is true, Mailer is even more closely related to Lawrence, who in the voice of Rupert Birkin of *Women in Love* discerned among the "marsh-flowers" of "destructive creation" certain blossoms that while they were spawned by the all-enveloping historical process of "universal dissolution" were not *"fleurs du mal,"* but rather "roses, warm and flamy." Lawrence himself was one of these exotic exceptions. And so is Mailer. If the roots of both writers necessarily nourish upon the food of darkness, the blossoms produced are bright with the warm colors of life, and grow toward the light. In Lawrence the blossom is the "man who has come through," the separate natural self released through the death of the conventional social self into a living and changing "star-equilibrium" with the otherness of nature and woman. In Mailer it is all this and a bit more: history, impelled by the American dream turned to nightmare, is a third constituent of the otherness, and the reborn self becomes an "existential hero."

* The Poirier essay is included in this collection. [Ed.]

*Advertisements for Myself* (1959) and *The Presidential Papers* (1963) are large and various but nevertheless unified collections of pieces, mostly nonfiction, written during the dozen years following Mailer's tentative effort and partial failure to achieve a new form in *Barbary Shore*. As books principally about their author, *Advertisements for Myself* and *The Presidential Papers* taken together have the shape, like *Barbary Shore* and *The Deer Park*, of a single action, the complex and difficult action of "sloughing off" the "old consciousness." "The existential hero," first coming to full life in *An American Dream* and *Why Are We in Vietnam?*, is Mailer's realization of this new style of consciousness. And *Advertisements for Myself* and *The Presidential Papers* are the record of its gestation in the mind of its creator, and of the large and small deaths prerequisite to its coming to birth.

Mailer uses his own "personality," he tells us, as the "armature" of *Advertisements* — an image aptly descriptive of both its form and its impact. The reciprocal emotions of dread and determination whirl at the center of the book, as its author frankly appraises, at mid-career, his qualified victories and larger defeats during more than a decade of trying to live up to his potenitals and ambitions as a man and writer. The pieces collected in *Advertisements* — stories, essays, and poems; polemics, meditations, and interviews; fragments of plays-in-progress and novels-to-be — are the measure of the worth of the life being lived, the substance of the tale being told. It is a tale, like Fitzgerald's in the *Crack-up* essays, of early success, subsequent failure and demoralization, and the reflexive counterthrust of self-regeneration and re-creation. *The Naked and the Dead*, which catapulted him to sudden and youthful fame, had, as he tells us in *Advertisements*, been "easy to write." But nothing would be so easy again, for this success was the beginning of his "existentialism," which was "forced upon [him]," as he says, by his finding himself "prominent and empty," a "personage," at twenty-five. He must justify the prominence and fill the emptiness. With such heroic models before him as the life-style of Hemingway and the *oeuvre* of Malraux, he thrusts experimentally into new territory with *Barbary Shore*, "the first of the existentialist novels in America." The hostility and ridicule with which it is greeted in 1951 knock him down. Deflated, ill, and anxious, he turns to writing "respectable" short stories in the earlier manner and jaunty sociopolitical polemics for such magazines as *Partisan Review* and *Dissent* (of which he also becomes an editor). All this is a sort of distraction and temporizing in the face of the big comeback, the planned colossal counterpunch which might dazzle the world with a starfall and revelations: a projected eight-volume novel of cosmic proportions whose framing consciousness, a minor man and an artist *manqué* named Sam Slovoda, has an alter-ego dream hero named Sergius O'Shaugnessy. The great work hovering in the wings refuses to emerge. But two related fragments appear, both of them again in the new manner: the story "The Man Who Studied Yoga," which is to be the great work's prologue, and a protracted but relevant detour from the main route, a novel called *The Deer Park*.

The story of the vicissitudes accompanying *The Deer Park's* publication and reception, most of it recounted in *Advertisements*, could itself be the stuff of a novel. The bad reception of *Barbary Shore* in 1951 and Mailer's divorce in 1952 are elements of a continuing pattern of gathering personal distress which characterize the years of *The Deer Park's* composition. These distresses reach a penultimate crisis when *The Deer Park*, already in page proof, is suddenly held up by its publisher: Stanley Rinehart finds in it something unacceptably obscene. Just recently Mailer has accepted the challenge of writing an essay called "The Homosexual Villain" at the invitation of the magazine *One*, an undertaking which has blown up a "log jam of accumulated timidities and restraints" in him. Partially as a consequence, he refuses to make the change in *The Deer Park* for Rinehart, and the deal is off. The next ten weeks, at the end of which *The Deer Park* will be accepted by Putnam after refusal by several other houses, is a time of crisis for Mailer. He has undergone another death — the death of certain illusions about himself as "a figure in the landscape," and about the "honor" of publishers and writers in the American present — and feels himself becoming a "psychic outlaw."

Drawing his powers now from forays into the worlds of jazz, Harlem, and marijuana, he sees that the style of *The Deer Park* is wrong for the narrator he wants to create — it is too poetic, in the vein of Fitzgerald's Nick Carraway. He begins to rewrite from page proof, thirsting for the kind of self-redemptive success which would change the world a little, and at the same time dreading the possibility of a bad reception and low sales. The revised *The Deer Park*, once published, is only a "middling success." And Mailer measures the quality of its success not only by sales and reviews but by the glimpses of possibility that have begun to emerge for the harried author with his last-minute impetus to rewrite it. Though tentative and incomplete, the accomplished changes adumbrate a new hero: the tender, wounded, and detached observer of the earlier version has begun to turn into a Sergius O'Shaugnessy who is not only "good" but also "ambitious"; a Sergius who, instead of virtuously spurning Hollywood's offer to film his life, might have taken the bait in a spirit of adventure and run it to some perilous triumph. The published book, its author laments, is but a hint of what might have been: the masterpiece in Mailer's generation equivalent to *The Sun Also Rises* in Hemingway's. As a "middling success," *The Deer Park* represents to its author his gross failure to bid on "the biggest hand" he had ever held, and a discovery that after all he hadn't the magic to "hasten the time of apocalypse."

But even so, this fumble, this failure, is no dead end. Like the emptiness of his success with *The Naked and the Dead*, and the fullness of his failure with *Barbary Shore*, it is a threshold to possibility. He has a vision, now, of what he must try to be and do as a writer, and of how considerable are the odds ranged against him. And like Sergius, who takes up bull-fighting at the end of *The Deer Park*, he moves directly into the arena of the world's action as a matador of existential polemics — a rebel general of "Hip" — in the pages of *The Village Voice*, which he helped found in 1955. Though a fresh excursion into novel-writing is delayed by these side trips into journalism, *The Village Voice* pieces are important as snap-shots of the "new" Mailer soon fully to emerge as exemplar and spokesman of the needed "new consciousness." His first important effort in the new mode is the essay "The White Negro," written in 1957 and first published, by City Lights, in 1958 (it was reprinted in *Advertisements*).*

A speculative psychocultural essay on the modern predica-ment, "The White Negro" is a paradigm of the vision, the ideas, the motifs and symbols that will shape all of Mailer's future work in whatever form. The Hipster refuses to capitu-late to the repressive denaturing, dehumanizing death-force of a "totalitarian" society. But because he is active — unlike the bourgeois "beat" who withdraws and passively sublimates in the surrogate quasi-life of song, flowers, meditation, hal-lucinogens, and "love" — he is confronted by the immediate dangers of physical violence and death. Like the Negro he is an *un*citizen (hence the label "white Negro") and danger is the medium of his life. Pleasure is his end; energy, courage, and wile are his means. The dynamic poise of his life-style implies the constitution, in microcosm, of a whole culture: decorums of manners, dress, language; an ethic; an aesthetic; even, finally, a metaphysic and a theology. The philosophy of the Hip, Mailer reflects, is the former insight of a "radical humanist" "brooding" on the energizing phenomenon of the Negro revolution in contemporary America.

The Hipster is, of course, only one of many possible realiza-

* "The White Negro" was first published in *Dissent* in 1957. City Lights Bookstore published a reprint, in pamphlet form, in 1958. [Ed.]

tions of the "new consciousness" of which Mailer is the prophet. He is but one version of the idea of the existential hero, whose incarnation not only *may* but *must* be limitless and unpredictable. For the existenital hero is the Dostoevskian underground man come aboveground into the Tolstoian mainstream of history. It is not known what he will be there, only that he will *do* — his being a function of his acting, rather than the other way around. He is a Sisyphus released from the stone of his dogged abstract commitment, a Hemingway galvanized into new life by the very terrors that threaten paralysis and death. Evading the fateful impasse between heroic "intactness" and human "completeness" that destroyed Fitzgerald's Dick Diver, he is a vital synthesis of the polar values of self-control and spontaneity represented in *The Deer Park* by Marion Faye, the black puritan of moral scruple, and Don Beda, the rosy orgiast of the senses. Extensively educated in anguish, division, and impotence, Sergius O'Shaugnessy has just touched the regenerative power of that synthesis when the book of his salvation closes. The same efflorescence in his creator, which achieves full bloom in *The Presidential Papers*, seems to have been nourished by a similar curriculum, as recounted in *Advertisements*, of prior defeats and despairs. *Advertisements*, in contrast to its successor, *The Presidential Papers*, is a book in the mode of elegy, recording in lyric regret and anger the difficult passing of romantic idealism and the death of youth's illusions. But *Advertisements* also has elegy's *dramatic* mode, being shaped as a total action embodying patterns of divestment and purgation which yield up at last a clear prospect of fresh possibilities: "Tomorrow to fresh woods, and pastures new." "The White Negro," which Mailer tells us was written in the depths of "fear that I was no longer a writer," turns out to be the bright and central song of a "man who has come through." It is after all, he sees, one of his "best things." In it, and in the two late stories in the "existential" mode, "The Time of Her Time" and "Advertisements for Myself on the Way Out," published at the close of *Advertisements*, can be found, as he says, "the real end of this muted autobiography of the near-beat adventurer who was myself."

The end of a life, whether well or badly lived, Mailer writes in *Advertisements*, is "seed." The "seed" of the agonies survived by the hero of *Advertisements* is *The Presidential Papers*, in which the author steps forth, re-created as public man and existentialist prophet, to address America and its leaders on the exigent realities of the age.

The "armature" of this book is not the author's personality in crisis, but rather an *idea* — the idea of "existential politics": "Existential politics is simple. It has a basic argument: if there is a strong ineradicable strain in human nature, one must not try to suppress it or anomaly, cancer and plague will follow. Instead one must find an art into which it can grow." In *The Presidential Papers* the pattern of personal crisis and salvation of self traced in *Advertisements* has been transmuted, by the chemistry of analogy so characteristic of Mailer's imagination, into the public terms of politics and history. But though the drama is now public rather than private, Mailer's self is no less central to the action. In the preface to *The Presidential Papers* he defines his role: to infuse John F. Kennedy, whose glamour and magnetism give him the potential of an "existential hero" in the arena of politics, with the requisite "existential" political consciousness. Mailer's commitment here is to steal back, for the languishing forces of "God," some of the energies of life which have passed over to the forces of darkness. But because history has moved so far on the downward path of de-creation, he must do it as a kind of undercover agent: he must perforce speak as a "devil." His first success as a metaphysical Robin Hood is his brilliant *Esquire* piece on Kennedy's nomination by the 1960 Democratic convention, which was written, despite his candidate's moribund "liberal" program, for the purpose of getting this rare man, so blessed "with a face," elected. For it is Mailer's belief that this essay, a product of his "Faustian" pact with "Mephisto," was the generative cause of Kennedy's small plurality over Nixon in the election. The rest of *The Presidential Papers* is a contemporaneous critique (with the blood, sweat, and tears of immediate response staining the pages) of "the Kennedy years," that ambiguous and perhaps despair-making historical return on its author's original existential wager.

Of all the fine pieces following, perhaps the most memorable is the essay on the Patterson-Liston fight, subtitled "Death." This essay is many things: It is a skillful piece of evocative journalism about an actual event; a symbolist's reading of the forces at war in the submerged psyche of America; a strange, oblique prophecy, through a poet's analysis of the attrition and inevitable doom of the spirit of American liberal idealism, of Kennedy's assassination. It is also a gaily profound exploration of the absurdity, and perhaps the peril, awaiting the writer as performing tragic-comedian whose ambition is to ride at the same time both bright Pegasus and the dark horses of wrath. But if the end — or "seed" — of life is life itself, then that effort must be made in spite of all hazard: "To believe the impossible may be won," Mailer writes elsewhere in *The Presidential Papers*, "creates a strength from which the impossible may be attacked." And in our time, though the memory of "God" and the light may shape ultimate heroic purpose, the hero draws nourishment for his "humanism" (a favorite recurring word of Mailer's) from the devil's realm, venturing ever more deeply — as Mailer does in the barbarous poems and scatological dialogues collected in *Cannibals and Christians* — into the territories of darkness.

*Cannibals and Christians*, published in 1966, is not so good a book as its two omnibus predecessors, though it has its bright spots, such as the piece on Goldwater's nomination and the temptation it wakens in its author to ride this newest bandwagon of the devil. The drama of self-discovery and re-creation, which gave unity to the brilliance and variety of *Advertisements* and *Papers*, is slowed and muffled in *Cannibals* by the didactic accents of the guru who gazes upon a vision that is cooling toward dogma and repetition. But it is perhaps understandable that the imaginative breakthrough represented by *An American Dream* should be followed by a somewhat studious contemplation of the truths revealed, for something more than half of the stuff of *Cannibals* was written shortly after *Dream*. Mailer himself seems to be aware of the condition. Written in a time of "plague" and under a lurid cloud of apocalyptic expectations, the collection is concerned with themes, he says, more appropriate to a novel. He feels again the impulse to "go back to that long novel, announced six years ago, and changed in the mind by all of seven years." *Cannibals*, he reflects, may be the last such collection for a while.

Since *Cannibals*, in addition to publishing *Why Are We in Vietnam?* Mailer has produced off Broadway his dramatization of *The Deer Park*, a crisply successful play in which a much clearer and more effective Sergius O'Shaugnessy has been purchased at the expense of the novel's richly internal realization of Eitel and Elena. He has also directed, produced, and starred in two full-length "existential" films of his own conceiving. The requisite honors have begun, belatedly, to come his way: in 1967 he was elected to the National Institute of Arts and Letters. And in October of the same year, this author of twelve books, father of six children, and veteran of four wives — "heroines all," he has gallantly affirmed — proved his continued interest in the public life of his time by getting himself arrested, jailed, and fined for an act of civil disobedience in the great Washington demonstrations against the war in Vietnam.

The immediate result of this was *The Armies of the Night*, published in the spring of 1968, a kind of autobiographical novel with a protagonist called "Mailer" who is at once an absurd citizen of "technology-land" in crisis and a bard of the bright dream that lies behind the thickening miasmas of the betrayed and perishing republic. It is unquestionably one of Mailer's best books — passionate, humorous, acutely intelligent, and, as always, eloquent in its empathy with the drift of history. It has new riches in it, too, of a more incidental kind, such as a gallery of sharply intimate verbal cartoons, highlighted with the reflected pigments of Mailer's own uniquely anxious self-image, of such primary men of our moment as Robert Lowell, Dwight Macdonald, and Paul Goodman. But most striking of all are its undercurrents of a softer emotion than we have been used to finding in Mailer, a new tenderness for life that lets him muse warmly along the way on his troubled love for his wife, his children, his mythic America. There is even a touch of nostalgic religious craving in it, a small recurring thirst for "Christ." But though the texture of feeling is more varied, the old Mailer, familiarly gravid with the epic furies and ambitions of a diminutive Brooklyn Achilles, still prevails:

> Mailer, looking back, thought bitter words he would not say: "You, Lowell, beloved poet of many, what do you know of the dirt and the dark deliveries of the necessary? What do you know of dignity hard-achieved, and dignity lost through innocence, and dignity lost by sacrifice for a cause one cannot name? What do you know about getting fat against your will, and turning into a clown of an arriviste baron when you would rather be an eagle or a count, or rarest of all, some natural aristocrat from these damned democratic states? No, the only subject we share, you and I, is that species of perception which shows that if we are not very loyal to our unendurable and most exigent inner light, then some day we may burn. How dare you condemn me! . . . How dare you scorn the explosive I employ?"

Lowell falls backward at this moment in the narrative, a noble Hector going bump on his head, as if toppled by the lightning bolt of his adversary's thought. Though *The Armies of the Night* is tempered with new softnesses and warmths, such passages would deter one from concluding too easily that Mailer may be getting ready to write his hymn of reconciliation–his *Tempest* or "Lapis Lazuli," his *Billy Budd* or *Old Man and the Sea.*

Good as *The Armies of the Night* is, and prolific in a variety of media as Mailer has been in the last decade, the great opus so long ago announced remains unachieved. Are such varied and frequent detours from the high road of novel-writing threatening, at this prime of his creative life, the ultimate dissipation of Mailer's talent as a major writer? This already familiar question was raised yet again by an interviewer in *Playboy* for January 1968.* Mailer answered that the pattern of his career was dictated by his instinctive feeling that "the best way to grow was not to write one novel after another but to move from activity to activity, a notion that began with Renaissance man." He does not mention the example of Milton, but he might as well have. Then, coming down off the high horse of the moment's rhetoric, he adds genially, "It's not my idea, after all."

He is, of course, right both about himself and about "the tradition." With the romantic movement the imaginative writer became alienated from public life. Next, under the neoclassical reactive pressure of modernist formalism, he became in a sense alienated even from his work — which was not to be an utterance but an object, a product of the "impersonal" operations of imagination. With this background in view, it is clear that Mailer's uniqueness as a mid-century writer lies in his conscious cultivation, in the manner of Yeats, of a dynamic interrelation between his art and his life-style. Intensely himself, he is nevertheless the writer reborn in the dimension of public man. Engorged with the inclusive themes of his age and his nation, his work is nevertheless deeply personal. "I've been working on one book most of my life," he

* Published in this collection. [Ed.]

told the *Playboy* interviewer. "Probably since I started with *Barbary Shore*, certainly with and since *The Deer Park*, I've been working on one book." As he tells us in the introduction to *Cannibals and Christians*, he is, like Lawrence, Henry Miller, and Hemingway, writing "one continuing book . . . of [his] life and the vision of [his] existence." He might also have mentioned Fitzgerald, whom he resembles in this respect as well as in many others, including his sense of the integral relation between the moral health of the artist and the quality of his art conceived as "style." "A really good style," said Mailer in his *Paris Review* interview of 1964, as if in echo of a dozen similar testimonies by Fitzgerald, "comes only when a man has become as good as he can be. Style is character."

"Style," broadly understood as the individual humane stance a writer chooses to take in relation to his material along its whole spectrum from language to vision, is perhaps the judgmental critic's most useful tool in approaching such a writer. For both the strengths and weaknesses of Mailer's work are the products of his unique commitment to being as "good," and thus as creative, a man as he can.

As recently as the early sixties, fairly literate people — often critics and teachers — were still saying that though Mailer certainly had a novelist's gift he "couldn't write." He was in their minds a kind of James Jones who, with no appropriate arsenal of sophistication, had gone adventuring into frontier territories of the imagination and was never heard of again. "I can't read him any more," they would say; and it was at least evident that these people who made themselves responsible for keeping up with Bellow and Malamud, Styron and Barth — current writers favored with recognition by the critical establishment — *weren't* reading him, whether or not they *couldn't* read him. To them he was at once nuttier than D. H. Lawrence, dumber than Sinclair Lewis, artistically more unselective even than Thomas Wolfe, these faults clumsily wrapped in a style a good deal more wooden and awkward than Dreiser's. Because they weren't reading him it wasn't possible to argue with any hope of success that his "beliefs" were the poetical vehicles of a metaphysician's speculative insights; that he was the only important novelist on the American scene who was also an authentic and sophisticated intellectual; that if he was temperamentally the inclusive artist, he was also deftly capable of the lean and compact virtuoso performance; and that his style — ranging the spectrum from slang to sublimity — was a distillate of all the rest into a shimmering and variegated brilliancy of words. An example from *The Armies of the Night*:

> There was an aesthetic economy to symbolic gestures — you must not repeat yourself. Arrested once, TV land would accept him (conceivably) as a man willing to stand up for his ideas; get busted twice on the same day, and they would view him as a freak-out panting for arrest. (Mailer's habit of living — no matter how unsuccessfully — with his image, was so ingrained by now, that like a dutiful spouse he was forever consulting his better half.)

This is the style incisive, the author cutting an idea down to the gem of epigram at its center. An example from *The Presidential Papers*:

> It is the wisdom of a man who senses death within him and gambles that he can cure it by risking his life. It is the therapy of the instinct, and who is so wise as to call it irrational? Before he went into the Navy, Kennedy had been ailing. Washed out of Freshman year at Princeton by a prolonged trough of yellow jaundice, sick for a year at Harvard, weak already in the back from an injury at football, his trials suggest the self-hatred of a man whose resentment and ambition are too large for his body. Not everyone can discharge their furies on an analyst's couch, for some angers can be relaxed only by winning power, some rages are sufficiently monumental to demand that one try to become a hero or else fall back into that death which is already within

the cells. But if one succeeds, the energy aroused can be exceptional. . . . One thinks of that three-mile swim with the belt in his mouth and McMahon holding it behind him. There are pestilences which sit in the mouth and rot the teeth — in those five hours how much of the psyche must have been remade, for to give vent to the bite in one's jaws and yet use that rage to save a life: it is not so very many men who have the apocalyptic sense that heroism is the First Doctor. . . . With such a man in office the myth of the nation would again be engaged. . . .

This is the style progenitive, the author pushing out from the central root-and-trunk idea a branch-bud-and-leaf exfoliation of confirmatory images.

Mailer's style is a style of eddying gusts and pointed audible silences textured on a background of the musing, ruminating, wondering human voice. Voice is the style's medium; its creative means are the instrumentalities of wit and amplification. Its end is to disclose, through dynamic interplay of the reciprocal rhetorics of incision and proliferation, the submerged realities of experience. Through implosion and explosion of the facts and patterns of common life, it intends to force a new vision upon the reader — to transform him, galvanize him, free him to become the vehicle of apocalypse. It is predictable that an imagination so metaphysically ambitious as Mailer's should generate fictions which, though open-ended and loosely shaped, contain a dense internal unity of interlocking analogies, and that that unity should be mirrored in a prose coordinately dense with analogizing metaphor.

Mailer's style of imagination is a *forcing* style: it exerts *force* upon reality; it seeks to *force* reality into the matrix of an idiosyncratic vision. This *urgency* is the key to Mailer's most prominent strengths: the relentless energy of desperation which makes *An American Dream* a single breathless action, and gathers the many moods and modes of *Advertisements* into a sharply unified portrait of the artist as a young man fighting the demons of crack-up; the monumentality of certain of his chief theme-bearing characters — John F. Kennedy and Herman Teppis, Sonny Liston and Deborah Kelly Rojack — who remain in the memory as vivid larger-than-life creatures of myth; and the fluency everywhere, from the close, sharp lash of the goading scatologist to the barrel-toned magniloquence of the bard.

But these strengths are shadowed by related weaknesses: a dulling of awareness through a persistence in urgency that is too relentless; a flatness, stockness, vagueness in characterization often, when the fictionist in the author inevitably capitulates to the didact; and a tendency to flatulence, garrulousness, clotted heaviness, that threatens to choke the naturally vigorous life of the prose. One is irritated, and finally deafened, by the sadomasochistic acid-head bebop and chowder mannerisms of D. J. Jethroe's nonstop answer to the question, Why Are We in Vietnam? — though there are "good things" in this work, and tightened up it might have made a memorable short story or novella. Sergius O'Shaugnessy is disastrously vague, and Marion Faye is flat; their central moral significance in *The Deer Park* is diminished to abstraction and formula by their failure to be as human as the roundly conceived moral cripples surrounding them in the populous world of Desert D'Or. (Collie Munshin is a pretty bloom of humanity by comparison.) And the ingenious dialogues on the metaphysics of death and excrement in *The Presidential Papers* and *Cannibals and Christians* are, when all is said and done, overextended and boring. And boring is, of course, one of the most undesirable things you can be in the Mailer canon of humane values. These qualities represent a temptation perhaps innate to Mailer's kind of sensibility. In *The Armies of the Night*, for example, he is attracted by the idea of "a short novel about a young American leading a double life in college as a secret policeman." Such a novel might be somewhat less vulnerable to prefabricated literary patterning than *Vietnam* (father-son tensions, heterosexual-homosexual tensions, man-beast tensions, all framed in a "significant" Texas-Alaska polar symbology); but even so it would threaten to become an "idea for a novel novel" (a useful phrase adapted from Donald Hall) — something quite "made up" and possibly *forced*.

Toward the end of *The Armies of the Night*, Mailer writes of his feelings upon his release from jail after the demonstrations in Washington: "yes, in this resumption of the open air after twenty-four hours, no more, there was a sweet clean edge to the core of the substance of things — *a monumentally abstract remark which may be saved by the concrete observation* that the air was good in his lungs . . . [my italics]." The bard, perhaps wearied by labor too large and prolonged, has mauled a small bright human fact with the dull brutality of abstraction; and "Mailer," throwing off the robes of office, rebukes his alter ego for this crime against nature.

Mailer once wrote a story called "The Paper House," one of the conventionally "realistic" stories of the early 1950's that he does not take very seriously now, which is all about how reality takes its vengeance upon the criminal abstractionist. The setting is Japan. An arrogant, boorish, and selfish GI named Hayes is unsparingly loved by Yuriko, a geisha uncommonly endowed with dignity as well as tenderness. By night he nourishes upon her love. By day he is the thorough cynic: "crap" is what he calls the unhappy story of her family's misfortunes, her indenturing to training and service, and her final and staunch pride in earning the status of "first-class geisha." Crap: she is a common whore. He subconsciously wants to marry her, the natural concomitant in him of her unqualified love. But instead he drunkenly jeers at her: she is a common whore, and he will return to the States without her. When she responds by claiming him with increased vigor, he strikes and strips her, brutally humiliating her before her peers and their clients. Later, when he meekly returns, she is as warm with him as ever, but sad and a bit withdrawn. What does this mean? She must go on a journey very soon, somewhat before his own departure for the States. Where? he persists. Why? What sort of journey? Finally he learns: because she, a first-class geisha, has been publicly dishonored by her lover, she will commit hara-kiri. Crap! he cries in irritable disdain. He will speak no more of it. A whore is a whore! But through the days that follow, her familiar tender attentions are touched with silent grief. Though he does not deign to speak of her threat, inside he aches with dread. And on the appointed day he cannot hold himself back from going to her. He finds her dressed in white, "without ornament, and without makeup," pleased that he has come after all to say "Bye-bye." As she turns to go to her self-appointed justice, he catches her by the arm, crying, "You got to stop this. It's crap." "Crap-crap," says Yuriko in answer, giggling. And hidden all around, the other geishas echo, "Crap-crap." Hayes retreats, and the girls follow him, a massed march of laughing, bright-kimonoed angels of derision jeering the conquered bully through the town to the chorused tune of "Crap-crap, Crap-crap."

A memorably fine story in its own right (Mailer acknowledges indebtedness to Vance Bourjaily for the anecdote on which it is based), it is also a model of Mailer's vision of marriage (in the soul-dimension Hayes and Yuriko are already "married") as the ultimate battleground of the laws of strife that govern love and sexuality, and in turn all of life. Alternatively turned on its side, upended, and inverted, "The Paper House" becomes a paradigm of the love-as-soulmaking-or-soulbreaking-combat themes of *The Deer Park*, "The Time of Her Time," and *An American Dream*. But it can also be read as a paradigm of the larger operations of a yet more ultimate law. In sharp contrast to his tender and humane buddy who narrates the story, Hayes is terrified of empathy. His is the naturally totalitarian temperament, bellowing, pounding, *forcing* reality to the shape of his belief. But Yuriko, whose unreasoning love frightens him into his worst brutality, *is* reality. The dignity of her otherness will not bend; she will not, finally, be forced. Her suavely just humiliation of her lover is so satisfying because it is a *natural* justice. A perfect illustration of the penalties which in the natural scheme of things are levied against unrepentant abstractionists who sin, through violence or neglect, against the actual.

This formula may provide one explanation of why it is that some people "can't read" Mailer anymore, and why even those who can and do read him find themselves at times, especially when reading his fiction, fatigued, irritated, hankering after something which the apocalyptic apparatus of his imagination quite purposely extracts and draws off from his material so that no dilution will threaten the strong potion of his vision. Perhaps it is thanks to the just and beneficent workings of Yuriko's law that Mailer cannot finally succeed in this effort. Perhaps this explains why his best work, the work that moves as well as amazes, is his most "impure" — as in *The Deer Park,* where the mere presence of Charles Francis Eitel and Elena Esposito mocks, with the awesome poignant reality of their flawed selves and failed love, the unreality of Sergius O'Shaugnessy and Marion Faye, those stiff and faceless standard-bearers of the author's abstract redemptive "truth."

While Mailer has steadfastly refused to be apologetic about his journalism, he has equally steadfastly identified his highest goals as a writer with some major achievement as a novelist. In *The Armies of the Night* he is quite openly if good-humoredly annoyed by Robert Lowell's insistent praises of him as our greatest "journalist" at the same time he envies Lowell's quiet authority in the role of "poet." It is a fact, I think, that the large and responsive audience Mailer has now won at the close of the sixties would tend to agree, no doubt to the writer's chagrin, that his "best" work has been in nonfiction. In putting forth my own concurrence I would want to make clear that while I view *Barbary Shore* and *Why Are We in Vietnam?* as inferior achievements (they are "abstract" in my sense of the word: they busy themselves making points rather than peopling a world; and the mannerisms of their prose, portentous in one case, ranting in the other, are dubious compensation for this impoverishment), they nevertheless have interest and deserve respect in the total picture of Mailer's career as honorable attempts at experiment and innovation.

Granting the solid excellence — its truth of substance and feeling, as well as its art — of *The Naked and the Dead*, and the breathless virtuosity of *An American Dream*, only *The Deer Park* remains in the running for honors as a "great" novel. Its depth and breadth of imaginative engagement with our time, its acute and inclusive sensing of the way we live now, through deft selection of setting and symbol and deft portraiture of a dozen varied secondary characters that are real as well as symptomatic, make it impressive. But as we move toward the core of this book — the affair between Elena and Eitel — surely we move from the impressive into the field of force of something like "greatness." Eitel, the hero-gentleman demeaned by history, is a complex character of almost tangible reality; he has all the fullness of being that Fitzgerald could not finally give to Dick Diver. Elena, the soiled broad and dumb waif of petty disasters, is rich with an inner gift of instinctive warmth and natural dignity worthy of Cleopatra; she is one of the few great woman characters in American fiction after James. The delicate, tender persistence of Mailer's articulation of the life of their affair, its growth, flowering, deterioration, and crippled resolution, is rare and magnificent. It is the *real* "armature" of the book, despite Mailer's efforts to give that power to his prophets of new consciousness, Marion Faye and Sergius O'Shaugnessy. Because Sergius, like Lovett in *Barbary Shore*, seems neither intelligent nor sensitive nor good enough, nor even *visible* enough, to attract the friendship and confidence of a man like Eitel, we do not believe in him. But we cannot quite console ourselves by saying, with Lawrence, "Never trust the author, trust the tale," because we are distracted and fatigued as we read by the badgering of Mailer's forcing style of imagination — and the book's armature slows, finally, and falters. *The Deer Park*, one can say (Mailer's exactly opposite account of its shortcomings notwithstanding), was a potentially great novel flawed by an authorial excess of misled good intentions. It is perhaps yet another validation of Yuriko's law that what remains persistently alive in one's memory of *The Deer Park* is Eitel and Elena, and the real world, intimate and at large, of which they were the vital center.

In the middle 1950's Mailer professed a credo that would still seem to hold for him in the late 1960's:

> I suppose that the virtue I should like most to achieve as a writer is to be genuinely disturbing. . . . It is, I believe, the highest function a writer may serve, to see life (no matter by what means or form or experiment) as others do not see it, or only partially see it, and therefore open for the reader that literary experience which comes uniquely from the novel — the sense of having one's experience enlarged, one's perceptions deepened, and one's illusions about oneself rendered even more untenable. For me, this is the highest function of art, precisely that it is disturbing, that it does not let man rest, and therefore forces him so far as art may force anything to enlarge the horizons of his life.

It is clear that most of his work to date has been done in the light of this statement of principle, and it seems probable that it will continue to be, if only because it is the kind of principle that any serious novelist of whatever artistic or philosophic persuasion would be likely to subscribe to with dedication. But it could be argued that in his fiction, at least, Mailer has yet to write a book worthy of the strictest interpretation of his principle. If he eventually completes the multivolume quasi-epic of neo-Joycean structure and Burroughs-*cum*-Tolstoian substance that he has been promising these many years, it probably will not be the novel, any more than his others have been, that fulfills the high aims of this credo. If he is to write a truly "great" novel, it will be the product of some new, subtler, and perhaps unimaginably humbler synthesis of the gifts for which he has now come to be appreciated. Perhaps he will learn something from his readers' obstinate tendency to prefer his nonfiction, where, with no sacrifice of his skills and all benefit to the power of his vision, he is happily mired in reality, hobbled to the facts of time, place, self, as to an indispensable spouse of flesh and blood who continually saves him from his other self that yearns toward wasteful flirtations with *Spiritus Mundi*. In any case, he will have to come to know truly, if in his own way, the "Thou" to which the "I" of Martin Buber's world is inexorably wedded, and he will have to find his own style of that "negative capability" which Keats identified as the root of true imagination.

Perhaps Mailer would dismiss such cavils as typical of the solemnly moribund mentality of official literary criticism. And yet he might be reminded that the newly respectful concern with his work, represented even by such exceptions as these, is the natural harvest, sought or not, of his maverick persistence in his calling — and for Mailer writing has always been, literally, a "calling" — despite the years of criticism's ignorant undervaluation of him. He has finally forced criticism, which once dismissed him as a sensationalist barbarian egomaniac who couldn't write, to eat its own words, salted and spiced with the true savor of his actual achievements. Criticism has been made to confess at last that Mailer is a symbolist and mythmaker, the alchemy of his imagination being capable of turning excrement, madness, and perversion into lambent revelations of the condition of man and God; that he is a true intellectual — acute, sophisticated, and dead serious in his probing criticisms of the life of his time; that he is an extraordinary prose stylist in the big-voiced American tradition of Melville and Faulkner; and that he is fortunately endowed, as most apocalyptics are not, with the easing human graces of wit and humor. Even such a book as *Advertisements for Myself*, which at the time of its publication so outraged and embarrassed the critics with its naked revelations of its author's wounds and vanities, has now come to seem, in the manner of Fitzgerald's *Crack-up* essays, a nobly original undertaking of self-definition, moving in content and daring in execution. *Advertisements* represents the invention, furthermore, of a new form (let's call it, to borrow a current term that has been misapplied elsewhere, the "nonfiction novel"), a form that has since served him well in *The Presidential Papers, Cannibals and Christians,* and *The Armies of the Night,* and will no doubt continue to do so.

But if his readers continue to feel, with some validity, that in the light of "the tradition" Mailer is not the finished and fully responsible writer-as-*artist* that many of his peers are, it has become easier lately to answer with equal validity that he nevertheless satisfies again and again, as they do not, by surprise. Where critics once measured his failings by the more finished accomplishments of his peers, it is now possible to suggest measurement of the shortcomings of his peers by citing the obstinate vigor of Mailer's restless creativity. For example: we are now capable of thinking (however our words are chosen to express the thought) of Mailer's imaginative ingenuity, that it is never so depthless as Barth's can be; of his ambitious fluency of expression, that it is never so hollow and self-serving as Styron's penchant for "style" can become; of his ideas and his humanity, that they do not seem borrowed or "literary" as do, respectively, a large portion of Bellow's and Malamud's.

It may be that Mailer has succeeded in enlarging a little the range of literature in his time, and that in so doing he has measurably modified our view of "the tradition." What is at least certain is that simply by persisting in being what he must be, writing as he must write, he has taught many of his critics to think more justly about his work, to respond more accurately to it. And a friendly commentator, taking all these facts and speculations into account, could hope that the work Mailer does in the future will fully justify what a young English instructor, whose equivalent only a few years ago would have turned the corners of his mouth down at the mere mention of Mailer's name, said to me only days before these sentences were written — "He's about the best we've got going for us now."

# Norman Mailer: The Embattled Vision

## by Norman Podhoretz

Norman Mailer is one of the few postwar American writers in whom it is possible to detect the presence of qualities that powerfully suggest a major novelist in the making. Anyone trying to describe these qualities would be likely to dwell on Mailer's extraordinary technical skill, or on the boldness and energy of his mind, or on his readiness to try something new whenever he puts pen to paper. What seems even more remarkable, however, is that his work has responded to the largest problems of this period with a directness and an assurance that we rarely find in the novels of his contemporaries. Mailer is very much an American, but he appears to be endowed with the capacity for seeing himself as a battleground of history — a capacity that is usually associated with the French and that American writers are thought never to have. He is a man given to ideologies, a holder of extreme positions, and in this too he differs from the general run of his literary contemporaries, so many of whom have fled ideology to pursue an ideal of sensible moderation both in style and philosophy. To follow Mailer's career, therefore, is to witness a special drama of development, a drama in which the deepest consciousness of the postwar period has struggled to define itself in relation to the past, and to know itself in terms of the inescapable, ineluctable present.

Now for many people the only Mailer worth considering is Mailer the realist, and for these *The Naked and the Dead* is the only one of his three novels that matters at all. It is true, I think, that Mailer's phenomenal talent for recording the precise look and feel of things is his most impressive single gift, and there is some ground for arguing that in deserting realism he has made insufficient use of this power. But it was not by arbitrary choice that Mailer abandoned realism, any more than it was by arbitrary choice that he wrote as a realist in the first place. Far from merely being a technique selected for its suitability to the author's talents, the realism of *The Naked and the Dead* is in itself an expression of his response to a certain structure of experience. The world of *The Naked and the Dead* is one in which a varied group of clearly defined individuals are pitted in a very direct and simple way against two allied enemies — the army and nature. Nature brings violent storms and intolerable heat, it provides jungles to be crossed and mountains to be climbed, and it also sets limits to the physical strength of the men exposed to its rigors. The army, on the other hand, is a society, tightly organized, efficiently ruled, and almost as confident of its power as nature itself. From the point of view of the individual, driven by a hunger for absolute freedom, hardly any distinction can be drawn between them. Just as nature threatens him with pain and fear and death, so the army threatens him with moral destruction, aiming finally to destroy his will altogether and reduce him to a mere servant of its own ends. To keep himself alive physically, he must be strong, resourceful, and determined; to keep himself alive spiritually, he must have enormous reserves of inner resistance.

This was an ideal situation for a writer with Mailer's natural gift of observation. Something palpable was there to describe and he described it brilliantly, down to the last quiver of a particular muscle in a man's thigh as he was climbing the face of a rock, down to the last twitch of temptation as he was saying no to an offer of promotion. The availability of a great literary tradition — a tradition which had itself developed out of just such situations in an age when society seemed as solid and substantial and unshakable as the army is in *The Naked and the Dead* — certainly helps to explain how it came about that a first novel by a young man of twenty-five should have exhibited mastery of so high an order. But there is more to the success of the best passages in *The Naked and the Dead* than a happy confrontation of talent, circumstance, and tradition. The rainstorm that descends on Anopopei shortly after the division has landed, the episode in which the platoon drags four huge guns through the muddy jungle in the black of night, the climb up Mt. Anaka — all these are so good and so moving because they are written by someone who in the deepest reaches of his being believes that the world is made up exclusively of stone walls and that life consists in a perpetual crashing of the head against them. It is as though the war provided Mailer with a never-ending succession of examples that confirmed everything he had ever felt or thought about human existence, and one can almost detect the relish with which he piled up the evidence in scene after astonishing scene.

*The Naked and the Dead*, however, cannot simply be read as an expression of Mailer's feelings about life in general; it also attempts to make certain specific statements about World

War II, the American army, and the character of American society. In 1948 Mailer — who was shortly to become a leading figure in Henry Wallace's campaign for the Presidency — subscribed to the notion that our postwar difficulties with Russia were the sole responsibility of American capitalism. We had gone to war against Hitler not because the American ruling class was antifascist, but because Hitler had shown himself unwilling to play the capitalist game according to the rules, and the next step was to dispose of Russia, the only remaining obstacle on the road to total power. World War II, then, was the first phase of a more ambitious operation, while the army had been used as a laboratory of fascism, a preview of the kind of society that the American ruling class was preparing for the future. These ideas are brought into *The Naked and the Dead* in various ways. Some of them emerge from the long discussions between General Cummings (the commander of the division that has invaded the island of Anopopei) and his young aide Lt. Hearn (a rich Midwesterner whose political sympathies are with the left and whom Cummings is trying to convert to his own special brand of fascism). Another channel is supplied by the "Time Machine" flashbacks, which are there partly in order to demonstrate Mailer's contention that American society is essentially a disguised and inchoate form of the army. But it is in the main line of the plot that the politics of the novel are most heavily emphasized. The scheme of *The Naked and the Dead* is to follow a single campaign from the preparations for invasion to the mopping-up operation, and the technique is to shift back and forth between command headquarters and one small platoon in the division. This enables Mailer to observe the campaign both through the eyes of the man who is running it and in terms of the day-to-day fortunes of those who are affected in the most immediate way by his every move. The experience of the enlisted men serves throughout as an ironic commentary on the general's behavior, but the irony becomes most pronounced in the last third

*63*

of the novel when Cummings decides to send a patrol to the rear of the Japanese positions for the purpose of determining the feasibility of a daring new plan that he has just conceived. This decision, prompted not by the interests of victory but by vanity and opportunism, results in the death of three men and in immeasurable misery for several others — all of it wasted. Even after the Japanese have surrendered, the patrol (which has not yet heard the news) is still being dragged up Mt. Anaka, again ostensibly in the interests of victory but really in order to further the mad ambitions of the platoon sergeant, Croft.

The army, then, is evil and the individual caught in its grip has only two basic choices: he can either submit without resistance (and eventually be led into identifying himself with his persecutors) or he can try to maintain at least a minimum of spiritual independence. To be sure, there are many degrees of submission, from Stanley's abject brownnosing to Wilson's easygoing indifference, but only one character among the enlisted men in the book is still completely unbroken by the time we come upon them: the ex-hobo Red Valsen. As for the officers, they are all (with the exception of Hearn) willing instruments of the evil power embodied in Cummings. Like Cummings and Croft, Hearn and Valsen represent the same principle on different levels of articulation and self-consciousness: they are rebels who do what they have to do but who will not permit their minds or their feelings to be drawn into collaboration with the system. The army proves too strong even for them, however, and ultimately both men are beaten down in much the same fashion.

Mailer's intentions are thus perfectly clear. Cummings and Croft exemplify the army's ruthlessness and cruelty, its fierce purposefulness and its irresistible will to power, while Hearn and Valsen together make up a picture of the rebellious individual who, for all *his* determination and courage, is finally defeated in an unequal contest. But no sooner do we become aware of this intention than we notice that there are forces at work in the novel whose effect is to subvert the general scheme. The most insidious of these, perhaps, is Mailer's tone: *The Naked and the Dead* simply does not *sound* like a book drawing up an angry indictment, though the things it says explicitly provide plenty of ground for indignation. The tone, indeed, is rather more disinterested than partisan; it is the tone of a man whose capacity for political indignation is inhibited by a keen sense of the world as a very complicated place, not easily to be understood by grand formulas. And the strength of this sense manifests itself unmistakably in Mailer's treatment of Valsen and Hearn, who turn out to be less sympathetic than their role in the general scheme would seem to require, just as Cummings and Croft somehow develop into more admirable figures than they were ever meant to be.

Hearn, the rich Harvard graduate, and Valsen, the penniless hobo, have a great deal in common. They are both incapable of attaching themselves to anything or anyone, and they share the nihilistic belief that "everything is crapped up, everything is phony, everything curdles when you touch it." Their rebellion against the system is sterile and ineffective, for it involves nothing more than a determination to preserve their "inviolate freedom," as Hearn puts it, "from . . . the wants and sores that caught up everybody [else]." What Mailer tells us in a key passage about Hearn is also true of Valsen: "The only thing to do is to get by on style. He had said that once, lived by it in the absence of anything else. . . . The only thing that had been important was to let no one in any ultimate issue ever violate your integrity." Style without content, a vague ideal of personal integrity, a fear of attachment, and a surly nihilistic view of the world are not enough to save a man in the long run from the likes of Cummings and Croft, and certainly not enough to endow him with heroic stature — and Mailer knows it. His desperate effort to redeem Hearn toward the end comes too late and in any case lacks conviction: perhaps the weakest passage in the whole novel is the one dealing with Hearn's decision on the night before he is killed to resign his commission and take a principled stand against everything that Cummings represents.

The same desperation shows through Mailer's effort to deflate Cummings and Croft. Like Valsen and Hearn, the platoon sergeant and the general have so much in common that they seem to be the same person in two different incarnations. They are both immensely competent; they are both very brave; they are both contemptuous of weakness; they both suffer from a sexually determined hunger to dominate. Most important of all, what they are both pursuing is the dream of absolute freedom, the dream of exercising will without obstruction or limit. Man, Cummings tells Hearn, is a being "in transit between brute and God," and his deepest urge is to "achieve God." It is this urge that drives Croft to drag the platoon up Mt. Anaka, just as it provokes Cummings to feats of military brilliance. But it is also what establishes the two men as the *natural* heroes of *The Naked and the Dead*. If life is truly what *The Naked and the Dead* shows it to be — a fierce battle between the individual will and all the many things that resist it — then heroism must consist in a combination of strength, courage, drive, and stamina such as Cummings and Croft exhibit and that Hearn and Valsen conspicuously lack. Moreover, Cummings and Croft are the only characters who point to anything like an adequate response to life as we see it in the novel. They are, of course, reactionaries, but they demonstrate (as reactionaries often do) the workings of the radical spirit — which is to say that the principle of their behavior is a refusal to accept the limitations inherent in any given situation as final, a refusal stemming from the conviction that the situation itself need not be regarded as final in advance. The trouble with Hearn and Valsen is their inability to transcend the terms of the given; they know perfectly well that these terms are intolerable, yet they cannot envisage any conditions other than the ones before their eyes, and therefore they are reduced to apathy, cynicism, and despair. Croft and Cummings also know that the terms are intolerable, but the knowledge acts as a stimulus to their energies and a goad to their imagination. Though the laws of nature seem to prohibit a man from climbing to the top of Mt. Anaka, Croft, who cannot bear to remain imprisoned within the boundaries of what has already been accomplished, dares to attempt the climb, while Hearn and Valsen shrug helplessly at the sight of the peaks: like liberalism itself, they lack the vision and the drive to push toward the top of the mountain. All this being the case, Mailer either had to give up his liberalism or forcibly prevent Croft and Cummings from running away with *The Naked and the Dead* altogether. Because he was not yet ready to write liberalism off and because it seemed impossible to find virtue in Cummings and Croft without also finding virtue in fascism, he had no alternative but to violate the emotional logic of his novel by destroying them as best he could. The destruction of Croft is spread thin throughout the novel, but the disposal of Cummings is only effected at the end, when Mailer contrives by a shocking twist of plot to rob him of credit for winning the campaign.

*The Naked and the Dead,* then, shows an exceptionally gifted young writer in the years immediately after the war discovering what he did not know he knew — that American liberalism is bankrupt because it cannot provide an answer to the challenge with which history has presented it. Not only does liberalism confine itself to the terms of the given at a time when there can be no hope of working within these terms, but it is animated by a vision of the world that neither calls forth heroic activity nor values the qualities of courage, daring, and will that make for the expansion of the human spirit. In the "absence of anything else," however, and out of his awareness that it was impossible to "get by on style" as so many intellectuals of his generation were trying to do, Mailer held on stubbornly to his liberal views, even as he was beginning to recognize that his real values tended in an antiliberal direction. So little, indeed, did liberalism affect his deepest judgments that the most compassionate writing in *The Naked and the Dead* is devoted to the tribulations of the pathological anti-Semite Gallagher when he receives the news of his wife's death in childbirth. Fascist or no fascist, Gallagher is a violent, passionate man, and this was enough to turn the balance in his favor, just as the timidity and mediocrity of Roth, Wyman, and Brown are the decisive factors in the adverse judgment Mailer passes on them. Ultimately what Mailer was looking for — and has continued to look for — is not so much a more equitable world as a more exciting one, a world that produces men of size and a life of huge possibility, and this was nowhere to be found in the kind of liberalism to which he committed himself in the earliest phase of his literary career.

It is characteristic of Mailer — and, I believe, of the essence of his strength as a novelist — that he never pays much attention to intellectual fashion. In 1948, when everyone of any sophistication understood that Henry Wallace had been duped by the Communists, Mailer was campaigning vigorously for the Progressive party, and if this amounted to a confession of political naïveté, it also exhibited a healthy reluctance on his part to be guided by the experience of others. He must always work everything out for himself and by himself, as though it were up to him to create the world anew over and over again in his own experience. He abandoned what was then being called "unreconstructed" liberalism only when he could see at first hand why it was wrong to support it, and even then he did so in his own good time and for his own special reasons. Certainly he must be the sole American example of a liberal who responded to the cold war by rushing to embrace revolutionary socialism. There was nothing "nostalgic" about Mailer's new radicalism; only a man who had been affected by Marx and Trotsky down to the core would have been capable of writing *Barbary Shore*, and it is because he was so profoundly affected that he could blithely ignore all the good arguments against Marx and Trotsky that were in currency at the time. It would be impossible to guess from a reading of this novel that the case it constructs with such loving care had ever been challenged or refuted or in the least damaged. Nor would it be easy to guess that objective conditions played their own imperturbable part in the breakup of revolutionary socialism as an active political movement. Everything in *Barbary Shore* seems to hang on the will of the people involved, and in this sense Mailer is right to describe the book as "existentialist" in spirit.

In Marx and Trotsky, Mailer found a system that brought the courage, vision, and uncompromising determination of Cummings and Croft into the service of freedom and equality rather than class and privilege, and consequently there is no conflict between idea and feeling in *Barbary Shore* of the kind we have seen operating in *The Naked and the Dead*. But if *Barbary Shore* exhibits an almost perfect internal coherence, it also suffers from a certain straining for effect, a certain shrillness and melodramatic solemnity of tone often verging on the pretentious that contrast very sharply with the flawless pitch of *The Naked and the Dead*. The source of this trouble seems to be Mailer's unwillingness to make any use whatever of the techniques he learned to handle so well in *The Naked and the Dead* and his attempt to write in a completely new style. Here again we see him beginning from scratch, repudiating the help of his own past as vigorously as he repudiates the help of everyone else's. But there is more to Mailer's desertion of realism than that. To write realistic fiction a novelist must believe that society is what it seems to be and that it reveals the truth about itself in the personalities it throws up, the buildings it builds, the habits and manners it fosters; all the writer need do is describe these faithfully, selecting whatever details seem to him most sharply revealing and significant, and the truth will be served. But Mailer's point in *Barbary Shore* is precisely that our society is *not* what it seems to be. It seems to be prosperous, vigorous, sure of itself, and purposeful, whereas in fact it is apathetic, confused, inept, empty, and in the grip of invisible forces that it neither recognizes nor controls. To write about this society as though the truth of it lay embedded in its surface appearances would be to endow it with a solidity and substantiality that it simply does not possess. The only hope of making any sense of such a society is with reference to the invisible forces that work in and through it and that cannot be described but that can be talked about abstractly and pictured allegorically. In delineating the world of the cold war, then, what Mailer tries to do is convey a sense of the strangeness of the way things are and to evoke a feeling for the overpowering reality of the invisible forces that supply a key to this strangeness.

Since an extremely bad press and a climate unfavorable to political radicalism resulted in a tiny readership for *Barbary Shore*, let me summarize its plot briefly before making any further observations. Most of the action takes place in a rooming house in Brooklyn Heights which turns out to be the refuge of a man calling himself McLeod, who — we eventually learn — had once been notorious throughout the world as the "Hangman of the Left Opposition." After breaking with the Communist party on the signing of the Nazi-Soviet pact, McLeod had come to the United States to work for the State Department and had subsequently run off again, this time to devote himself to a Marxist analysis of why the revolution went wrong. An FBI agent, Hollingsworth, is also living in the rooming house under an assumed identity, and the plot centers around his efforts to recover a mysterious "little object" which had disappeared from the State Department along with McLeod. Neither Hollingsworth nor anyone else knows what the "little object" is, but he assumes that it must be worth a fortune and is planning to steal it himself once he gets it away from McLeod. The landlady, Guinevere, a former burlesque queen secretly married to McLeod, is in league with Hollingsworth, and he also has the help of a girl named Lannie Madison who had literally been driven out of her mind by the assassination of Trotsky and who hates McLeod because he is the "undertaker of the revolution." The story is told by another tenant, Michael Lovett, a would-be novelist who is a victim of total amnesia and so can remember nothing whatever of his past but who, it develops, had been almost as deeply involved in the Trotskyite movement as Lannie. In the end, Lovett decides to devote his life once again to the hopes that had been shattered for him by the wartime collapse of revolutionary socialism, and this decision makes it possible for McLeod to pass the "little object" on to him instead of surrendering it to Hollingsworth, as he had finally agreed to do. In a rather hasty climax, McLeod commits suicide, Hollingsworth runs off with Guinevere before the police arrive, and Lannie is taken into custody. Lovett is left alone with McLeod's will and the "little object," charged with the responsibility of keeping the flame of "socialist culture" alive while he waits for the apocalyptic war that is inevitably to come, hoping against hope that out of the conflagration a new opportunity may arise for realizing the goals that were betrayed in the first great revolution of this century.

*Barbary Shore* is obviously an allegory, but of what? Most of the reviewers in 1951 took it to be an extravagant view of McCarthyism, but McCarthyism as such is actually a negligible element in the book. Mailer's real subject is the effect on modern life of the failure of the Russian revolution, and if there is an extravagant assumption at work in *Barbary Shore*, it is that *all* our difficulties (political, spiritual, psychological, and sexual) are directly traceable to this failure. "The growth of human consciousness in this century demanded — for its expanding vitality — that a revolution be made," Mailer

wrote some years later, and in this sentence, I think, we have
the key to *Barbary Shore*. The Russian revolution figures here
not as one important historical event among many but (in the
words of Lovett) as "the greatest event in man's history," the
culmination of an evolutionary process dictated by the inner
necessities of the human spirit. The race, in Mailer's view,
must either grow into greater possibilities or retreat into less;
there can be no stagnation. But the retreat into less is not
merely a matter of shrinking or cowering; it involves a disrup-
tion of the whole organism, a radical dislocation — it is a
disease that infects the life of individuals no less than the
behavior of nations. *Barbary Shore* is an investigation of this
disease, a pathology of the modern spirit.

The two characters in the book who have been most directly
affected by the failure of the revolution are Lovett and Lannie. After his first political discussion with McLeod, Lovett
begins to recall his days as a member of a Trotskyite study
group, and he describes them in a remarkably evocative passage:

> I was young then, and no dedication could match mine. The
> revolution was tomorrow, and the inevitable crises of capi-
> talism ticked away in my mind with the certainty of a time
> bomb, and even then could never begin to match the ticking
> of my pulse. . . . For a winter and a spring I lived more
> intensely in the past than I could ever in the present, until
> the sight of a policeman on his mount became the Petrograd
> proletariat crawling to fame between the legs of a Cossack's
> horse. . . . There was never a revolution to equal it, and
> never a city more glorious than Petrograd.

Lovett's amnesia is the consequence of the death of this passion, and its effect has been to cut him off from everything,
including his own experience. He represents the modern consciousness, and the weird unfamiliar world that we see
through his eyes is in fact intended as a picture of the world
we all inhabit. In Lannie, we get an image of the modern

72

consciousness in its most violently pathological aspect. The loss of hope in her case has taken the form of guilt for having presumed to think "that there was a world we could make," and her insanity consists in a total surrender to the given — submitting herself with grim enthusiasm to the brutal handling of Hollingsworth and to the bewildered narcissism of Guinevere. This surrender constitutes insanity because the given (as Lannie herself says in an extraordinary outburst to Lovett) is a world whose nature has been most sharply revealed in the Nazi death camps. What follows from the surrender, moreover, is a frantic attempt to reinterpret the moral meaning of things: "There is neither guilt nor innocence," she tells Lovett, "but there is vigor in what we do or the lack of it," and it is in Hollingsworth and Guinevere that she imagines she sees vigor. Hollingsworth she believes to be strong and purposeful, for to her he is the embodiment of those who now rule the earth, while to the raucous, grotesque, and vulgar Guinevere she makes her sick love, calling what Guinevere symbolizes good and beautiful and begging it to discover its goodness and beauty in her eyes, just as she wants only for the powerful to discover their strength in exercising it upon her.

If Lannie and Lovett together make up a picture of the modern consciousness, Guinevere and Hollingsworth must be regarded as different aspects of the disease engendered by the failure of the revolution. Nothing could be more fantastic than the way everyone takes Guinevere to be the fulfillment of his own special desires. Her vitality, however, is only superficial, the air of abundance about her is a lie, and she lacks the wherewithal to deliver on her vast promise. Given all this, I would suggest that she figures in the allegorical scheme as an image of the life outside politics, the attempt to live by and for self, the purely private life, and that she is Mailer's comment on the sorry possibilities of such a life in America today.

Hollingsworth's role is easier to formulate, since it is described explicitly by McLeod in an analysis of the forces that make the Third World War inevitable. Today, he says, "the aim of society is no longer to keep its members alive, but quite the contrary, the question is how to dispose of them." This is "the first stage of cannibalism" in a process leading inexorably to the destruction of the world, and it expresses itself initially in the rise of a class of bureaucrats who come to power "at the very moment they are in the act of destroying themselves." Far from being strong and purposeful, then, Hollingsworth is the creature of conditions he neither controls nor comprehends and the victim of inner compulsions he neither respects nor recognizes. Sick with greed and with homosexual longings, he can only find relief in outbursts of petty sadism and in the symbolic seduction of McLeod (whose crimes, Lannie declares at one point, were responsible for his very existence). Mailer, however, gives him a moment of genuine self-consciousness in which, like a character in poetic drama, he is suddenly permitted to enunciate the principle of his own being with force and conviction:

> More modesty. We ain't equipped to deal with big things. If this fellow came to me and asked my advice, I would take him aside and let him know that if he gives up the pursuits of vanity, and acts like everybody else, he'd get along better. Cause we never know what's deep down inside us . . . and it plays tricks. I don't give two cents for all your papers. A good-time Charley, that's myself, and that's why I'm smarter than the lot of you.

This is the doctrine by which the disease being investigated through Guinevere and Hollingsworth calls itself health and by which the blindness to reality that is one of its major symptoms claims the right to be known as "realism."

At the center of *Barbary Shore* stands McLeod, the incarnation of the revolutionary spirit itself. His biography amounts to a moral history of that spirit — its early achievements, its subsequent crimes, its temporary abdication, and then its agonized attempt to find new strength by a humble return to "theory." The "little object" that McLeod has stolen from the State Department is never identified, but we can be fairly confident in thinking of it as Hope or Dedication or Vision or a "coagulation" of all three — the loss of it is what accounts for the gradual and subtle derangement of the system and the possession of it by this lone individual entails the most fearful of responsibilities. Vision and hope and dedication, at any rate, are the qualities that separate McLeod from all the other characters and that finally enable him to jolt Lovett out of his stupor and to win the support of Lannie. By the rigorous terms set up in *Barbary Shore* he points to the only possible course left to the modern consciousness — which is to hold on with all its might to the "little object" while crying a plague on both your houses to the two contending powers in the cold war who are irrevocably committed to the cause of death. The heritage McLeod passes on is a feeble thing, but it means feeling for Lovett where there was apathy before and relatedness where there was absolute isolation.

What it meant for Mailer, however, was another matter entirely, since the grand heroic life he was looking for could no more be found in revolutionary socialism than in liberalism. If the one is bankrupt in drive, vision, and imagination, the other is dead in practice, frozen in outworn categories, and cut off from the living realities of the present. Several years after the appearance of *Barbary Shore* Mailer declared (in replying to Jean Malaquais' attack on his *Dissent* article "The White Negro") that Marxism had failed in application because it was "an expression of the scientific narcissism we inherited from the nineteenth century" and motivated by "the rational mania that consciousness could stifle instinct." One might almost take this as a criticism of the cold, tense, claustrophobic brilliance of *Barbary Shore* itself; and indeed,

Mailer's abandonment of revolutionary socialism in favor of the point of view he calls "Hip" was as much a repudiation of ideological thinking in general as of Marx and Trotsky in particular. Here again we have an example of the curious relation to intellectual fashion that appears to mark the movements of Mailer's mind. Just as he remained untouched by all the sophisticated arguments against "unreconstructed" liberalism that were circulating so energetically through the intellectual atmosphere of 1948 until he had discovered their truth for himself and in his own good time, so he had to go through a period of revolutionary fervor and ideological rigidity before beginning to yearn (as so many former radicals had done before him) for a breath of fresh air and a supple, openended point of view. Unlike the great majority of his literary contemporaries, who knew all about the deleterious effects of ideological commitment without ever having tasted the accompanying passion, Mailer was able to experience both the passion and the rigidity on his own pulses, and when he finally turned against ideology it was with the roar of a man betrayed, not with the complacency of the wise at one remove. And again — as in the case of his shift from liberalism to revolutionary socialism — he followed a wholly unexpected path in making his escape from the constrictions of ideological commitment.

In the Hipster (whom he calls the American existentialist) Mailer believes he has found an effective mode of rebellion against the terms of the given neatly combined with the flexibility and openness to life that were lacking in revolutionary socialism. In contrast to Lovett — who had nothing to do once he accepted the "little object" from McLeod but drift from one back alley to another while waiting for the apocalypse to come — the Hipster has developed a strategy for living fully and intensively in the present. He too refuses to have any truck with the world around him and he too recognizes that collective death is the goal toward which our society is moving, but he differs from Lovett in the further refusal to pin his hopes on the future. Having no future, he cares nothing for the past, and therefore he is totally consigned to the fluctuating dimensions of the "enormous present." In effect, the Hipster as Mailer describes him in "The White Negro" is a man who follows out the logic of the situation in which we are all presumably caught: a man who, faced with the threat of imminent extinction and unwilling to be a party to the forces pushing toward collective death, has the courage to make a life for himself in the only way that conditions permit — by pursuing the immediate gratification of his strongest desires at every moment and by any means.

The full consequences of this new position for Mailer's work are yet to emerge, but several results have already become visible in *The Deer Park* — which, though written before "The White Negro," belongs to Mailer's Hip phase — and in the completed sections of the ambitious novel on which he is currently engaged. The most important consequence, perhaps, is that Hip, with its "burning consciousness of the present" and the "terribly charged" quality of experience it involves, has allowed Mailer to make a more intensive use of his great powers of observation than he has done since *The Naked and the Dead*. Whereas *Barbary Shore* seems to have been produced by a mind shut in upon itself and glowing with the febrile intensity of a lonely intellectual passion (it is a book such as might have been written by one of those brooding, distracted students who haunt the pages of Russian literature), *The Deer Park* exhibits a newly liberated capacity for sheer relish in the look and feel and sound of things. Mailer is now back in the world that he deserted in *Barbary Shore*, though it is by no means the same world that he evoked in *The Naked and the Dead*. What he sees in Hollywood is the image of a society that has reached the end of its historical term, a society caught between the values of an age not quite dead and those of a new era that may never crawl its way out of the womb.

The defining characteristic of such a society is a blatant discrepancy between the realities of experience and the categories by which experience is still being interpreted — a discrepancy that can make simultaneously for comedy and horror. The reality is that the scruples, inhibitions, and conventions which were once effective in restraining the natural egoism of the individual no longer work very well because the values from which they drew their strength no longer command much respect. No one, however, is willing to admit this, and they all go on talking and sometimes acting as though what they "really" wanted were the things that people used to want when their basic psychological drives were still roughly in harmony with their professed values — when, that is, these values were powerful enough to create internal needs that became almost as pressing as the primary needs themselves. This situation reveals itself in every department of life, but it is in sex that its contours are most clearly defined, and therefore it is on the sexual affairs of his characters that Mr. Mailer concentrates in *The Deer Park*. What he gives us is a remarkable picture of people saddled with all the rhetoric of the monogamous while acting like some primitive tribe that has never heard of monogamy and is utterly bewildered by the moral structure on which this strange institution rests. It is a world of people who talk incessantly about being in love and craving "decent, mature relationships" but who are in fact tightly imprisoned in their own egos and who have no true interest in anything but self. For them sex has become a testing ground of the self: they rate one another on their abilities in bed, and the reward of making love is not so much erotic satisfaction or spiritual intimacy as a sense of triumph at being considered "good." Mailer's attitude toward all this — I mean the attitude built into his tone and his emphases — is very tricky. There is an unmistakable note of shocked disapproval at many of the things he is describing, yet he insists on treating them with the respect due a major fact of experience. What follows from that respect is a highly disciplined refusal to dismiss the "decadent" narcissistic sexuality of his characters either as immoral or (what comes to the same thing) immature, either as sinful or unhealthy. It would be difficult to exaggerate the originality of this approach, for it is almost impossible to think of another serious American novelist who has even so much as attempted to study contemporary sexual life on its own terms, let alone one who has brought to the subject anything resembling Mailer's readiness to find the organizing principle, the principle of meaning, that may be implicit in these terms.

*The Deer Park* takes place largely in Desert D'Or, the favorite resort of the Hollywood movie colony, and it centers mainly on Charles Francis Eitel, a famous and very talented director who has been blacklisted for refusing to cooperate with a congressional investigating committee and who, after holding out for a whole year against all the pressure to capitulate, finally collapses and gives in. This, of course, is the standard Mailer situation — the rebellious individual crushed by the powers that be — but we do not have to read very far into the novel before we realize that Mailer's view of the nature of the conflict has changed considerably since *The Naked and the Dead*. Hearn and Valsen were defeated in a contest against a hopelessly strong adversary; it is not, however, the strength of his adversaries that defeats Eitel. The two producers Teppis and Munshin are formidable enough in their own way but they are also — what Cummings and Croft could never be — figures of comedy and objects of ridicule. For the first time in Mailer, then, victory over the system has become possible to those who can see through it and who are sufficiently brave to act on what they see. Eitel, a sensitive and intelligent man, understands the secret of the system quite as well as the two characters in the novel who succeed in overcoming it — the narrator Sergius and the diabolical young pimp Marion Faye — but he fails because he lacks the courage to disregard "all the power of good manners, good morals, the fear of germs, and the sense of sin," and to turn himself into a complete and ruthless egoist.

Sergius and Marion are thus the natural heroes of the world of *The Deer Park*, as Cummings and Croft were the natural heroes of *The Naked and the Dead*, and since Mailer is aware of this, there is no need for him to wrench our sympathies in a direction that the novel itself refuses to support. He does, however, make several positive assertions about Sergius and Marion that are as unwarranted aesthetically as the negative assertions made in *The Naked and the Dead* about Cummings and Croft. It is impossible, for example, to believe that the Sergius we see moving around in *The Deer Park* could ever have developed into the author of this novel.* Not only is he simpleminded, unimaginative, affected, and basically senti- mental, but (what is perhaps more to the point) utterly dis- missing in his view of other people. When Eitel, who has been his good friend, finally capitulates to Teppis and Munshin and the committee, Sergius cuts him off brutally — he has failed and is therefore entitled to no further consideration. There is no question that this is the final judgment Mailer himself passes on Eitel, but it is only a final judgment and it is qualified and complicated by the rich, full picture we get of the process that brought Eitel to the painfully sorry pass in which we see him in the last chapter of the novel. Now it is hard to credit that the man who could respond so insensitively to his friend's failure would ever have been able to summon up the subtlety and the insight to understand how a failure of this sort comes about. Nor could such a man conceivably have produced the account of Eitel's affair with Elena, where every nuance in the progress of a vastly complicated relationship is

* To forestall the obvious objection, I ought to explain that Sergius's role as narrator is comparable not to Nick Carraway's in *The Great Gatsby* but to Marcel's in Proust. Moreover, he is an active character in the story, one of whose purposes is to explain why he rather than Eitel must be considered the true artist.

registered with a delicacy and a precision that recall Proust himself. He would also have been incapable of the brilliant comic portraits of Munshin and Teppis, which are so good precisely because they are *not* dismissing — Mailer devastates the two producers while allowing them their full due. Nothing we see of Sergius in the novel could explain how he might have come to compose the marvelous letter of self-justification that the drunken Elena sends to Eitel after she has gone to live with Marion — that letter in which a girl who has been universally snubbed and patronized because of her social crudity suddenly bursts forth with astonishing power as a woman of feeling and perception.

But if Sergius could not conceivably be the author of *The Deer Park*, Eitel very easily could; what Mailer has done here is to endow Sergius with Eitel's sensibility, just as he tries to endow Marion's nihilism with grandiose theological significance. The reason, I think, can be found in "The White Negro," where Mailer tells us that the nihilism of the Hipster is really a creative force. In Hip "incompatibles have come to bed, the inner life and the violent life, the orgy and the dream of love, the desire to murder and the desire to create." Yet the curious thing is that the Hipster who "lives out, acts out, follows the close call of his instinct as far as he dares," who is the herald of a revolution moving "backward toward being and the secrets of human energy," and whose subversiveness takes the form of a constant pursuit of immediate gratification — the curious thing is that this "adventurer" of the night is deeply suspicious of feeling and mortally afraid of passion. The nihilism of Marion Faye, for example, amounts to a rebellion *against* feeling, a kind of Nietzschean repudiation of his "civilized" or Christian self. Everything he does is done precisely because it is repugnant to him, and he believes that "there is no pleasure greater than that obtained from a conquered repugnance." He is not naturally cruel and therefore he forces himself to be hideously cruel; he is not naturally vicious and therefore he cultivates the vices with the grimness of a hermit scourging himself in the desert. Similarly with Sergius, who bends all his efforts toward the perfection of a style based on the suppression of spontaneous feeling: above all he wants to be *cool*.

The irony is that with Sergius and Marion we are back again to Hearn — and he is still trying to get by on style and an ideal of personal integrity. It is much the same style and derives from much the same source (the unavailability of radical political solutions), but in the rank atmosphere of cold-war stalemate it has grown and matured and begun to mistake itself for a portentously weighty philosophy. At the time of the Korean War, when the apocalypse seemed about to descend at any moment, Hearn (who had been killed off in *The Naked and the Dead* before his newly formed resolve to throw off his surly nihilism could be tested) reappeared in *Barbary Shore* split into the amnesiac Lovett and the madwoman Lannie. The loss of the political faith that would have sustained him in the thirties was now seen by Mailer as worse than simply a sign of spiritual inadequacy — it was a sickness of the mind and a disease of the soul. But his brave attempt to recapture that faith proved to be only a dramatic gesture in the face of a dramatic situation; when the situation lost its drama and settled into the dull round of aimless anxiety that has marked the Eisenhower years, the gesture lost its air of glory, as all apocalyptic gestures inevitably do when the apocalypse itself takes too long in coming. Under these circumstances, Mailer turned back to the old Hearn and began to cast about for hidden resources of creativity where before he had seen only the emptiness of mere style, and for stature where before he had perceived only a well-intentioned mediocrity. In identifying himself finally with Hearn, he has in effect acknowledged his kinship to the intellectuals of his own generation — that generation of whose failings he has always been the most intransigent critic and whose qualities he has always tried so hard to extirpate from his own character. His espousal of Hip indicates that he is still trying — for what else is Hip as he defines it but a means of turning away in despair (as most of his contemporaries have done) from the problems of the world and focusing all one's attention on the problems of the self without admitting that this must automatically entail a shrinking of horizons, a contraction of the sense of possibility, a loss of imaginative freedom?

One can only sympathize with Mailer's latest effort to maintain a sense of huge possibility, even if one is totally out of sympathy with some of the doctrines he has recently been preaching. In my opinion, his great mistake is to attribute direction and purpose to the Hipster (and I think that the weakness of Sergius and Marion as imaginative creations indicates that the novelist in Mailer is once again resisting the commands of the theoretician). Hipsterism, it seems to me, is a symptom and not a significant protest, a spasmodic rather than an organized response. The Hipster is the product of a culture (exemplified beautifully in the Hollywood of *The Deer Park*) whose official values no longer carry any moral authority, and he reacts to the hypocrisy, the lying, and the self-deception that have contaminated the American air during the cold-war period by withdrawing into a private world of his own where everything, including language, is stripped down to what he considers the reliable essentials. To this extent, his response to the America of Eisenhower bears a certain resemblance to Hemingway's response to the America of Woodrow Wilson. As many critics have pointed out, Hemingway's prose was generated by the wish to liberate language from the fine lying rhetoric in which Wilsonian idealism had cloaked the horrid realities of the First World War; like the personal style Hemingway elaborated in his stories — the code of courage and craft in the face of a constantly threatening universe — the prose style itself was the expression of an effort to establish a truth of human experience that would be proof

against the distorting incrustations of "culture" and "civilization," a truth (as it were) of the state of nature, a truth at
rock bottom. But the difference between Hemingway and the
Hipster is the difference between mastering a bad situation
and being victimized by it, between exercising intelligence,
sensibility, and discipline in order to overcome the rot of history and seizing upon the rot of history as an excuse for resign-
ing from the painful responsibility to exercise the mind at
all.

If it is true that Mailer has been reading things into Hip
that are simply not there — and just those things that Hip
would need to satisfy his demand for size and importance and
a sense of huge possibility — then we can be fairly certain that
sooner or later his restless imagination will light out for some
other territory. Indeed, he has already shown signs of an impulse to drop his original emphasis on the political significance of Hip in favor of what he takes to be its theological
implications. The idea, apparently, is that God is "no longer"
omnipotent and therefore needs the help of man to fulfill the
"enormous destiny" with which He has been charged (by
whom, Mailer does not say). Here is how he put it spontaneously to an interviewer:

> . . . I think that the particular God we can conceive of is a
> god whose relationship to the universe we cannot divine;
> that is, how enormous He is in the scheme of the universe
> we can't begin to say. But almost certainly, He is not all-
> powerful; He exists as a warring element in a divided uni-
> verse, and we are a part of — perhaps the most important
> part — of His great expression, His enormous destiny; per-
> haps He is trying to impose upon the universe His concep-
> tion of being against other conceptions of being very much
> opposed to His. Maybe we are in a sense the seed, the seed-
> carriers, the voyagers, the explorers, the embodiment of that
> embattled vision; maybe we are engaged in a heroic activity,
> and not a mean one. . . .

The attraction of this fantastic collection of ancient Christian heresies for Mailer comes out explicitly a little later in the interview:

> This involves new moral complexities which I feel are far more interesting than anything the novel has gotten into yet. It opens the possibility that the novel, along with many other art forms, may be growing into something larger rather than something smaller, and the sickness of our times for me has been just this damn thing that everything has been getting smaller and smaller and less and less important, that the romantic spirit has dried up. . . . We're all getting so mean and small and petty and ridiculous, and we all live under the threat of extermination. . . .

We get some notion of what Mailer means by these "new moral complexities" from the prologue to his novel-in-progress which was published in the Fall 1958 issue of *Partisan Review* under the title "Advertisements for Myself on the Way Out." The reader, he announces, must be prepared "for a dissection of the extreme, the obscene and the unsayable" in this "tale of heroes and villains, murderers and suicide, orgy-masters, perverts, and passionate lovers," and it is abundantly clear that the exploration of these "mysteries" is to be made without the help of any traditional moral assumptions. Murder is not necessarily to be regarded as evil, perversion is not necessarily to be considered perverse, suicide is not necessarily to be looked upon as an act of simple self-destruction, and so on. We can now only wait to see what comes of all this, and Mailer being so unpredictable a writer, the one safe guess we can make is that it will turn out to be very different from what many readers of "Advertisements" have assumed — very different and very much more exciting than most of the fiction that is being produced by most of the other novelists of his sorely beleaguered generation.

# PART TWO:

# Books and and Issues

# How Good Is Norman Mailer?

### by Alfred Kazin

Perhaps more than any other book since Scott Fitzgerald's *The Crack-up*, this book (*Advertisements for Myself*) reveals how exciting, yet tragic, America can be for a gifted writer. It is a remarkably full book; all of Mailer up to now is in it; and that is exactly what is wrong with it. For at thirty-six, after following up *The Naked and the Dead* with an artistic failure, *Barbary Shore*, and one ambiguous *succès de scandale*, *The Deer Park*, Mailer (now embarked on a very long and extremely ambitious novel that may take many years) has obviously been hungry to make his mark again in one big smashing outrageous way. He has put together an anthology of all his works, from undergraduate short stories to two sections of the novel in progress, that includes his columns from a Greenwich Village weekly, social

This essay originally appeared in *The Reporter* (November 26, 1959) and is reprinted here with the permission of Atlantic–Little, Brown and Company (Inc.) from *Contemporaries* by Alfred Kazin. Copyright © 1959, 1962 by Alfred Kazin.

and political comment, his now famous essay on "The White Negro" and other sociosexual themes, stories, spoofs, interviews, poems, and some shrewd but essentially subjective evaluations of his literary generation. In the "advertisements" to the different works he talks about himself and Hemingway, himself and marijuana, himself and sex, himself and Eisenhower's America. By the time you get through what is often a very brilliant if screamingly self-conscious book, you feel that Mailer has worked so hard to display everything he has done and everything he knows that it has all collected on the surface. Mailer's permorance here reminds me of the brilliant talker who impresses the hell out of you at a cocktail party but who, when he turns his back to go home, seems vaguely lost.

## 2

Yet *Advertisements for Myself* is a remarkable performance, and it is clearer to me than ever that Mailer is a powerful, courageous talent admirably provoked by our culture. I admire him because he is naturally a radical, strong, and exuberant talent; this book is full of more penetrating comment on the America of Eisenhower, television, suburbia, and J. D. Salinger than anything I have seen in years. But as Mailer says, "I have been running for President these last ten years in the privacy of my mind," and he is probably the only Jew who has been. He wants to be not just a good novelist but the Hemingway of our period. Hemingway obsesses him (and ignores him); Faulkner once made fun of him for saying that whites are always jealous of Negro sexuality; the publisher who made so much out of *The Naked and the Dead* finally turned down *The Deer Park*; there are actually good writers in America who pay no attention to him.

In short, like many another American radical, desperado, Reichian stalwart of sexual frankness, Norman Mailer has been driven crazy by an affluent and greasily accommodating society which not only doesn't oppose him but which turns even his disgust and frankness into a form of literary capital. Just as the hipsters, whom Mailer admires, are not outlaws, not radicals, but the slobs and remittance men and spoiled brats of a society so wasteful and indulgent and satiated with normal sex that it has to discover new thrills all the time, so the secret burn of Norman Mailer is that a book like this, which is meant to slap respectable America in the face, may not sell as much as it could. Like every American writer whose name is an instant password, who can support himself by his writing, who knows himself a celebrity because he moves largely in the company of celebrities, Mailer can no more stay off television or move back to Brooklyn than, being an honest and intransigent spirit, he can admire television or sentimentalize the Brooklyn which, as he says, is not the center of anything. Anyone who reads this book with as much attention and admiration as I have just done can, nevertheless, see that what obsesses Norman Mailer is not just the swarminess of our culture, the repressiveness of our official morals, the flabby gentility of our ruling intellectuals, but the fact that this same America is itself constantly coaxing Norman Mailer to share in the take and join the fun.

What makes this society so marvelous for the gifted rebel, and so awful, is that, lacking all standards by which to counter or to question the new, it hungrily welcomes any talent that challenges it interestingly — but then holds this talent in the mold of its own shapelessness; the writer is never free enough of his neighbors and contemporaries to be not simply agin the government but detached from it. Mailer, who like all his generation has had to work against the overpowering example of Fitzgerald and Hemingway and Faulkner, now thinks that these older fellows had it easier, that our society did not drag them into its maw as compulsively as it does present writers. When I recall how desperately out of fashion Fitzgerald and

Lewis and Anderson and Cather felt at the end of their careers, I doubt that the literary competition has ever been less punishing than Mailer obviously feels it to be. What has changed since the 1920's is first that there are more and more writers, as there are more and more people. Even "advanced" literature is beginning to get as crowded as the mass media, and Mailer cannot be sure, now that he has dismissed Bellow, ignored Malamud, and ruled out all women writers as unreadable, that there isn't someone in South Dakota who may yet outdistance him.

More important, Hemingway (of whom Mailer seems constantly to dream and to curse in his dreams) was still based enough on the old "inner-directed" Protestant culture to measure his need of courage against the moral abstractions of courage, duty, grace, etc. Mailer measures himself against others. Symbolically, Hemingway got his great experience in the first world madness by volunteering for the Italian army long before Americans were in the war. Mailer in 1943 had to keep from becoming a clerk, for only as a rifleman could he collect the experience for the great Hemingwayish novel about the war that he was already prepared to write. And only in the Pacific, as he brilliantly estimated again, would he be able to gather experience for a really provocative novel, since there the growing reactionary tendencies in American life would be manifest.

Without his egotism, no writer is likely to carry much weight. But granted that he must fight for himself and push himself, what reserves of thought and imagination are left? A writer is not only what he knows himself to be, what he consciously fights for and hates and loves — he is the book he makes, the book that must surprise him in the making, the book that somewhere within itself is always greater than he is. Scott Fitzgerald's *The Crack-up*, moving as it may be, has less of Fitzgerald than *The Great Gatsby*. The question all over this book is: How good is Norman Mailer? — and the trouble is that Mailer thinks that he can answer it in terms of available competition. Only a highly self-conscious and rather stormily competitive fellow would have tried so hard to win the prize by dismissing so many writers whose books he hasn't read. This performance calls up the comment on the famous French writer who boasted in his journal that sexually he was more gifted than other men: "How does he know?"

Still, *we* have a right to ask, How good is Norman Mailer? How good are his books? Quite apart from the deleterious influence of our government, our publishers, our official morals — and apart from all the obscene words about television and the cowardice of the "squares" and the marvelous sexuality of Negroes and the necessity of Hip — how good are Norman Mailer's novels? My answer would be that *The Naked and the Dead* is a good novel, though too literary, with worked-up army detail that is thin compared with James Jones's *From Here to Eternity*, and with only one real character in it, the General, who is too obvious a villain; that *Barbary Shore* is hysterical politically and a bad novel by a writer of obvious talent and guts, so that everything in it makes its mark, but not as a work of art; that *The Deer Park* is an extraordinarily uneven and somehow sick book with something peculiarly closed and airless about it. I felt this painfully when I read the novel, and Mailer says in *Advertisements* that he rewrote the novel under marijuana. I am neither shocked by this nor moved to admire Mailer because of it; I do think that *The Deer Park* is not what Mailer thinks it is. It seems to me ridiculous for Mailer to push his novel so hard in this book, since the question is not what Rinehart or the critics did to the book but what Mailer did.

How good is Norman Mailer? The answer varies from work to work, sometimes from page to page. Some of his new work, particularly a torrid story wholly about sexual intercourse, "The Time of Her Time," seems to me remarkable; the opening of his new book, "Advertisements for Myself on the Way

Out," a lot of wind. Not only can Mailer not know how good he is; he is himself one of the most variable, unstable, and on the whole unpredictable writers I have ever read. He has a remarkable intelligence, and this book shows it; a marvelously forceful and inventive style; great objective gifts as a novelist. On the other hand, his intelligence, though muscular, has no real ease or quietly reflective power; he is as fond of his style as an Italian tenor of his vocal cords, and he sometimes tends to overpower when the more manly thing — if I may touch on a major concern in this book — would be to convince; his sense of reality, though boldly critical, is often obsessive in its self-consciousness. On the whole, Norman Mailer is very, very good indeed — not better than ten million other fellows, as he thinks one has to be, but good.

But what will become of him God only knows, for no one can calculate what so overintense a need to dominate, to succeed, to grasp, to win, may do to that side of talent which has its own rule of being and can never be forced.

# Norman Mailer: The Angels Are White

## by Gore Vidal

I first heard of Norman Mailer in the spring of 1948, just before *The Naked and the Dead* was published. He was living in Paris or had been living there and just gone home when I arrived in France, my mood curiously melancholic, no doubt because of the dubious fame I was enjoying with the publication of a third book, *The City and the Pillar*. At twenty-two I should have found a good deal more to please me than I did that spring and summer in the foreign cities. I do recall at one point Truman Capote telling me about *The Naked and the Dead* and its author, a recital which promptly aroused my competitive instincts . . . waning, let me say right off, and for reasons which are relevant to these notes. Yet at that time I remember thinking meanly: So somebody did it. Each previous war had had its big novels, yet so

This essay was first published in *The Nation* (January 2, 1960) under the title "The Norman Mailer Syndrome." It is reprinted here with the permission of Little, Brown and Co. (Inc.) from *Rocking the Boat* by Gore Vidal. Copyright © 1960, 1962 by Gore Vidal.

far there had been none for our war, though I knew that a dozen busy friends and acquaintances were grimly taking out tickets in the Grand War Novel Lottery. I had debated doing one myself and had (I still think) done something better: a small cool hard novel about men on the periphery of the action; it was called *Williwaw* and was written when I was nineteen and easily the cleverest young fox ever to know how to disguise his ignorance and make a virtue of his limitations. (What an attractive form the self-advertisement is: one could go on forever relighting one's image!) Not till I began that third book did I begin to get bored with playing safe.

I took to the field and have often wondered since, in the course of many excursions, defeats, alarums and ambushes, what it might have been like to have been a safe shrewd custodian of one's talent, playing from strength. I did not suspect then that the ambitious, rather cold-blooded young contemporary who had set out to write the big war novel and who had pulled it off would one day be in the same fix I was. Not safe. Not wise. Not admired. A fellow victim of the Great Golfer's Age, then no more than a murmur of things to come in the Golfer's murmurous heart.

My first reaction to *The Naked and the Dead* was: it's a fake. A clever, talented, admirably executed fake. I have not changed my opinion of the book since, though I have considerably changed my opinion of Mailer, as he himself has changed. Now I confess I have never read all of *The Naked and the Dead*. But I read a good deal of it. I recall a fine description of men carrying a dying man down a mountain. Yet every time I got going in the narrative I would find myself stopped cold by a set of made-up, predictable characters taken, not from life, but from the same novels all of us had read, and informed by a naïveté which was at its worst when Mailer went into his Time-Machine and wrote those passages which resemble nothing so much as smudged carbons of an early Dos Passos work.

Sourly, from a distance, that year I watched the fame of Mailer quite surpass John Horne Burns and myself, as well as Truman Capote, who had made his debut earlier the same year. I should explain for those who have come in late or were around then but inattentive that the OK List of writers in 1947 and 1948 was John Horne Burns, Calder Willingham and myself. Capote and Mailer were added in 1948. Willingham was soon dropped; then Burns (my own favorite) sank, and by 1949 in the aftermath of *The City and the Pillar* I too departed the OK List.

"I had the freak of luck to start high on the mountain, and go down sharp while others were passing me" — so Mailer wrote, describing the time after *Barbary Shore* when he unexpectedly joined the rest of us down on the plain. Now the descent, swift or slow, is not agreeable; but on the other hand it is not as tragic as Mailer seems to find it. To be demoralized by the withdrawal of public success (a process as painful in America as the withdrawal of a drug from an addict) is to grant too easily a victory to the society one has attempted to criticize, affect, change, reform. It is clearly unreasonable to expect to be cherished by those one assaults. It is also childish, in the deepest sense of being a child, ever to expect justice. There is none beneath our moon. One can only hope not to be destroyed entirely by injustice and, to put it cynically, one can very often flourish through an injustice obtaining in one's favor. What matters finally is not the world's judgment of oneself but one's own judgment of the world. Any writer who lacks this final arrogance will not survive very long, especially in America.

That wide graveyard of stillborn talents which contains so much of the brief ignoble history of American letters is a tribute to the power of a democracy to destroy its critics, brave fools and passionate men. If there is anything in Mailer's new book* which alarms me, it is his obsession with public success.

* Vidal is reviewing *Advertisements for Myself* in this essay. [Ed.]

He is running for President, as he puts it. Yet though his best and most interesting works have been unjustly attacked, he should realize that in this most inequitable of worlds his one worldly success was not a very good book, that *The Naked and the Dead* is redolent of "ambition" (in the Mary McCarthy sense of the word — pejorative, needless to say) and a young man's will to be noticed. Mailer himself nearly takes this view: "I may as well confess that by December 8th or 9th of 1941 . . . I was worrying darkly whether it would be more likely that a great war novel would be written about Europe or the Pacific." Ambition and the day coincided and a success was made. Yet it is much less real a book than Burns's *The Gallery*, or even some of the stories of Robert Lowry, works which had the virtue of being felt, possessed entirely by the men who made them, not created out of stern ambition and dogged competence. But, parenthetically, most war books are inadequate. War tends to be too much for any writer, especially one whose personality is already half obliterated by life in a democracy. Even the aristocrat Tolstoi, at a long remove in time, stretched his genius to the breaking point to encompass men and war and the thrust of history in a single vision. Ernest Hemingway in *A Farewell to Arms* did a few good descriptions, but his book, too, is a work of ambition, in which can be seen the beginning of the careful, artful, immaculate idiocy of tone that since has marked both his prose and his legend as he has declined into that sort of fame which, at moments I hope are weak, Mailer seems to crave.

But it is hard for American writers not to measure themselves according to the standards of their time and place. I recall a conversation with Stephen Spender when I lapsed, unconsciously, into the national preoccupation. Some writer had unexpectedly failed, not gone on, blown up. Spender said rather pointedly, "The difference in England is that they *want* us to be distinguished, to be good." We order things differently; although our example is contagious, for in recent years the popular British press has discovered writers in a way ours never has. Outside the gossip column and the book page no writer except Hemingway is ever mentioned as news in the American press, but let the most obscure young English novelist attack the Establishment and there are headlines in London. Mailer can denounce Eisenhower as much as he likes in *Dissent* but the readers of the *Daily News* will never know the name of Mailer, much less the quality of his anger. Publicity for the American writer is of the "personality" kind: a photograph in *Harper's Bazaar*, bland television appearances . . . the writer as minor movie star, and as unheeded.

Mailer and I finally met in 1954. I had just published my last, or perhaps I should say latest, novel, *Messiah*, and it had sunk quietly into oblivion in America. (If it were not for the continuing interest of Europe, especially England, a great many of our writers would not survive as well as they do their various seasons of neglect.) I liked Mailer, though I am afraid my first impression of him was somewhat guarded. I am suspicious of people who make speeches at me, and he is a born cocktail-party orator. I have not the slightest recollection of what we talked about. I do recall telling him that I admired *Barbary Shore*, and he was shrewd enough to observe that probably I had been driven to read it to see if it was really as bad as everyone thought. Which it was not. Of his three novels I find it the most interesting and the least diffuse, and quite literally memorable. It is hallucinatory writing of a kind Mailer tried, as far as I know, only that one time; and though I think his talents are essentially naturalistic, he does seem again in his new novel (judging from the advance samples he displays in *Advertisements for Myself*) to be trying for that revelation through willful distortion which he achieved in *Barbary Shore*. One is curious to see the result.

I have gone into the chronology of Mailer's days and mine because they run parallel, occasionally crossing, and because the book he has just published is, in effect, an autobiography covering more or less his entire career with particular attention to the days of the Golfer's dull terror. Mailer gives us his life and his work together, and therefore it is impossible to review the book without attempting to make some estimate of both his character and the corpus of his work, the tension of his present and the shape of his future. Mailer is sly to get himself all this attention, but I must point out that it is a very dangerous move for an artist to expose himself so completely. Indeed, in other times it would have been fatal for an artist not yet full grown to show us his sores and wounds, his real and his illusory strength. Until very recently the artist was a magician who did his magic in public view but kept himself and his effects a matter of mystery. We know *now* of Flaubert's suffering, both emotional and aesthetic, during the days of his work, but it is hard to imagine what would have happened if the court which prosecuted *Madame Bovary* could have presented as evidence a volume of his letters. In effect, Mailer has anticipated his own posterity. He is giving us now the storms and the uncertainties, private and public, which he has undergone. He has armed the enemy and not entirely pleased his allies.

However, it may be possible to get away with this sort of thing today, for we live in the age of the confession. What Mailer has done is no different in kind from what those deranged and fallen actresses have accomplished in ghost-written memoirs where, with a shrewd eye on the comeback trail, they pathetically confess their sins to Demos, receiving for their tears the absolution of a culture obscenely interested in gossip. I suspect Mailer may create more interest in himself by having made this "clean breast of it" than he would have got by publishing a really distinguished novel. The audience no longer consumes novels, but it does devour personalities. Yet what happens after one is eaten? Is one regurgitated? Or does the audience move on to its next dinner of scandal and tears, its previous meal absorbed and forgotten?

Nevertheless, I am fairly certain that Mailer will survive everything. Despite a nice but small gift for self-destruction, he is uncommonly adroit, with an eye to the main chance (the writer who lacks this instinct is done for in America; excellence is not nearly enough). I noted with some amusement that, despite his air of candor, he makes no new enemies in this book. He scores off those who are lost to him anyway, thus proving that essentially the work is politic. His confessions, when not too disingenuous, are often engaging and always interesting, as he tries to record his confusions. For Mailer does not begin to know what he believes or is or wants. His drive seems to be toward power of a religiopolitical kind. He is a messiah without real hope of paradise on earth or in heaven, and with no precise mission except that dictated by his ever-changing temperament. I am not sure, finally, that he should be a novelist at all, or even a writer, despite formidable gifts. He is too much a demagogue; he swings from one position of cant to another with an intensity that is visceral rather than intellectual. He is all fragments and pieces. He appears to be looking for an identity, and often it seems that he believes crude celebrity will give it to him again. The author of *The Naked and the Dead*, though not the real Mailer, was at least an identifiable surrogate, and duly celebrated. But Mailer was quickly bored with the war-novelist role, and as soon as possible he moved honorably to a new position: radical politics, in the hope that through Marxist action he might better identify himself to us and to himself. But that failed him, too. Nor is it the new Mailer, prophet of Hip and celebrator of sex and its connection with time, apt to interest him or us for very long.

I also noted at moments toward the end of this book that a reaction was setting in: Mailer started using military allusions. "Back in the Philippines, we . . ." — that sort of thing. And there were references to patrols, ambushes. It was startling. Most of our generation was in the war, usually ingloriously, yet I have never heard a contemporary make any reference to it in a personal way. The war to most of us was a profound irrelevance; traumatic for some, perhaps, but for most no more than an interruption. When the 1959 Mailer reminds us that he was a rifleman on Luzon, I get embarrassed for him and hope he is not going back to his first attitude to get the attention he wants.

Now for the book itself. It is a collection of stories, essays, notes, newspaper columns, and part of a play. It begins with his first story at Harvard and ends with part of his new novel. The play, which I read in an earlier version, could be remarkable onstage. But the best work in this volume is two short stories. "The Language of Men" tells of the problems of an army cook who has an abstract passion for excellence as well as a need for the approbation of the indifferent men who eat his food. His war with them and himself and his will to excel are beautifully shown and in many ways make one of the best stories of its kind I have read, certainly preferable to Hemingway's *The Old Man and the Sea*, which it resembles in theme. But where Hemingway was pretentious and external, Mailer is particular and works with gentle grace from within his characters. The other story, "The Patron Saint of Macdougal Alley," is a wildly funny portrait of an archetypal drifter, and I think it is of permanent value: we have had this sort of fool in every age (Catullus and Juvenal each dealt with him), but I have not seen him done quite so well in our day.

By and large, excepting "The White Negro," I did not like the essays and the newspaper columns. Mailer is forever shouting at us that he is about to tell us something we must know or has just told us something revelatory and we failed to hear him or that he will, God grant his poor abused brain and body just one more chance, get through to us so that we will *know*. Actually, when he does approach a point he shifts into a swelling, throbbing rhetoric which is not easy to read but usually has something to do with love and sex and the horror of our age and the connection which must be made between time and sex (the image this bit of rhetoric suggests to me is a limitless gray sea of time with a human phallus desperately poking at a corner of it). He is at his best (who is not?) when discussing his own works and days. The piece about getting *The Deer Park* published is especially good, and depressing for what it reveals about our society. But, finally, in every line he writes, despite the bombast, there is uncertainty: Who am I? What do I want? What am I saying? He is Thomas Wolfe but with a conscience. Wolfe's motive for writing was perfectly clear: he wanted fame; he wanted to taste the whole earth, to name all the rivers. Mailer has the same passion for fame but he has a good deal more sense of responsibility and he sees that the thing is always in danger of spinning down into meaninglessness. Nothing is quite enough: art, sex, politics, drugs, God, mind. He is sure to get tired of Hip very soon. Sex will be a dead end for him, because sex is the one purely existential act. Sex is. There is nothing more to be done about it. Sex builds no roads, writes no novels, and sex certainly gives no meaning to anything in life but itself. I have often thought that much of D. H. Lawrence's self-lacerating hysteria toward the end of his life must have come out of some "blood knowledge" that the cruel priapic god was mad, bad and dangerous to know, and, finally, not even palliative to the universal strangeness.

Perhaps what has gone wrong in Mailer, and in many of our fellow clerks, is the sense that human beings to flourish must be possessed by one idea, a central meaning to which all experience can be related. To be, in Isaiah Berlin's bright metaphor, hedgehog rather than fox. Yet the human mind is not capable of this kind of exclusivity. We are none of us hedgehogs or foxes, but both simultaneously. The human mind is in continual flux, and personality is simply a sum of those attitudes which most often repeat themselves in recognizable actions. It is naïve and dangerous to try to impose on the human mind any system of thought which lays claim to finality. Very few first-rate writers have ever subordinated their own apprehension of a most protean reality to a man-made system of thought. Tolstoi's famous attempt in *War and Peace* nearly wrecked that beautiful work. Ultimately, not Christ, not Marx, not Freud, despite the pretensions of each, has the final word to say about the fact of being human. And those who take solemnly the words of other men as absolute are, in the deepest sense, maiming their own sensibilities and controverting the evidence of their own senses in a fashion which may be comforting to a terrified man but is disastrous for an artist.

One of the few sad results of the collapse of the Judeo-Christian ethical and religious systems has been the displacement of those who are absolutists by temperament and would in earlier times have been rabbis, priests, systematic philosophers. As the old Establishment of the West crumbles, the absolutists have turned to literature and the arts, and one by one the arts in the twentieth century have become hieratic. Serious literature has become religion, as Matthew Arnold foresaw. Those who once would have been fulfilled in Talmudic debate or suffered finely between the pull of Rome and the Church of England have turned to the writing of novels and, worse, to the criticism of novels. Now I am not sure that the novel, though it is many things, is particularly suited to didacticism. It is certainly putting an undesirable weight upon it to use it as a pretext for sermons or the resuscitation of antique religious myths. Works of fiction, at best, create not arguments but worlds, and a world by definition is an attitude toward a complex of experience, not a single argument or theme, syllogistically proposed. In the nineteenth century most of our critics (and many of our novelists) would have been writing books of sermons and quarreling over points of doctrine. With religion gone out of the intellectual world they now write solemnly and uneasily about novels; they are clearly impatient with the vulgar vitality of the better novels, and were it not that they had one another's books about books to analyze, I suspect many of them would despair and falter. The novelists don't seem very bright to the critics, while their commentaries seem irrelevant to the novelists. Yet each affects the other; and those writers who are unduly eager for fame and acceptance will write novels which they hope might interest "religious"-minded critics. The results range from the subliterary bleating of the Beats to Mailer's portentous cry which takes the form of: I am the way and the life ever after, crucify me, you hackers, for mine is a ritual death! Take my flesh and my blood, partake of me and *know* mysteries . . . ! And the curious thing is that they will crucify him; they will partake of his flesh; yet no mystery will be revealed. For the priests have created the gods, and they are all of them ritual harvest gods.

I was most struck by this remark of André Gide in the posthumous *Ainsi Soit-il*: "It is affectation that makes so many of today's writings, often even the best among them, unbearable to me. The author takes on a tone that is not natural to him." Of course it is sometimes the work of a lifetime for an artist to discover who he is, and it is true that a great deal of good art results from the trying on of masks, the affectation of a persona not one's own. But it seems to me that most of my contemporaries, including Mailer, are — as Gide suggests — desperately trying to convince themselves and the audience that they are something they are not. There is even a certain embarrassment about writing novels at all. Telling stories does seem a silly occupation for one fully grown; yet to be a philosopher or a religious is not easy when one is making a novel. Also, in a society such as ours, where there is no moral, political or religious center, the temptation to fill the void is irresistible. There is the empty throne, so . . . *seize* the crown! Who would not be a king or high priest in such an age? And the writers, each in his own way, are preoccupied with power. Some hope to achieve place through good deportment. Universities are filled with poets and novelists conducting demure and careful lives in imitation of Eliot and Forster and those others who (through what *seems* to have been discretion) made it. Outside the universities one finds the buccaneers who mean to seize the crown by force, blunt Bolingbrokes to the Academy's gentle Richards.

Mailer is a Bolingbroke, a born usurper. He will raise an army anywhere, live off the country as best he can, helped by a devoted underground, even assisted at brief moments by rival claimants like myself. Yet when all is said, none of this is the way to live. And it is not a way (at least it makes the way harder) to create a literature that, no doubt quixotically, remains the interest of each of us. I suppose if it helps Hemingway to think of literature as a Golden Gloves Tournament with himself pounding Maupassant to the mat or fighting Stendhal to a draw, then no doubt the fantasy has been of some use. But there is also evidence that the preoccupation with power is a great waste of time. Mailer has had the honesty to confess that his own competitiveness has wasted him as he worries about reviewers and bad publicity and the seemingly spiteful successes of other novelists. Yet all the time he knows perfectly well that writers are not in competition with one another. The real enemy is the audience, which grows more and more indifferent to literature, an audience which can be reached only by phenomena, by superior pornographies or willfully meretricious accounts of the way we live now. No serious American novelist has ever had any real sense of audience. C. P. Snow made the point that he would, given a choice, prefer to be a writer in England to a writer in America because, for better or worse, the Establishment of his country would read him and know him as he knew them, as the Greek dramatists knew and were known by their city's audience. One cannot imagine the American President, any American President, reading a work by a serious contemporary American writer. This lack of response is to me at the center of Mailer's desperation. He is a public writer, not a private artist; he wants to influence those who are alive at this time, but they will not notice him even when he is good. So each time he speaks he must become more bold, more loud, put on brighter motley and shake more foolish bells. *Anything* to get their attention, and finally (and this could be his tragedy) so much energy is spent in getting the indifferent ear to listen that when the time comes for him to speak there may be not enough strength or creative imagination left him to say what he *knows*. Exhausted, he becomes like Louis Lambert in Balzac's curious novel of the visionary-artist who, having seen straight through to the heart of the mystery, dies mad, murmuring: "The angels are white."

Yet of all my contemporaries I retain the greatest affection for Mailer as a force and as an artist. He is a man whose faults, though many, add to rather than subtract from the sum of his natural achievement. There is more virtue in his failures than in most small, premeditated successes which, in Cynic's phrase, "debase currency." Mailer, in all that he does, whether he does it well or ill, is honorable, and that is the highest praise I can give any writer in this piping time.

# The Moral Radicalism of Norman Mailer

## by Diana Trilling

In 1959, at the not very advanced age of thirty-six, Norman Mailer published what amounted to a grand view of his literary lifetime. In a single big volume, *Advertisements for Myself*, he not only reprinted virtually everything he had written except his three novels — and there are even excerpts from these — but also prefaced, or connected, his stories, essays, and journalism with an extended commentary in which he reported on his states of mind at various stages of his development as an author and public figure, on the reception given his work in the press and by his publishers, and on his present estimate of his earlier performances. A retrospective enterprise of such proportions is bound to tax

This essay was originally published in *Encounter* (November 1962) under the title "Norman Mailer." It is reprinted here by permission of Doubleday & Company, Inc., from *The Creative Present*, edited by Nona Balakian and Charles Simmons. Copyright © 1963 by Nona Balakian and Charles Simmons.

the generosity of the public. It assumes, for one thing, that its audience shares the writer's own sense of his importance in the record of his period — which indeed it may, but no public likes to have this certification demanded of it. It also presents its author as if in the absolving perspective of history. And it requires of its readers enough grace to forgive, if they cannot welcome, the persistent self-reference inevitable in such a sustained task of self-evaluation. For someone of Mailer's age and present uncertain place in the American literary scene, the undertaking was perhaps ill-advised. By most of its reviewers, *Advertisements* was received reservedly, or with condescension, or irony. The compelling force of the volume, its demonstration of the courage and complexity of Mailer's talent, was slighted in the apparent desire of its critics to separate themselves from his recent questionable, even distressing, moral positions.

This is unfortunate, and it perhaps constitutes one of those occasions when criticism has failed to live up to its responsibility of open-mindedness and has not met its claim of being able to adjudicate between the valuable and the inconsequent, or shoddy, or even out-and-out wrong in a man's work. But one cannot overlook Mailer's share in confounding criticism, even before the publication of *Advertisements*. We live, of course, in a period in which precocity is no longer regarded as it was in, say, Dickens's time, as the sign of a genius so deep-rooted and natural that it must surely augur long years of fulfillment. Instead, we take it as the portent of imminent extinction. While Mailer has neither stopped writing nor succumbed to the temptations of Hollywood, he has had his own gifted way of cooperating in our more cynical expectations for him as a novelist and of obstructing the development that might once have followed upon the early flowering of so much talent. After the extraordinary triumph of *The Naked and the Dead*, he not only deserted the "naturalism" of his first novel but more and more moved from fiction to nonfiction, and of a polemical sort. And increasingly he has offered the public the myth of the man rather than the work of the writer. When we add to this the nature of his present doctrine and the degree to which he has met the challenge of modernity by disavowing that considerable part of his sense of life which is traditional in favor of the more subversive aspects of his thought, it is scarcely surprising that his career is now shadowed in dubiety.

And yet, whatever Mailer's truancy from the novel, or his self-mythologizing impulse, or the violence he does to our traditional moral values, perhaps it is none of these but only the paradoxical character of his talent that finally creates his present equivocal situation. Where a writer exists in this much contradiction, the realization of his possibilities is always chancier than it would be in a more unitary talent, and it would be hard to name a writer of our or any time whose work reveals a more abundant or urgent endowment which is yet so little consistent with itself — so much moral affirmation coupled with so much moral anarchism; so much innocence yet so much guile; so much defensive caution but such headlong recklessness; so much despair together with so imperious a demand for salvation; so strong a charismatic charge but also so much that offends or even repels; so much intellection but such a frequency of unsound thinking; such a grand and manly impulse to heroism but so inadequate a capacity for self-discipline; so much sensitiveness and so little sensibility; so much imagination and such insufficient art. Contradictions like these no doubt contribute to Mailer's appeal; but they also make for his limitations. And they describe a talent which necessarily lives on the sharp edge of uncertainty.

Yet to trace the paradoxes in Mailer is not to figure an unknown constellation. It is to experience the shock of recognition, for in the sum of his contradictions he bears a striking resemblance to present-day America. What distinguishes him, however, from other contemporary American writers who also express their culture even while they reject it is the depth to which he is shaken by the crash of modernity against the poor bulwarks of Western tradition and, even more, his driving need to turn this experience to social use.

For the advanced writer of our time, the self is his supreme, even sole, referent. Society has no texture or business worth bothering about; it exists because it weighs upon us and because it conditions us so absolutely. The diverse social scene is homogenized into a force we feel only grossly, as a source of our horror or terror or emptiness. The job of literature in our period is thus more poetical than novelistic — our advanced fiction neither anatomizes the society that is nor conceives the society that might be; it deals merely with the massive brute social fact in its impress upon the individual consciousness. Where the novelist of an earlier day helped us to understand and master a mysterious or recalcitrant environment, the present-day novelist undertakes only to help us define the self in relation to the world that surrounds and threatens to overwhelm it. And this search for self-definition proceeds by sensibility, by the choice of a personal style or stance which will differentiate the self from, or within, its undifferentiated social context.

Mailer is no Balzac of the twentieth century. And he is engrossed in his own grim effort of self-validation. But he conceives society as being quite as actual as the self, and as much to be addressed. It is not so much that he thinks of the modern world as a world of negotiable particulars. But he believes the social totality generates a dialectic between itself and the individual; it is therefore not merely to be endured in self-pity, it can be faced up to and changed. For instance, in his fine story, "The Man Who Studied Yoga" — it is, I think, one of the best stories of our time and aesthetically Mailer's best-integrated piece of fiction — he has a would-be novelist protest to a friend that he "does not want to write a realistic novel, because reality is no longer realistic"; but Mailer's immediate riposte to this familiar statement is a description of the boring "petulance of their small voices" as the two young men luxuriate in their dreariness. Or, typically, he remarks of Beckett's *Waiting for Godot*:

> I doubt if I will like it, because finally not everyone is impotent, nor is our final fate, our human condition, necessarily doomed to impotence, as old Joyce knew, and Beckett I suspect does not. . . .

And in *The Deer Park*, where he momentarily borrows Hemingway's symbol of sexual impotence for his narrator, Sergius O'Shaugnessy, he has this predate the opening of the story; once the novel begins, O'Shaugnessy is active enough.

Mailer's temperament, in other words, is adversary not fugitive, hortatory not seismographic. Even his Hipsterism, concerned as it is with styles of personal being, rejects the premise of a self at the mercy of society, and refuses the sanctuary of sensibility. And no doubt this has much to do with the striking fact that big as Mailer looms as a personality of the literary left, one can name only a single serious critic of his general cultural persuasion, Norman Podhoretz in *Partisan Review* (Summer 1959),* who has written about him without embarrassment, as an author of stature. While he outrages conservative opinion by the ultimateness of his judgment upon modern life, he equally alienates radical literary opinion by his offense against the reality it is most disposed to acknowledge — that of our helplessness before Conditions.

"Hip is not totally negative," Mailer declares, "and has a view of life which is predicated on growth." And in the figure of the cool cat he projects an image of man as someone who, far from being inert before danger, is precisely poised for action against the enemy — it is a posture without great appeal to the contemporary distaste for "hostility." And despite Hipsterism's emphasis upon the self, it places on the self the largest possible responsibility for the "collective creation" (as

* Printed in this collection. [Ed.]

Mailer calls it) which is our culture. "If society was so murder-ous," he asks, "then who could ignore the most hideous of questions about his own nature?" There is, of course, menace in so primary an inquiry, and Mailer has himself been badly scarred in its pursuit. The question nevertheless carries us a salutary distance beyond our modern view of the individual as victim of a world he never made and cannot remake.

Mailer's adversary disposition recalls D. H. Lawrence, his predecessor in the line of literary minds dedicated to the reno-vation of society by means of a revolution in the individual consciousness. But of the two, Lawrence is actually closer to our present literary spirit, for he is not only the more subjec-tive writer but also the more abstract. Society exists in his novels only as an aggregate of unspecified destructive condi-tions. The most poetical of social revolutionaries, he scorned politics in their troublesome concreteness. But Mailer has al-ways carried the burden of social actuality of the intellectual thirties. He has engaged in politics — the politics of literary intellectuals — through his career, even in years when it has not been the literary fashion. At the time of the publication of his first novel, he was a Communist sympathizer and cam-paigned vigorously for Henry Wallace in that same year. Then, when Stalinism failed him, he turned to Trotskyism, and even today he still professes a modified allegiance to Marxism. For instance, in an interview with Mr. Richard Wollheim in England as recently as September 1961, Mailer describes the socialist preference which has remained to him from his old Communist commitment as now only a choice made *faute de mieux*, certainly with no passion of confidence. Of Marxism, however, he speaks like a man of honor who would not disavow a once-precious love. By and large, his criticism of socialism is much the same as his criticism of mod-ern civilization: just as it is the ugliness and minimalism of modern life that make him dissent from civilization and wish to prod it into a more conscious barbarism from which he can hope there will arise a revitalized way of personal being, just so he dissents from the ungenerosity, the uncourageousness, the lack of elegance and wit and charm, the personally minimal quality which he finds in socialism. Yet despite his belief that the Marxist economic emphasis is not adequate to the present crisis in world affairs, he still calls himself a Marxist, albeit in the tone of someone submitting to a rather tedious test of his integrity. What Mailer implies is that in a world as ripe for reaction as he thinks ours is, a man sticks to his guns even though they are obsolete.

This is a far cry from Mailer's younger Marxism. In fact, the single live line of connection between the monolithic doctrine of a book like *Barbary Shore*, which came out in 1951, three years after *The Naked and the Dead*, and his present merely vestigial Marxism is Mailer's continuing fear of political reaction in the democracies. For Mailer, as for so many Western intellectuals, political probity rests essentially in demonstrating one's anxiety about the threat from the right; the abrogation of human rights under the dictatorship of the left is allowed to disappear in a generalized disapprobation of Communism; or another way to put it is that the threat of armed conflict between the democracies and the Soviet Union overrides the principled opposition to Communist totalitarianism which, for the sake of convenience, as it were, is presumed to exist in a different moral context from any totalitarianism which might appear in the West. Even before the height of McCarthyism, as far back as his first novels, Mailer had arrived at this conviction that fascism is not merely a potential in America as in any modern capitalism but, what is quite another order of political hypothesis, that it is the most coherent and dominant force in American society. And this fear is apparently no less compelling in Mailer today than it ever was: as late as the spring of 1961, he published an open letter to Fidel Castro in which he addressed the Cuban dictator as "Brother" and elevated him to the rank of a born Hipster in order to sanctify his role as savior of the Cuban workers and peasants from American fascism. But then we must remember, of course, that John F. Kennedy also figures in Mailer's pantheon as a natural Hipster; at least he did at the time of his nomination.

Whatever our evaluation of Mailer's political predictions for America, the important point is that his work is not properly to be understood apart from his profound preoccupation with the idea that modern democratic man is about to yield his dignity, his freedom, his very manhood before the onslaught of political reaction. Second only to his religious zeal, it is Mailer's sense of himself as the heroic antagonist of a malevolent reactionary authority that has powered his fictional imagination.

*The Naked and the Dead,* published when Mailer was twenty-five, two years after his separation from the Army in which he served with credit in Leyte, Luzon, and Japan, was everywhere acclaimed as the best novel of World War II. And even as we read it today, knowing what the war brought as its aftermath of futility and desperation, it remains a remarkable document of the defeat inherent in any modern victory in war. Technically, his first novel advances no farther than Dos Passos, whose influence Mailer acknowledges in *Advertisements.* And in the main it relies on fictional materials which were well exploited in the first war. But it brings to a familiar subject the informing view of a new and radically altered generation. Our present-day belief that we stand outside the ordinary movements of historical evolution, the loss of faith in both the orderly and the revolutionary processes of social development, our always-increasing social fragmentation and our always-diminishing trust in individual possibility — it is these changes in consciousness that separate Mailer's war novel from the novels that followed World War I, as does, too, its drastically accelerated sense of time. Time is always running out on a soldier, in the midst of the inexorable tedium of his days, but this fact of experience is raised to a principle for Mailer's GIs. The hot breath of the future — one might better say, the hot breath of our expiring day — broods over the pages of *The Naked and the Dead* as foul and stifling as the surrounding jungle air.

Although even before Tolstoi literature had of course represented the common soldier as the victim of a force he could neither understand nor control, it is only in our time that the Army has become identified with the irrational and destructive authority of society itself. *The Naked and the Dead* incorporates this death-dealing power in two characters, General Cummings and Sergeant Croft. Cummings is a man of the rising middle classes whose overweening personal ambition, bolstered by great gifts for organization and by an imagination which knows no restraints of human feeling, leads him, for private reasons, to order a reconnaissance platoon on a tour of duty which must inevitably end in catastrophe. Croft is an illiterate Army regular, brave, skillful, and cunning, for whom the hieratical sanctions of war provide a nice measure of satisfaction of an unquenchable lust for conquest and blood. Cummings is sufficiently educated to bring the historical process and his own ambitions into working conjunction with each other; he has announced himself on the side of the future. He thinks of his men as the instruments of history and his own will — the two are synonymous. In Mailer's political scheme he is, simply, fascism, and Croft is his eager though unconscious collaborator. The suffering men in Croft's platoon, who endure unspeakable torments as they struggle through swamp and jungle on Cummings's order and who, without voice in their fate, stumble mindlessly in their sergeant's footsteps as he pits himself against the unscalable heights of Mt. Anaka, are the masses of mankind who lack the individual or collective will to resist being propelled to annihilation. This Army, which, in the name of historical necessity, captures, rules and destroys the common life of humanity, is modern society as Mailer sees it, and the presentiment of worse to come. And his introduction of Lieutenant Hearn, the intelligent, decent liberal whom Cummings cannot quite seduce and must therefore kill, completes his political indictment and prophecy.

The influence of Dos Passos' U.S.A. is obvious in Mailer's management of his fictional forces in *The Naked and the Dead* — his crowded canvas of GIs together with their officers, and behind them their families, their wives, their girl friends. Where his own young genius announces itself is in his dramatic inventiveness and, even more, in his feeling — unmatched in our time, even by Hemingway in *For Whom the Bell Tolls* — for topography, for the look of the natural scene. As a matter of fact, the two gifts are associated: the most dramatic moments in *The Naked and the Dead* are precipitated by intensities in nature. Indeed, this loyal delight in physical truth is what gives *The Naked and the Dead* its extraordinary distinction. It is therefore of some interest that Mailer's first novel is, so far, his last to be set outdoors — it would seem that his fiction must now be enclosed in walls in order to reproduce the strangling effects of modern life.

The bald schematic structure of Mailer's novels, starting with the first of them, suggests a paraphrase of T. S. Eliot's comment on Henry James, that James had a mind so pure that no idea could violate it: of Mailer we can say that his novelist's mind is peculiarly violable by idea, even by ideology. In *The Naked and the Dead* there is at least the battle of man against nature to excite the artist in Mailer; but even here the contest between man and society has already begun to make him its ideological prisoner. Despite its brilliant evocation of atmosphere, and its integrity as a story of war, *The Naked and the Dead* takes its ultimate stand, not in art, but in doctrine. As much as it is a drama of human motives, Mailer's first novel is a political document — the testimony of a young Marxist, or proto-Marxist, whose experience of war confirms his worst reading of history. If, however, *The Naked and the Dead* is to be understood as Mailer's forecast of the dreaded victory of fascism, we are bound to balk at the moral as well as political ascendancy of Croft at the end of the book. In Mailer's reading of the future, Croft is clearly the coadjutor of ruthless reactionary assertion. And yet, as the novel draws to its conclusion, Croft ceases to be one of its villains and usurps the place in his author's sympathies which we had thought was Hearn's. This curious shift in the moral focus of *The Naked and the Dead* perhaps adds to its fictional interest, but it remains unexplained in Mailer's system of thought until we meet Marion Faye, the Hipster hero of Mailer's third novel, *The Deer Park*, in whose resemblance to Croft we discover the ominous political implications of Mailer's criteria for heroism.

Mailer's disillusionment with Communism followed rapidly on the publication of *The Naked and the Dead*, but it was a break only with Stalinism, from which he moved to the Trotskyite Marxism of his second novel. In *Barbary Shore* (1951) Mailer attempted a new literary manner, and he paid dearly in popular success for diappointing a public eager for more of the seen and felt life of his first book. But as doctrine his second novel took up virtually where its predecessor left off — with liberalism dead and with the confusion and despair of the working classes sounding their dull prelude to the victory of the right; the fact that, between 1948 and 1951, Mailer had himself lost faith in the Communism of Soviet Russia simply reinforced his earlier perception of the hopelessness of the American proletariat rescuing itself from its bad situation. What had happened to Mailer's politics in the three years between his first and second novels shows itself, in fact, chiefly in the changed perspective of the two books. Whereas in *The Naked and the Dead* the historical process is viewed in terms of its effect upon the general run of mankind, in *Barbary Shore* Mailer writes out of the dilemma of the defeated radical intellectual. The great battle of history is now fought out, not on the wide "proletarian" front where his first novel had located it, but on the intellectual left flank where Mailer had been isolated by his inability to maintain his trust in Stalin's revolution.

In Mailer's second novel, fascism again trumpets its advance, but now it is personified in an FBI agent named Hollingsworth — the collocation is not absurd to Mailer nor, presumably, to his putative readers. As befits the representative of a social force that is already licensed to execute the political dreams of a Cummings, Hollingsworth has none of the human attributes of a mere novice in tyranny like Mailer's General; for all his shrewdness and sharp-wittedness, Hollingsworth moves through *Barbary Shore* robotlike, directed by a power remote from the scene of his activities. His assignment in the novel is to track down a "little object" stolen from the State Department by a man named McLeod, who had come to work for the Government after a considerable period as a Communist leader and then as a member of the Communist Opposition. When we meet McLeod in the surrealist Brooklyn boardinghouse which is the setting of *Barbary Shore*, even this recourse has failed him; he has nothing to which to dedicate himself except an intensive study of Marxism and the preservation of the Communist ideal which, detached from the Soviet reality which has betrayed it, persists in the form of the stolen token he has stashed away for use in an improbable future. As Mailer's highly allegorical story progresses, it turns out that this secret of our future rehabilitation is never recaptured by Hollingsworth, but the dark powers of reaction are nonetheless triumphant — the novel ends with Hollingsworth stealing, if not McLeod's key to the salvation of mankind, then at least his wife, who, in *Barbary Shore*, stands for pretty much what Mailer's GIs did in *The Naked and the Dead*: the common life of humanity but grown distinctly less human and more sinister with the passage of the years. McLeod commits suicide — we are reminded of Hearn's suicidal conspiracy with his murderers in Mailer's first novel — and the young narrator of the book, an amnesiac who has wandered by historical "accident" into this epochal war and been cast as McLeod's confidant and disciple, is left the guardian of our small unpromising legacy of political hope.

In spite of its many funny passages, most of which center around McLeod's mad wife, Guinevere, *Barbary Shore* is a web of finespun fantasies, as obscure as they are frightening, allowing us no connection with any recognizable world of feeling. Even Guinevere is drawn so outrageously and abstrusely that we can never be certain of the meaning Mailer attaches to this sharp, slobby lady who is always bartering or withholding her flyblown sexuality in some strange, awful enterprise of personal advantage. It is only at the last, when McLeod's wife chooses to run off with Hollingsworth, that we begin to understand her place in the ideological scheme of the novel. Greed, cupidity, sloth, a sporadic and wildly misdirected energy, spiritless lust, stupidity, and mean ambition — these, Mailer is telling us, are what today define democratic man, or woman; and in a society in which the masculine principle is reduced to an automaton like Hollingsworth, a woman perhaps best symbolizes our deteriorated situation. Guinevere is the civilization — or, if you will, the American masses — with whom the revolutionary idealist has perforce had to align himself, and to whose partnership with fascism his death must be witness.

McLeod dead, it is to a writer and intellectual — or Mailer's rather shadowy version of one — who has lost his memory except for vagrant recollections of having once been close to the radical movement, that our decent social values are bequeathed. Lovett, the amnesiac narrator of *Barbary Shore*, is of course the precursor of the orphaned Sergius O'Shaugnessy, Mailer's spokesman in *The Deer Park* and again in his most recent story, "Time of Her Time." Both men are without tie to the past; both inhabit a universe without historical precedent or direction. Both of them announce, that is, Mailer's own thoroughly democratic stance of the self-made man, and his detachment from cultural tradition — Harvard to the contrary notwithstanding. Certainly in view of Mailer's obsessive interest in history, it is remarkable how little reference there is in his work to anything — political, philosophical, or literary — that happened day before yesterday; there is only now and tomorrow. Even when Mailer alludes to such towering figures as Hemingway or Faulkner in the generation before his own, they are introduced like parents into a gathering of contemporaries and friends. It is only when he writes about his literary siblings — Bellow, Styron, Jones, Capote, Vidal, Baldwin — that we feel the direct fire of his personal and literary judgment. Mailer's concern with history, in other words, is a concern with history-in-the-making. It is the Marxist's preoccupation with present-day action in the light of future necessity.

Implicit in Marxism as a method of historical analysis there is always this assumption that if we correctly track the movements of history we can foretell future developments and put ourselves in accord with them; we can then aid prophecy in fulfilling itself. But in Mailer there is an unusual collaboration between the higher and lower arts of prognostication: the Marxist's prophetic faculty can regularly call upon the assistance of irrational intuition and even downright superstition. For example, in the early pages of *The Naked and the Dead*, when we first meet Sergeant Croft, he is playing poker and has had a run of bad hands, but firm in his belief that "whatever made things happen was on his side," he waits the better luck that he is certain is in store for him, and soon he is the winner. Then, later the same day, Croft correctly predicts that before nightfall a boy named Hennessey will be dead, and Mailer tells us of this accurate prevision that it fills the Sergeant with a sense "of such omnipotence" and "such portents of power" that his life is as if magically altered. What happens, obviously, is that, by imagining himself in alliance with fate, Croft marshals a will he otherwise lacks, which does indeed alter his fate. General Cummings, too, exemplifies Mailer's providential view of the relation between destiny and perspicuity: "The fact that you're holding the gun and the other man is not," he explains to Hearn, "is no accident. . . . If you're aware enough, you have the gun when you need it." Thus the rationalistic Marxist, the wily general, and the ignorant superstitious sergeant are all blood brothers in their ability to envision and foster what anyway lies ahead. The Marxist determinist who charts the inevitable course of events so that we can put ourselves on the side of history is of the same family with the military tactician or the gambler whose correct hunch puts him on the winning side of fate.

The fate Mailer's Marxism foretold with the completion of *Barbary Shore* was of a society whose determining forces produced only its dissolution, never its reconstruction along the hoped-for revolutionary lines, and the publication of his second book therefore marked a turning point in Mailer's career. If the alternative to a fascist triumph was so remote from political actuality that it could be represented in an unnamed little lost object, then clearly the political solution had failed. From this point forward, Mailer has sought salvation elsewhere than in politics — in Hipsterism, a mode of being that will re-energize a worn and perverted civilization irresistibly drawn toward reaction.

Hipsterism — or Hip, as Mailer sometimes calls it in a discrimination whose meaning is uncertain — is, we are told, an American existentialism designed to return man to the center of the universe and to bring the individual into direct and vital communication with the self and its needs. It is the doctrine which, enshrined in the place that Marxism once had in his system of thought, allows Mailer to probe modern society on a level deeper than that of political and economic determinism. Since it is manifestly man's destiny in our century to live with death and destruction, then the only life-giving answer is to accept the terms of death, to live with death as immediate danger, to divorce oneself from society, to exist without roots, to set out on that uncharted journey into the rebellious imperatives of the self.

God is in danger of dying — this, in fact, is the "single-burning pin-point of the vision in Hip." Because God is no longer all-powerful, man must take His place at the center of the universe and become the embodiment of His embattled vision.

The original settler in this terrain which lies beyond the demands of society, the guide Mailer offers us in our unmapped journey of self-exploration, is not the dark primitive of Lawrence, but he is similarly alien to a white Protestant middle-class culture. He is the Negro; and Mailer makes his most complete statement of the meaning of Hipsterism in his essay, "The White Negro." The Negro, says Mailer, "has the simplest of alternatives: live a life of constant humility or ever-threatening danger. In such a pass where paranoia is as vital to survival as blood, the Negro has stayed alive and begun to grow by following the need of his body where he could." So we, too, must know our impulse as it speaks to us of a true need of the self. "One must know one's desires, one's rages, one's anguish, one must be aware of the character of one's frustrations." And we must be prepared to act on the mandate of the self. "Whether the life is criminal or not, the decision is to encourage the psychopath in oneself, to explore that domain of experience where society is boredom and therefore sickness, and one exists in the present. . . . One is Hip or one is Square. . . . One is a rebel or one conforms."

Although "The White Negro" appeared in 1957, two years after *The Deer Park*, Mailer's third novel already contained in embryo the chief ideas Mailer would develop in his celebrated essay. Among the rebellious imperatives of the self, none is more exigent than sex, and surely the novelist who would treat this aspect of the modern consciousness not, like

Lawrence, as a sacred lost essence but as existential fact cannot do better than to turn to Hollywood. But Mailer would seem to have come to the sexual theme of *The Deer Park* only secondarily, or even incidentally, while embarked upon a political novel along familiar simplistic lines, about a liberal movie director, Charles Eitel, who is blacklisted in the studios for his refusal to talk before a congressional investigating committee but who then capitulates to the joint pressure of authoritarian government and ruthless finance and is reinstated in his job. It would appear, that is, that the sexual life of the movie colony originally served somewhat the same function as the tropical setting of *The Naked and the Dead*, of providing the context for a political drama, but that by the time Mailer was fully launched in his story, he realized that politics was failing him as the material of fiction, as it had failed him as a means of saving the world; Eitel's crisis of political conscience had turned out to be but a dim counterpoint to the larger crises of personal feeling in which he and the people around him were involved. The sexuality of Hollywood, once intended as merely the ambiance in which political hope is defeated, became then the drama itself — the account of a last-ditch fight on behalf of a personal destiny that could no longer be sought in politics.

Considering his sensational material, Mailer is notably neutral in his report of the Hollywood sexual scene. This neutrality of voice must be understood, however, as an aspect of his aesthetic procedure rather than of his moral judgment. Although nothing could be less conventionally censorious than Mailer's investigation of the diverse sexual tastes and deportment of his stars and their hangers-on, of his movie moguls and their call girls, *The Deer Park* is finally as charged with morality as *Lady Chatterley's Lover*. For Mailer, as for Lawrence, sexual activity is never its own justification; its good is measured by the quality of the emotions it produces or expresses. The moral platform of Mailer's Hollywood novel reveals itself from behind the apparent irony of its epigraph — a quotation from a shocked description of the sexual life in the Deer Park of Louis XV — and is clearly argued in every line of Mailer's portrait of a society which manufactures the American mass sexual dream. Here is truly our jungle within walls, a miasma of desire fulfilled and yet always unfulfilled, as torturing as the burning, tangled, insect-infested jungle of *The Naked and the Dead*. The inhabitants of Mailer's Hollywood are wracked by a fever without cure; in their freedom from conventional sexual restraint there sounds the rattling of the chains of a bondage as awful as that of the Army. Only love and tenderness, only the terrible self-denying imperatives of feeling can release these victims from the tyranny of their unimpeded sexual compulsions — and their search for feeling is their futile struggle toward the unattainable heights of an emotional Mt. Anaka.

"The only revolution which will be meaningful and natural for the 20th century," Mailer has said, "is the sexual revolution one senses everywhere." And as one reads his account of the free sexual life of Hollywood, one might perhaps be misled into thinking that this is the revolution to which he is referring. But Mailer is more complex than this. While he recognizes that the Hollywood life of free sexual impulse does indeed constitute a major rebellion against conventional sexual morality, his novelist's eye for truth has searched out the frenzy and emptiness in the lives of his sexual freebooters. Mailer has a predilection for last-minute heroes; just as Croft's sudden triumph at the end of *The Naked and the Dead* suggests the changes in feeling that Mailer was experiencing in the course of composing his first novel, so the replacement of Eitel by Faye as the most significant figure in *The Deer Park* indicates the dramatic evolution of Mailer's thought while writing his Hollywood novel. In Marion Faye we discover the distinction Mailer makes between a sexuality which, like that of the movie colony, appears to be free but is really an enslavement, and the sexuality of Hipsterism which expresses a new, radical principle of selfhood. The difference is not one of behavior but of consciousness. Whereas all the other characters in the novel, whether in their political decisions or their sexual conduct, follow the worn paths of consciousness laid out for them by an exhausted civilization, Mailer's incipient Hipster hero has settled the new direction the world must take to save itself: it is the direction of purposeful, as opposed to purposeless, death. Faye is not God the Father, but he is unmistakably in training to be God the Son. Dying for us, the Hipster becomes our savior; he is the resurrection and the life in a society of Eitels and call girls who, will-lessly submitting to their poor destinies, can promise us nothing but further desperation and enervation.

Faye is a young, elaborately sadistic pimp who closely conforms to Mailer's anatomy of the white Negro several years later. He is totally bored by society, paranoically alert to danger, and he lives in an acute intimacy with the criminal and the psychopath in himself. This intimacy has, in fact, the charge of a mystical fulfillment: it is when Faye is most wholly possessed by his psychopathic needs that he achieves his strongest sense of spiritual exaltation. As jealous of his freedom of will as Dostoevski's Underground Man, he finds the assurance of his autonomy in a strenuous rationalism — his reiterative reminder to himself that he is master of his fate, unconditioned by the moral values of his culture. And the question seems never to enter his or his author's mind whether a man is any the less a victim for being at the mercy of his own psychopathology rather than that of his society.

In Faye, then, we are introduced to the new hero of Hip. And yet he is of course not a wholly new figure in Mailer's work: he has made a premonitory appearance as Sergeant Croft in *The Naked and the Dead*. The single indispensable ingredient Mailer has added to Croft in creating Faye is the consciousness that his program of cruelty and self-imposition has a large social and spiritual meaning. The passage of nearly a decade, in other words, has brought Mailer full circle to the exposure of the unresolved conflict which already existed in his first novel — between his overriding fear, in politics, of an authority which makes its law in defiance of the decent social values and his powerful attraction to the same authority in the personal or spiritual realm.

The conflict is not without literary precedent: the modern imagination apparently takes the heroic leap only at some cost in moral logic. But writers like Lawrence or Yeats had the advantage, we now see, of living in a time when they were not required to give public account of their political preferences, and we can suppose that had Mailer been of their period instead of ours, he would have similarly avoided the predicament of presenting us with a hero not easily distinguishable from his named political enemy. He would have been able to evade the political consequences of consigning the future of civilization to a personal authority morally identical with the dark reaction from which it is supposed to rescue us. Or, to put the matter in even cruder terms, he would not have exposed himself to our ridicule for offering us a God who is a fascist.

But the situation has changed: today Mailer is guilty of a mortal fallacy in his moral-political thought. And yet, even as we trap him, we realize that our whole "enlightened" culture is caught in the same inconsistency. No less than Mailer, we all of us who accede in the moral implications of modern literature but continue to make our political choices on the basis of traditional moral values exist in ambiguity. It is quite a long time now since Conrad asked us to choose between his Kurtz and his "Pilgrims," between a heroic principle of evil and a seedy, hypocritical bourgeoisie that lacks the courage of its inherent malevolence. And once we received such an alternative as really our only option, we accepted the premise of a civilization intolerable to itself; we concurred in the negation of the moral values on which we had established our enlightened political ideals. The very notion of a hero of liberalism, or a hero of antidictatorship, or a hero of social justice becomes absurd, even unimaginable, in a literature whose moral habitude it is to assign personal grandeur to the demonic and destructive. If Mailer's dual wish — to preserve us from the malign forces of political reaction but also to give civilization another push toward the extinction to which it seems inexorably drawn — leads him into moral and political self-contradiction, he is not alone in this dilemma. It is the dilemma of anyone of high political seriousness who also identifies himself with the characteristic moral tendency of our literature.

And the moral tendency of contemporary art is not isolated in our culture. Everywhere in Western society there is an erosion, if not an entire sweeping-away, of assumptions once thought secure, which takes place not at the behest of reason but by an undirected tide of feeling, by what almost seems to be a psychological mutation. The psychologists may not be noting the change but the novelists record it even when they are not always aware of the significance in what they so circumstantially bear witness to. Where do we, where shall we, where can we derive our moral sanctions — from a failing tradition or from the wild free impulses of our racial infancy, from the Ego or the Id? This is the ultimate pressing question of our time, separating our historical period from any that came before it. And because Mailer not only knows the full force of the question but passionately dedicates himself to its answer, he transcends the follies and excesses which attend Hipsterism and claims his place in the forefront of modern writers.

Obviously in Mailer's application to this ultimate issue, far more than in his politics, we discover his radicalism, just as it is in their deep involvement with this large moral-cultural tendency of our period rather than in their newly fervid socialism or their disenchantment with the democracies that we locate the radicalism of his literary contemporaries. For Mailer, as for the whole of a new literary generation, politics is today the least revolutionary aspect of social protest.

That, despite the political struggles which fed his moral imagination, Mailer's present moral radicalism came to him only gradually and from such emotional sources as have always nourished the traditional novelist is plainly indicated in his story, "The Man Who Studied Yoga," written in 1952, shortly after the political disillusionment of *Barbary Shore* but well before the appearance of Marion Faye. Product of a moment of suspension between ideological engagements, this superb long story is singularly free of the restrictions imposed upon Mailer's fiction by his usual systematic thought. And it is also the warmest and most domestic of his fictional works, his sole excursion into the middle-class "normality" in which he, too, like the characters in his story, might have entrenched himself against the dangerous next steps in his development. In Mailer's brilliant description of Sam and Eleanor Slovoda we can examine the supposedly "mature" alternative our civilization offers those of us who scorn "regression" to the barbarism of infancy. Sam, an ex-radical and novelist *manqué*, earns his living writing continuities for comics; Eleanor, a painter *manqué*, is a suburban housewife and the dutiful jargon-driven mother of two fine modern-reared children. The course of their lives of quiet-desperation-cum-psychoanalysis is interrupted (but only for a day while the children visit their grandmother) by the showing of a pornographic film at a party. After ten years of marriage, the Slovodas and their friends are responsible citizens and parents, responsible matrimonial partners, responsible and tender, even humorous social companions. But they ache with the sexual longings that are never to be satisfied, and with the frustration of their dreams of themselves. They are the human counterparts of the charmless rational housing development their culture has provided for them. If this is what it means — and who can argue

129

the flawless truth of what Mailer shows us? — to take our due place in society without violating the established decencies, then Mailer is surely right that conformity is purposeless death. But at this point in his career Mailer has no taste for pressing the polemical issue. The story delivers its message without preachment and this is its triumph.

Sam Slovoda has turned to psychoanalysis for the deliverance that will never come, and from Mailer's satiric references we can take it that the therapy is orthodox, therefore, to him, especially suspect. In later essays, Mailer goes on to make Freudianism the target of some of his sharpest attacks on the modern dispensation; expectably enough, he by and large lines up with the Reichians. Jung, Fromm, Reich: it is among these analytical dissidents that protest now regularly seeks the psychology with which to replace the Freudian psychology which it believes lives too comfortably with the traditional attitudes of our society. Like Reich, Mailer rejects the idea of a self obedient to social law, and from Reich he takes his measure of instinctual gratification, the orgasm: it is in his orgasmic potency that the Hipster finds the best test of his capacity for self-realization. As a matter of fact, Mailer's most recent story, "Time of Her Time," carries this criterion of personal release to the amusing point where, notwithstanding the ingenious twists Mailer makes on his sexual theme, the orgasm plays the same tyrannous role in assessing psychic well-being that sexual "adjustment" does in the mental-health culture that has sprung from Freudianism.

In "Time of Her Time," O'Shaugnessy is returned to New York from Hollywood and Mexico. By day he teaches bullfighting; his nights are for lovemaking with an endless series of Village girls who prey upon his swaggering maleness. The epitome of these predators is a graceless, tight-knit, Jewish college student who defies him to give her the sexual satisfaction she has not yet experienced. Challenged, O'Shaugnessy finally accomplishes his grim mission by fiercely forcing upon her a reversion to a more primitive zone of feeling than the female genital; stripped of her defenses, the girl attains to womanliness — and she is not grateful. She must hit back at her despised savior, or master, with her own bleak, ugly attempt to rob him of his masculine pride. The story ends with both partners in this loveless battle worn and battered, both equally the victims of their excoriated egotism — and with the girl bound again for the Freudian couch where, so Mailer has it, she has learned the tactics of assault which are her civilized protection.

"Time of Her Time" is the crudest of Mailer's attacks upon Freudianism, and it is peculiarly anomalous that Mailer should deal with Freud this unworthily. For, although he is himself not aware of it, the fortitude which is implicit in the demand he makes upon the self is much closer to the Freudian than the Reichian temperament. Mailer's heroic assertion and his insistence upon the controlling power of man's consciousness have their antecedents not in the psychoanalysis that has diverged from Freud but in Freud himself; the Reichian psychology proposes a character considerably less valorous and self-contained. The heroism of Freud, however, was the heroism of endurance; he knew better than most the price that civilization exacts in denied instinct, and tragically, resentfully, he was prepared to pay it. Mailer's is the courage of nonacceptance; he refuses to sacrifice instinct to a civilization which is itself so little removed from savagery. But perhaps because of Freud's readiness to face into the issue as between civilization and instinct, Mailer does, in fact, direct his criticisms not so much to Freud himself as to his disciples today, where he stands on firmer territory. The unwillingness of contemporary orthodox analysis to take account of the actualities of a culture in significant transition, its unacknowledged acquiescence in a moribund middle-class morality, its reluctance to treat with the human personality apart from the limitations of social imperatives — these are the grounds of Mailer's adverse judgment upon present-day Freudianism. One could fairly put it that what Mailer attacks in Freud's followers is their passive or neutral assent in a choice which, as Freud made it, had such harsh resonances.

Naturally enough, of the various excesses into which Mailer is led by his own option against civilization, the most disturbing is his expressed tolerance of, even his partisanship with, extreme personal violence. And he is not speaking metaphorically; here, as elsewhere, he is announcing a program of action. What is worse, he speaks of violence in a language of love learned in the moral culture he undertakes to dismiss in its entirety. For example, in a statement which he made in the course of an interview in *Mademoiselle* (February 1961), he has this to say about a brutal gratuitous murder:

> Let's use our imaginations. It means that one human being has determined to extinguish the life of another human being. It means that two people are engaging in a dialogue with eternity. Now if the brute does it and at the last moment likes the man he is extinguishing then perhaps the victim did not die in vain. If there is an eternity with souls in that eternity, if one is able to be born again, the victim may gets his reward. At least it seems possible that the quality of one being passes into the other, and this altogether hate-filled human, grinding his boot into the face of someone . . . in the act of killing, in this terribly private moment, the brute feels a moment of tenderness, for the first time perhaps in all of his experience. What has happened is that the killer is becoming a little more possible, a little bit more ready to love someone.

This is of course monstrous and intolerable. We recall, however, that the statement was made at a time of great personal stress, and we are relieved to counter to its enormity the modified terms in which Mailer, but a few months later, discussed the violence of Hipsterism with Richard Wollheim in England.

> I don't see the real choice as one between violence and non-violence. It's rather between the violence of the individual and collective violence. . . . [Whether or not protest needs to take such a total form as that of Hipsterism] depends on whether one thinks a society can solve its problems rationally. If one thinks it can, then hip will go nowhere. But if one thinks it can't, and that barbarism is closer, and that violence is in the seed, then at least hip introduces the notion of art into barbary.

We might reply to a formulation like this that barbary is precisely where art is not and never can be; that art and civilization are genetically inseparable. But no one who admits into the record of contemporary civilization the savagery of nazism, or the spiraling success of Communist totalitarianism or, at a perhaps absurd extreme, even the gruesome spectacle of professional wrestling, can evade the validity of the problem Mailer poses for us when he asks that we look at the collective violence we call our moral order and, in the light of what we see, decide whether we can exempt the individual of responsibility for our degradation, and continue, as a culture, to feel morally superior to our collective conduct. While Hipsterism's conspiracy with the vicious in man's nature suggests a "cure" which certainly is little better than the disease for which it is prescribed, Mailer at least presses upon us an effort of honesty without which we live in moral delusion.

And yet is it not enough that he tell us what we must learn instead of telling us what we must do?

Clearly, this is the chief pitfall Mailer has contrived for himself as a writer — his neglect of the metaphoric character of the literary endeavor. For it is here that his espousal of violence ceases to be a strategy by which we are shorn of the hypocrisies and self-delusions with which we surround our participation in a violent civilization and becomes so gross an offense against the decency we still cherish both in our personal and in our collective lives. But if Mailer's actualization, even in his own conduct, of ideas that, for another writer, would remain simply figures of speech, has had its inevitable effect of nullifying some of the difficult truth with which he is dealing, it may also in the long run protect his radical insights from being so quickly and easily absorbed that we make no use of them. "The world doesn't fear a new idea. It can pigeon-hole any idea. But it can't pigeon-hole a real new experience." This is D. H. Lawrence speaking, who produced a body of work which is entirely metaphoric. And Lawrence left the world, certainly not untouched by his urgent insights, but sadly unaltered in its main course.

But Mailer's impulse to break the metaphor-barrier and himself act out, or ask that we act out, his ideas would now appear to have another, much deeper source than his impatience with the ability of art to achieve its tangible miracle of renovation. Intense as his literary dedication unquestionably is, his religious mission is now infinitely more compelling. Just as he writes in order to preach the word of God, he acts in order to attain to God, by whatever thorny path. And when he invites us to follow his example he literally means us to join a religious crusade.

Even as a young writer and young Marxist, Mailer's vision carried him beyond a world of simply defined or materially determined notions of good and evil. We look back upon his first novel from our present vantage to see that Sergeant Croft's ascent of Mt. Anaka must be interpreted as the ascent of the Cross, and that Croft's triumph at the end of *The Naked and the Dead* represents a transcendence not merely over his own poor character, as we would judge it, but over an inglorious mankind which presumes to pass moral judgment and which fails to realize that God may appear to us in the strangest of disguises. And similarly with Marion Faye: while so far we see only the stigmata, we can suppose that in the long novel on which Mailer is working, in which Faye is said to have a leading part, Mailer's Hipster will come into the fullness of his spiritual blessedness. Nor is Mailer's invitation to sin so that we may find grace an unfamiliar heresy. If there has always been missing from Mailer's writing any true perception of the mysterious circuitous paths by which literature accomplishes its improving work, undoubtedly this is because he has always been occupied with the mysterious circuitous ways in which God performs His work. His moral imagination is the imagination not of art but of theology, theology in action.

This defect in Mailer's artistic imagination has many corollaries, of which the most obvious are his small fictional concern with the complexity and variety of human responses and, even more disabling, the absence of a prose adequate to the larger intentions of literature. If we were to conceive of Hemingway offering us his heroic choice and his disenchantment with the hollow idealisms of modern life in a language which was sufficient to propagate a doctrine but no more than that; which failed to be its own quintessential comment on the modern world and which exposed us to the crude manipulations of ideology, without those areas of retirement and indecision and even discordance which are so perfectly re-created for us in the subtle tones and rhythms of Hemingway's best writing — this would approximate Mailer's situation as a novelist. For the life-giving subtleties of style, Mailer substitutes a generosity of words. Like Thomas Wolfe before him, like Saul Bellow in his own generation, he has a giant energy of vocabulary with which he undertakes to make his discriminations of meaning. But his taut strings of noun upon noun, adjective upon adjective, intended to sharpen our response to reality, in fact sharpen only his own act of assertion.

Of some (superficial) aspects of his stylistic problem, Mailer is himself aware. Often in *Advertisements* he refers to his continuing effort to achieve a prose which will support his vision of modernity and forbid us our easy evasions and falsifications.

But if, so far, his endeavor has largely missed its goal and indeed has had the perverse effect of reinforcing Mailer's rhetoric of will, this is by no means an inappropriate outcome. To a greater extent than he perhaps recognizes, Mailer is an anti-artist, deeply distrustful of art if only because it puts a shield between the perception and the act. His writer's role, as he conceives it, is much more messianic than creative. While it was in the very nature of Hemingway's literary vocation that even in the moment of his most urgent masculine assertion he was able to keep in abeyance the impositions of the merely personal masculine will, it is in the nature of Mailer's social and spiritual vocation that he should wish to challenge, even personally dominate, his reader.

But if we listen closely, we perhaps hear his insistence as less the expression of personal authority than a call to a time when religion was still a masculine discipline — a call, that is, to a Hebraic world, still molded in the image of the stern father, Moses. From Moses to Marion Faye, with a stopover at Marx: Mailer's religious route is surely a strange one. But the braver efforts of culture are not always straightaway and simple.

# Mailer's Campaign

## by Midge Decter

Norman Mailer's *Presidential Papers* is a collection of much of his occasional writing of the last few years. There are the epic essays on the 1960 Democratic convention and the first Patterson-Liston fight; some poems; a couple of interviews, one real, one imaginary; a chapter from a novel in progress; some columns done for *Esquire* and *Commentary*; a speech delivered in debate with William Buckley; and a few assorted sundries. The pieces are of varying lengths, intensities, and postures, held together by the kind of introductory comments Mailer originally fashioned for *Advertisements for Myself*. Unlike the earlier collection — which spanned many more years and several turnings in his career — the *Papers* are all products of a single and ever-intensifying preoccupation: that vision of men and society

This essay originally appeared in *Commentary* (February 1964) and is reprinted here by permission of Midge Decter. Copyright © 1964 by The American Jewish Committee.

for which Mailer has (not entirely arbitrarily) preempted the name of existentialism.

The book, like so many of its author's public performances, will not fail to outrage (and all the more since the assassination of President Kennedy). For one thing, because it is exactly that, a public performance. Mailer is a writer who has not for one moment allowed his contemporaries to forget the impulse to seduction by exhibition that trembles beneath the written word. But more important, I think, is that throughout the *Papers* Mailer's cheekiest and gaudiest moments are precisely his most serious ones; he therefore cannot be taken seriously except in his own way on his own terms — which is a form of tyranny that few writers are not either too timid or too well-mannered to impose.

Consider the shocking liberty of these pieces. Norman Mailer sets out to define the application of his existentialist notions to politics; this definition is extracted and formulated out of his own writings; and the whole thing is then consecrated to the education of the President of the United States. What is more, his address to Mr. Kennedy is undertaken in no mere spirit of fun — with little of that ebullience which derives from the new dispensation to make clean sport of public affairs — but for the purpose of being listened to and even wielding some influence. He has himself photographed for the dust jacket seated on an old-fashioned platform rocker; even this is only half a joke, one can see it in his eye — he has considered the position. And taking for himself the ear of the President, what does he offer? The gleanings of three years' insistent and childlike spiritual adventuring, which involves him in considerations of the nature of God and the Devil, magic, violence, cancer, and excrement. What impudence!

To judge from past responses, however, what most of Mailer's confreres are apt to find being violated here is not their sense of the sanctity of John F. Kennedy (though now, of course, that too) but rather their traditional commitment to what should be the sanctity of *Norman Mailer*. Those liberties of his that have always been most violently objected to are not the liberties taken at the expense of public propriety and responsibility but the ones that threaten certain hard-earned pieties of the literary community itself. The truth is that a writing man may with impunity act out just about anything in relation to the society out there — complacency, cynicism, destructiveness, even criminality — anything, that is, except a simple desire to be implicated in its power.

The trouble with Norman Mailer as a literary figure, then, is that he is always, in the radical sense of the word, so unruly. No sooner is he settled among us at peace, holding our major concessions to his talent and achievement and promise, than he is off again, setting up the next test of his personal strength — and of our willingness to venture. For where he goes he must take everyone, must have confirmation, assent, bigger and newer concessions. When he should be gratified, he turns out to be restless; when he is engaged in what would go down as interesting play, he turns out to be in dead earnest, demanding of us an answering dead earnestness. When he should above all be consolidating his position as a Leading American Novelist, he announces that he is running for President, or mayor of New York, or whatever. He is, in short, an altogether untrustworthy citizen of the Republic of Letters.

One always speaks of him this way, as a figure, a citizen, instead of merely as a writer; it is really impossible to separate the two. Nor does Mailer himself do so. He gives over his personal gestures and his prose equally to the judgment of the age. For what he is seeking at every moment is the *effect*, the visible effect of his power to create new possibilities, to work what he has called "a revolution in the consciousness of my time." Therefore everything about him is made to matter: not only his books and pieces and poems, but his discoveries of mood as well; or that he beat William Buckley in debate and the New York *Times* failed to record his victory; or that he had divined a victory for Patterson in the sixth round, who never even made it through the first; or that he had on a certain occasion not been smoking; or that, to take the matter about as far inside as it can go, some of the body cells had probably expired as a result of a given spiritual onslaught. Now it would not be politic to ignore the fact that such pressure on the material of experience can also be called by a simple, ugly, clinical term. But clinical terms are not so much beside the point as beneath it. For the real point is not that Mailer defines a world over which his being is sovereign, but rather that he risks finding all the dimensions of the real world in himself. He is to be the social microcosm — and thus our voluntary scapegoat for weaknesses and corruptions and inadequacies. This is not a modest or endearing ambition. Its stakes are murderously high. But on the other hand, were Mailer to win, he would win all.

It is important to remember about Norman Mailer that though his gestures can be foolish — in the sense of being wasteful, disruptive, misplaced — they are almost never without the grace of consciousness. (As it often works out, he comes under indictment for just those aspects of his behavior and attitudes that he himself finds it necessary, for the sake of what he would assert, to expose. I am thus-and-such a kind of fool, he says, and those who cannot really bear his disorderliness tend to accept at face value this offering of his self-irony.) The closest he has ever come to being utterly graceless is in his piece on Jackie Kennedy. He tells us that after the appearance of his essay on the convention that nominated her husband, she sent him a letter, clearly full of praise. In his answer to her he announced that he was contemplating a work on the Marquis de Sade, and later tried to explain this egregious blunder on grounds of inaccurate sociology. But when a gentleman tries to interest a distant, beautiful, and famous lady in *his* interest in the Marquis de Sade, he is obviously making love to her. And in Mailer's case the love he was making — just like the whole misbegotten impression he presented of the lady in the first place — was merely the expansion of some feeling of pleasure with himself. It was unintelligent of him not to know that; he deserved her silence.

But such lapses are rare. Considering the particular fates chosen for tempting by this man, and the number of temptations offered them, it seems something of a miracle of the spirit that they are so rare. He manages, for instance, to swagger through his introductions, propose solutions to the problems of juvenile delinquency and capital punishment, discuss his hatred of masturbation, analyze the cause of cancer, or even mount a poetic attack on the book reviewers of *Time* — all without making himself look the least bit prettier. He distances himself from nothing, and he withholds nothing. In the shattering account of his almost diabolically perfect louse-up at the famous Liston press conference, one comes upon the denouement — Mailer, a parched beggar, finally wringing one moist "I like this guy" from the world champ — knowing that no matter what his pose of the moment, he will never allow one to be deceived in him. Whether or not he is making a revolution in the general consciousness, he has, perhaps alone in this country, succeeded in investing public unruliness with a serious style. At the very least, then, he may effect a permanent improvement in the manners of radicalism.

The seriousness with which he faces up to his personal demands on this society — and with which he is therefore able to count their cost to the soul — is not merely a matter of bravery (though it is a measure of the corruption of thought and feeling just how brave a man has to be to get down to things so self-evidently simple as wanting to be a member of a world championship). Partly Mailer's daring has to do with something not, I think, sufficiently taken into account about him, and for which *The Presidential Papers* brings massive evidence. And that is how *American* he is. By "American" I do not mean anything literary-metaphysical. I mean quite simply that he owns America. He unquestioningly and unambiguously belongs here; and the whole country gives itself up to him in a range of natural assumption and reference that seems, in its ease and artlessness, quite unavailable to the rest of the special community he inhabits. The America of the essay on Kennedy is not a thought-out or striven-for place but an experienced one, geographically, socially, and culturally. It is a country which by virtue of its solidity, rather than its abstractness, lends itself to subtle analysis — and by the same token, to real subversion. Probably a lot of this has to do with the fact that Mailer as a very young man experienced an enormous American-style success, virtual movie-stardom. But whatever the reason, one thing is clear; he has not the slightest doubt, and therefore needs not the slightest justification, of his right to be important. He calls himself an existentialist, but he is no snob of existences. If he is alienated (sanctified condition), it is an alienation from within, the kind one suffers in relation to one's family rather than to one's neighbors. The difficulty, of course, is that his own family has the power to make even the soberest and most mature of men misbehave. But on the other side, no one can have more power than he to hit them where they live.

This freedom to take for granted the terms of his own culture without flinching has made of Mailer a very earnest man. He forever takes one by surprise with his earnestness. It is a quality not much associated with sophistication or subtlety: passion, yes, and even a capacity for murderous reduction — but not the kind of dogged, megalomaniacal earnestness that was meant earlier by the word "childlike." In this book, for example, the Devil, plastic, and cancer, his three main symbols for the totalitarianism he maintains is threatening to swallow up man's being, are not interesting or illuminating metaphors for evil; they are the actual, material conditions of evil. The God described by Mailer as dependent for his continuing sovereignty on the strategic successes of his human troops is the living God in Mailer's firmament. The waste that results from people's inability to make heroic acceptances and undergo heroic assimilations is — their excrement. At least half of *The Presidential Papers* is taken up directly, and the rest indirectly, with relating these conditions to a varying group of subjects (one should really say objects) ; from Fidel to birth control to Hasidism; sometimes with blinding brilliance; sometimes with great wit and spirit; sometimes with the kind of clumsiness that comes with bearing down too hard on one's words and being too solemn in one's soul. Only a very reckless man would be in such a hurry to convert his images into new categories of thought. And only a very generous one would leave it so obvious where these categories do and do not work.

I think it is safe to assert that Mailer will not, at least in his own terms, win all. No one less than a major philosopher could succeed in synthesizing what are so far only the bits and pieces of the revolution he means to achieve. And Mailer is no philosopher: his "philosophy" is poetry, requiring always his discrete and precise perceptions of the moment to persuade us. Partly from intellectual brashness and partly from a novelist's habit of thought, he is in the end not sufficiently respectful toward the history of man's difficulties with the problem raised in this book. When he writes discursively of the possibility that there are extranatural connections between natural phenomena, for instance, he manages only to convince us of how sincerely he believes in them. But when he works his willingness to consider the power of magic against something he has actually seen or known — when, in short, he acts the observer he supremely is — he is able to provide all the evidence needed for the truth and rightness of his own sense of things. His *Commentary* column on dread and the absolutely breathtaking description of Patterson's defeat are examples of how Norman Mailer can illuminate those things on heaven and earth our philosophy has not lately bothered to dream of. The man in the state of existential dread and Floyd Patterson are not appropriate figures for a universal discourse, but they are, inescapably, one's fellow Americans. Whatever else Mailer may have failed to do, he has, by a grand fidelity to the character of his own perceptions, given these men's experience a necessary new dimension. If he has not earned the right to deal with the universe, natural or otherwise, no one is currently telling us more about the United States of America.

# A Nightmare

# by Norman

# Mailer

## by Elizabeth Hardwick

*An American Dream* by Norman Mailer is a fantasy of vengeful murder, callous copulations and an assortment of dull cruelties. It is an intellectual and literary disaster, poorly written, morally foolish and intellectually empty. Must we, backing away from the hole this new novel represents, remind ourselves once more how good a journalist Mailer has been elsewhere; must we bring up again his Sonny Liston piece, his archetypal paranoia about the Kennedys, his brilliant account of the Goldwater convention? Yes, it is well to have at hand the consolation of his cameo WASPs with their "five-year subscription to *Reader's Digest* and *National Geographic*, high colonics and arthritis, silver-rimmed spectacles, punched-out bellies, and that air of controlled

This essay was originally published in *Partisan Review* (Spring, 1965) under the title of "Bad Boy," and is reprinted here by permission of Elizabeth Hardwick and *Partisan Review*. Copyright © 1965 by *Partisan Review*.

schizophrenia which is the merit badge for having spent one's life on Main Street." Bear in mind the squalid humor of "The Time of Her Time" and "The Man Who Studied Yoga." Remember the white Negroes and the old starlets on producers' laps in *Deer Park*. We have always said to ourselves that NO MATTER WHAT Mailer had humor, a free, radical spirit, and remarkable literary gifts.

Where have they gone? At the moment we have only a bombed-out talent, scraping in the ashes. *An American Dream* is a very dirty book — dirty and extremely ugly. It is artless, unmysterious and so there is no pain in it, no triumphant cruelty or instructive evil. Begin with the title. "An American dream" promises our national unconscious surprised in sleep. The phrase is used to signify the aspirations of the immigrant and so there is a briefly echoing irony. Our hero's aspiration is the strangulation of a pop-fiction heiress wife, a poor unreal creature brought to rest in her own filth for reasons known only to the odor- and anal-obsessed author. The dreamer has come to bring us noxious fornications, to vomit our cocktails, to bear the world's orgastic bites and bruises, to trade wisecracks with the cops. The hero is Stephen Richards Rojack: Harvard, war hero, Phi Bete, professor of existential psychology (author of "the not inconsiderable thesis that magic, dread and the perception of death were the roots of motivation") — and TV star. Rojack begins his story with the exhausted Mailer-Kennedy joke: "I met Jack Kennedy in November, 1946. We were both war heroes, and both of us had just been elected to Congress. We went out one night on a double date and it turned out to be a fair evening for me. I seduced a girl who would have been bored by a diamond as big as the Ritz."

The forebodings of the beginning are sustained throughout the book, except for a few brilliant diversions, such as a scene with the Negro singer, Shago, that do most movingly testify to Mailer's old power. Perhaps it is the very environment of this new novel that so viciously betrays. The environment is made up of a crippling wife-hatred, degrading sexual boasting, and a determination to produce a novel, to gain or regain power thereby. (The inability to write a novel has been one of Mailer's themes.) Somehow these private obsessions would take on significance, tell us about ourselves, expose the wife-killer in every husband. The excremental, the sadistic, the hideous would frighten us into self-knowledge — and so on. How strange it is, though, that ugly and meanspirited as this book is, no heat arises from its many brutal couplings, no real sense of danger from the heedless cruelty. You do not feel confronted with some unpleasant but original force. What appears is an uglier, smellier pop-fiction. This, in the end, is the shock of *An American Dream*.

Stephen Rojack kills his wife, Deborah, with a crack, crack, crack of her neck. If you look for the motivation of the murder, you will find it written in the cement of a typical speculation, such as the following: "I hated her more than not by now, my life with her had been a series of successes cancelled by quick failures, and I knew so far as I could still keep any confidence that she had done her best to birth each loss, she was an artist at sucking the marrow from a broken bone, she worked each side of the street with a skill shared only in common by the best of street-walkers and the most professional of heiresses." Rojack strangles his wife and then throws her body out of the window of her plush [sic] East Side apartment. But while the body is still on the floor, he seduces, in a particularly loathsome and ridiculous scene, the German maid: ". . . as abruptly as an arrest, a thin, high constipated smell (a smell which spoke of rocks and grease and the sewer-damp of wet stones in poor European alleys) came needling its way out of her." Then there is the singer, Cherry, friend of gangsters, and some cops and more and more of the same. Rojack does not have to bear any responsibility for the murder of his wife because his story of her suicide is made more plausible by the discovery that she had cancer — and also because her death is OK to the police. It seems she had a thing for secret agents and was herself mixed up with them.

What can have been Mailer's intention in this novel? The characters cannot really be looked at because they are almost classically unconvincing — tough rich girls, sexy New York playboy, the usual cops. *An American Dream* is not a parody; one of its oddities is that there is very little humor in it. Perhaps, Mailer meant by his sadistic eroticism to write something like those "crimes" in Sade. But the perverse power Sade has over the erotic impulse of the reader comes from his fanatical involvement in his own fantasies. There is in Mailer none of the concentration that would make "good" pornography. He seems, instead, tired, distracted, vengeful — and what is fatal for the perverse writer, to be merely showing off, pretending. The incredibly poor quality of the composition, the incoherent mixing of cheap effects, pulls almost every page down into fatuity. Consider the description of Deborah:

> That was love with Deborah and it was separate from making love to Deborah; no doubt she classified the two as Grace and Lust. When she felt love, she was formidable; making love she left you with no uncertain memory of having passed through a carnal transaction with a caged animal. It was not just her odor, that smell (with the white gloves off) of the wild boar full of rut, that hot odor from the gallery of the zoo, no, there was something other, her perfume perhaps, a hint of sanctity, something as calculating and full of guile as high finance, that was it — she smelled like a bank.

This passage — and it is not untrue to the composition of the book as a whole — gives the clues to Mailer's failure. Carelessness, indifference and some inexplicable distance from the characters produce "the white gloves off" as an image for day-to-day respectable, deceptive life; pretentiousness and again indifference mix Grace and Lust, and the fumes of the zoo with sanctity. Of course we don't accept any of it because we have not seen or felt any sanctity in Deborah and so the image offends more than the wild boar's rutting, which we recognize as a trick from pornography, where the waning lustfulness of the male is always being pepped up by the imposition of wild, jungle insatiability on the part of the female. Every kind of banality meets in this short description of Deborah: banalities of expression as much as of feeling. She is the center of the novel's action, the object of Rojack's lengthy speculation, the whole reason, we feel, for the book itself. And she is either lamely generalized or preposterously unconvincing.

Mailer's attention has never been fully given to this novel. His indolent style, way below anything he has written previously, trivializes everything from death and murder to love. He makes very little effort; the words simply flow, and the images — and worse, the thoughts — nearest to hand are accepted one after another. Rojack puts on his shirt after the murder "with the devotion of a cardinal fixing his hat." When he thinks of punishment — and there is no guilt in this fantasy — he writes, "Yes, I could go to prison, spend ten or twenty years, and if I were good enough I could try to write that huge work which had all but atrophied over the years of booze and Deborah's games." (I cannot imagine what Mailer had in mind here. The only image that came to me was a sort of Nehru, under colonial rule, producing in prison the story of his life — and that is singularly inappropriate to the novel's circumstances.) Graphic images are also nearly always trite or unexceptional. "Her nose was a classic. It turned up with just that tough tilt of a speedboat planing through the water."

Stephen Rojack lives by the clichés of pop-cruelty, but he has a strangely old-fashioned "smell" about him. He does not appear to feel anything, and yet he has none of the sleek, new affectlessness of the young people in French movies. He is ineffably corny, native, mean, messy, unattractive. He is only pretending, wretchedly *hoping* to be an evil spirit. Mailer has not been able to transform Rojack or his murder. They come to us without art and without inspiration — and yet they do not represent even a minimal truth. What was meant to be a black pearl, evilly shining, is just a pile of dust. And perhaps Mailer's mistake has been to think that he should be, in his writing, a new Lucifer. The odd thing is that his best gifts are often genial. Those gifts are serious ones, always unexpected and original. That they are still his we know from the extraordinarily vivacious piece about the Republican convention, written after *An American Dream*.

# Son of Crime and Punishment

## by Tom Wolfe

Or: How to go eight fast rounds with the heavyweight champ — and lose

Norman Mailer announced in the December 1963 issue of *Esquire*, in a column he had in there called "The Big Bite," that he was going to write a serialized novel under the old nineteenth-century pop magazine conditions, namely, in monthly installments, writing against a deadline every month. A lot of *pressure* and everything. Mailer worked the whole thing out with the editor of *Esquire*, Harold Hayes. The idea was to write the first chapter and then, after that went to press, he would write the second chapter; and after that one went to press, he would write the third one, and so on, through eight chapters, turning out one every thirty days, writing right up to the press time all the time.

The idea stirred up a lot of interest among literati and culturati in New York. For one thing — daring! — it was like *Dickens* or something. That comparison came up quite a

This essay originally appeared in *Book Week* (March 14, 1965), and is reprinted here by permission of Tom Wolfe, c/o International Famous Agency, Inc., and The Washington Post Company. Copyright © 1965 by The Washington Post Company.

bit — Dickens. It was going to be interesting to see if Mailer could voluntarily put himself inside the same kind of pressure cooker Dickens worked in and not merely endure but thrive on the pressure the way Dickens did. *Tour de force! Neo-Dickens! Courage under fire!* Actually, looking back on it, everybody should have figured out at the time that it really wasn't Dickens that Mailer had in mind. Any old epopt of the Harvard EngLit like Norman Mailer would consider Dickens a lightweight. The hell with Charles Dickens. The writer Mailer had in mind was a heavyweight, Dostoevski. I will try to show in a moment, in the scholarly fashion, how specifically he had Dostoevski in mind.

The other thing that stirred up a lot of interest in this prospect of Mailer's was his personal history. Mailer had not written a novel in practically ten years when he started on this serial. Seventeen years ago, in 1948, Mailer had published a highly praised first novel, *The Naked and the Dead*. Among the military novels of the period, I would say it ranked second only to James Jones's *From Here to Eternity*. Mailer published his second novel, *Barbary Shore*, in 1951. The critics really bombed it. Somebody called it "a 1984 for D train winos." The D train on New York's IND subway line runs all the way from 205th Street in the Bronx to Coney Island and is great for sleeping it off. Mailer published his third novel, *The Deer Park*, in 1955. The critics bushwhacked him again. They cut him up, they *tenderized* him.

Mailer stopped publishing novels at that point, although he did try to write one, a kind of windy one, judging from excerpts. Yet during the next ten years, from then to now, Mailer became a bigger public figure writing no novels at all than he had by writing them. He was on television all the time and wrote articles here and there. He hung around with prizefighters the way Hemingway hung around with bullfighters, and he tried pot and existentialism and Negroes and did a great deal of brooding over God, freedom and immortality and the rest of it. He had a lot of good roughhousing ego and anger and showmanship and could always get an audience, even among people who didn't want to listen. *Happy Chutzpah!*

In 1960 his life really began to pick up momentum. He started to write articles for *Esquire*, reportage, which were by far his best work since *The Naked and the Dead*. The first big one was on John Kennedy's nomination. Mailer, like Gore Vidal and James Michener, had gotten very much wrapped up in politics and gotten a mystic crush on Kennedy, much the way the stock liberals of another generation had fallen for the first American "left aristocrat," Franklin Roosevelt. Mailer announced on TV that he was going to run for mayor of New York.

He also committed a number of acts that firmly established him in the Wild Boy of Western Literature tradition. Holy Beasts! That wasn't why he committed them, but that was the upshot of it. First off, in June 1960, he was arrested in the boho resort of Provincetown, on Cape Cod, for getting drunk and hailing a police car with the cry "Taxi! Taxi!" because it had a light on top of it. His head was cracked open in a fracas at the station house, but he got some revenge on the police by acting as his own lawyer at the trial and giving the police a going-over on the stand. On November 14, 1960, he was arrested about 4 A.M. in Birdland, the Broadway jazz club, after an argument over a check. Six days later he stabbed his second wife, Adele, after a party in their apartment on Ninety-fourth Street. She refused to press charges, and he got off with a suspended sentence, but the case got a lot of mileage in the papers.

He was all over the papers again in 1961 when they pulled the curtain on him during a poetry reading at the Young Men's Hebrew Association because his poems were getting too gamey for even that liberal atmosphere. In 1962, more headlines — Mailer married Lady Jeanne Campbell, daughter of the Duke of Argyll and granddaughter of Lord Beaverbrook. Their courtship, their marriage, their breakup, their divorce in 1963, the old Juarez route — people were fascinated by all this and talked about it all the time. The pace kept picking up and picking up, even to the point where Mailer hired a hall, Carnegie Hall, in 1963 and got up on a podium and orated, read from his own works, preached, shouted, held colloquies with the audience, great stuff. He also started writing his *Esquire* column, "The Big Bite," which kind of flamed out — but then — brave bull! — he began his serial novel, *An American Dream*, in *Esquire*'s January 1964 issue.

The story, as it unfolded, ran like this: Stephen Rojack, war hero, ex-congressman, author, professor, television star, and accomplished stud, is separated from his wife, Deborah, a forceful woman who has noble blood in her veins and an English accent. He loves her but he hates her, because she is all the time humiliating him. He visits her apartment one night, they exchange their usual venomous *mots*, he gets mad and strangles her to death. He throws her body out the window onto the East River Drive, where it causes a five-car pile-up. Brought to a halt by the whole mess is a car bearing Eddie Ganucci, the Mafia boss, and Cherry, nightclub singer and Mafia love slave. Rojack and Cherry fall in love more or less at first sight. Rojack claims his wife committed suicide right in front of his eyes. The bulk of the story concerns whether or not the police can pin the murder on Rojack and, more important, whether or not he is strong enough to withstand the various pressures the whole thing puts on him. The police put him through an ingenious interrogation, but he maintains his cool and is released for the time being. He turns to Cherry, takes up with her, and beats up her Negro ex-lover, one of America's great popular singers, Shago Martin. Rojack is now ready to face up to his dead wife's father, fabulously wealthy, powerful Barney Oswald Kelly. They have a talk-out in Kelly's Waldorf Towers apartment and a climactic ordeal-by-courage.

The scramble to meet the deadlines in writing the serial was just as wild as Mailer himself had predicted it would be. Hayes, *Esquire*'s editor, kept the layout forms open for Mailer's installments practically up to the morning of the day the presses had to run. A lot of roaring around, one understands, gasps, groans, desperation, but even in all that Mailer wasn't really doing things the Charles Dickens way. Dickens was rather cool about the whole process. Sometimes Dickens used to come down in the living room and write down there with four or five guests sitting around and talking with his wife. He would put his head up from time to time and interject a remark when something in the conversation caught his ear. That cool, hip Dickens. But Mailer wasn't even thinking about Dickens. He was going to take on Dostoevski.

Mailer has always been measuring himself against other writers. He has been saying, Is Jones, Willingham, Capote or Kerouac or whoever as good as me, long after most literati regarded Mailer as no longer even in the competition. In one essay, "The Other Talent in the Room," he managed to tell off most of the prominent novelists in the country as inferior men — weaklings mostly, no guts, no cool, can't drink, you know? — as well as artists. Well, here he had demolished all his contemporaries, and so now he had nothing but a few dead but durable giants to look to. Hemingway, with whom Mailer identifies quite a bit, had the same streak. Hemingway once announced that he had beaten Turgenev's brains out and there was only one champ left to take on, Tolstoi. Mailer has even stronger motives, personal ones, to look to Dostoevski.

Dostoevski, like Mailer, had a solid decade in his young manhood when he didn't write a thing. In 1849 Dostoevski was convicted as a revolutionary and sent to Siberia. He didn't return to St. Petersburg and start writing until 1859, at the age of thirty-eight. Mailer had a hiatus almost that long, 1954 to 1964. Nobody sent Mailer off anywhere, but the result was

*155*

the same. There he was, forty-one years old, and hadn't written a novel since he was thirty-one. Anyway, Mailer knew something about Dostoevski's comeback that isn't popularly known, namely, that Dostoevski did it all, suddenly burst forth as the greatest writer in Russia, by writing serialized novels under monthly deadline pressure. Dostoevski's greatest works, *Crime and Punishment*, *The Gambler*, *The Idiot*, *The Possessed*, *The Brothers Karamozov*, first appeared in magazines, most of them in *Russky Vestnik*.

Dostoevski wrote Katkov, the editor of *Russky Vestnik*, offering him the first in this incredible streak of magazine fiction, *Crime and Punishment*, one September (1865), the same month of the year Mailer picked to offer *An American Dream* to Hayes at *Esquire*. I haven't talked to Mailer about this, but I wouldn't be surprised if he didn't decide to follow Dostoevski's example just that closely. He has a great vein of nineteenth-century superstition in him, a lot of voodoo about *cancer*, for example, the personal outlook of the kidney cells, incredible gothic theorizing. Mailer apparently has read Dostoevski's letters and diaries. In his prospectus for the serial project in the December 1963 *Esquire*, he cites a passage from Dostoevski's journals telling how he used to work all night long, in the lucid moments between attacks of epilepsy, in order to keep going and meet the deadlines.

Dostoevski's performance in 1866, the year *Crime and Punishment* started appearing in *Russky Vestnik*, was prodigious. The first installment appeared in January — the month of the year Mailer's serial began — and there were eight installments in all — the same as with Mailer. In the same year (1866) Dostoevski also signed a contract to do a novel for another magazine by November 1. If he didn't make the deadline, he would suffer a heavy financial penalty, and the publisher, Stellovsky, would get the right to publish all of Dostoevski's novels, in book form, past and future, without giving him anything. As of October 1 Dostoevski still had about one-fourth of *Crime and Punishment* to write and hadn't written a line of the novel for Stelovski. On October 4 he hired a stenographer — later he married her — and started dictating *The Gambler* right out of his head. He finished it on October 30, a forty-thousand-word novel that is considered his most perfect novel from a technical point of view. The next day he sat down and started dictating the last two installments of *Crime and Punishment* and was home safe on both novels.

All of this must have had a double appeal for Mailer. First of all, here was a man who made his comeback in a big way through the magazine serial. Second, he did it through a *roman à thèse*, a philosophical novel. Mailer has a terrible hang-up on the *roman à thèse*. The reason for the failure of both *Barbary Shore* and *The Deer Park* was chiefly their soggy tractlike nature. But *Crime and Punishment* was a *roman à thèse* that did make it, and *An American Dream* — well, there are a great many things in Mailer's book that resemble *Crime and Punishment* in plot, structure, theme and detail.

Mailer's book, like *Crime and Punishment*, concerns a sensitive young man who murders a woman, and the story in each case hinges on whether or not the hero is going to have the existential — to use a term Mailer likes — the existential willpower, the courage, to weather the storm that follows. In each case, the hero turns to a quasi-prostitute for emotional sustenance immediately after the crime — Raskolnikov turns to Sonia in *Crime and Punishment* and Rojack turns to Cherry in Mailer's book. In both cases the hero comes together with the girl as the result of a wreck in the street. In both cases the hero confesses his guilt to the girl as a pledge of faith. In both books he undergoes a long, intriguing interrogation by the authorities, in which the questioner seems to know he did it and is trying to trap him emotionally and verbally into confessing. In both cases it is technically, circumstantially, within the power of the hero to get out of the whole thing without admitting his guilt. Most curiously of all, Mailer, like Dostoevski, has chosen to add to the story a short, final chapter, called "Epilogue" — rather weak and pointless in each case — in which the hero goes off into some kind of wasteland. Raskolnikov is sent off to Siberia, even though the book has a very powerful and dramatic natural ending with the confession itself. Mailer has Rojack drive off into the Nevada desert.

Dostoevski is not a great deal more profound than Mailer, but Dostoevski always had the good fortune of never being able to make his ideas dominate his characters. Dostoevski is always starting out to have some characters express one of his ideas and very quickly the whole thing gets out of hand, Dostoevski gets wrapped up in the character rather than the idea, as in Marmeladov's saloon scene. Dostoevski resembled Dickens in this respect. Both seemed to have such powers of imagination that characters grew in concept during the very process of the writing, with all sorts of baroque and humorous curlicues of the psyche coming out. Mailer's trouble is that whenever he has a theory, which is pretty often, he always kills some poor son of a bitch in his book with it. In *An American Dream* he crushes his hero, Rojack, with too much thinking in the first fourteen and a half pages and kills him off for the rest of the novel.

At the outset we get a picture of this brave, talented, and highly placed man — hero, author, scholar, TV star, socialite, sex maestro — who for some reason is in a hopeless funk, foundering, sinking down through a lot of rancid gothic metaphysics. One is reminded of a remark Turgenev made about Dostoevski's weakest novel, *Raw Youth*: "I took a glance into that chaos. God! What sour stuff — the stench of the sickroom, unprofitable gibberish, psychological excavation." By page 13 Rojack is out on somebody's apartment terrace thinking about jumping, and by then he is already so boring and logorrheic, one's impulse is to put the book down and say, Jump. Mailer was clearly trying to establish a Dostoevskian mood of the Troubled Genius in this passage. What

*158*

he does mainly, however, is give one the feeling that here is some old gasbag who doesn't know when he is well off. Rojack, like all of Mailer's people, doesn't know how to laugh. He opens his mouth and — aaaagh — just brays in a kind of sterile Pentecostal frenzy. Mailer could still have salvaged Rojack, I suspect, if he had only written the novel in the third person instead of the first. Use of the first person leads Mailer to have his hero think himself into all sorts of puling funk holes all the time.

If I were editing *An American Dream*, I would cut out the first fourteen pages and about half of page 15, through the sentence that ends ". . . they were flinching as the wind rode by." That sentence is too nineteenth-century gothic anyway, all this business of the wind riding by. The wind doesn't do much riding in this era of meteorology, it just blows. I would start the book with the next sentence, "A familiar misery was on me." That's a little Poe-like, but it's all right. If the book starts right there, no background information needs to be added. The whole thing starts off fast from that point and we have a good little action story going. One big advantage is that now, in the scene where Rojack starts having words with his wife, which is a fine scene, actually, we can have some kind of sympathy for him, because his wife is obviously such an accomplished bitch. We can even sympathize with his choking her to death and we can pull for the poor guy to outwit the police. As the book is actually written, however, one's first impulse is to hope that Rojack *gets his*, too.

The next passage that has to go is pages 41 through 46, which describes perhaps the most ludicrous love scene in fiction. Rojack starts *thinking* again, that is the trouble. He gets this *theory* that after he murders his wife he has got to make love to her maid, Ruta, by alternating, rapidly, from conventional copulation to buggery, back and forth. He does so, and he is *thinking* all the time. It is all wrapped up with God, the Devil, and the Proper Orgasm, and even aside from certain quaint anatomical impossibilities, it is all told in some kind of great gothic Lake Country language of elegance. It sounds, actually, with all these gods, devils, and orgasms running around, like some Methodist minister who has discovered orgone theory and, with a supreme ecumenical thrust, has decided to embrace both John Wesley and Wilhelm Reich.

If we get rid of that scene, we are quickly back into a stretch of fine fast-paced action, almost like James M. Cain. The spell breaks in the last chapter, however, when Rojack starts thinking his head off again during the confrontation with Barney Oswald Kelly. The scene bogs down further in another difficulty of the book, unreal dialogue. Kelly has a lengthy speech in this chapter and keeps slipping into such rhetoric as, "I thought myself a competitive fellow, just consider — I had to be nearly as supersensational with sex as with *dinero,* and Bess and I gave each other some glorious good times in a row; up would climb the male ego; applause from Bess was accolade from Cleopatra; then swish! she'd vanish."

Aside from the coy expressions, such as *dinero,* all this doesn't . . . *parse.* One reason, perhaps, is that Mailer brings his big characters on one by one in this book like cameo parts in a play like *The Days and Nights of Beebee Fenstermaker.* They have just one big scene each, and so they have to start talking like maniacs right from the word go and ricochet around all over the place and tell their whole life stories while Rojack, who is *thinking* all the time, lards up the scene a little more.

Even so, once the first fourteen and a half pages of the book are out of the way, Mailer exhibits much of the best things he has going for him, his drive, his pace, his gift of narrative, his nervous excitement, things Cain and Raymond Chandler had, but not too many other American novelists. Using the serial form — ending each chapter cliff-hanger style — Mailer creates excellent suspense — in fact, in much of the book Mailer moves, probably unconsciously, in the direction of

Cain and shows great promise. In the context of a Cain adventure, Mailer's gothic attitude toward sex — which Cain shares — a great deal of new-sentimental business about how making love to a broad is all mixed up with death and fate and how you can tell your fortune by the quality of the orgasm — all this is not embarrassing in the context of a Cain novel like *The Postman Always Rings Twice.*

Of course, Mailer cannot match Cain in writing dialogue, creating characters, setting up scenes or carrying characters through a long story. But he is keener than Cain in summoning up smells, especially effluvia. I think Norman Mailer can climb into the same ring as James M. Cain. He's got to learn some fundamentals, such as how to come out of his corner faster. But that can be picked up. A good solid Cain-style opening goes like this:

"They threw me off the hay truck about noon . . ."

# "Morbid-Mindedness"   by Richard Poirier

William James probably would have admired Norman Mailer's *An American Dream*. And since to read James is more instructive about contemporary literature than to read the reviews of Mailer's book, there's a chance that the novel will find the respected place in history that literary journalism refuses to give it. Defining (in *The Varieties of Religious Experience*) the necessary antagonism, even in 1902, between the "healthy-minded" and the "morbid-minded," James offers a fable for those reviewers — especially Joseph Epstein in the *New Republic*, Philip Rahv in the *New York Review of Books*, Elizabeth Hardwick in *Partisan Review*\* — who have found in this latest of Mailer's works a pretext for moralisms that are witty and articulated almost in direct ratio to their critical irrelevance:

\* Included in this collection. [Ed.]

This essay was originally published in *Commentary* (June 1965) and is reprinted here by permission of Richard Poirier. Copyright © 1965 by The American Jewish Committee.

To this latter way, the morbid-minded way, as we might call it, healthy-mindedness pure and simple seems unspeakably blind and shallow. To the healthy-minded way, on the other hand, the way of the sick soul seems unmanly and diseased. With their grubbing in rat-holes instead of living in the light; with their manufacture of fears, and preoccupation with every unwholesome kind of misery, there is something almost obscene about these children of wrath and cravers of a second birth. If religious intolerance and hanging and burning could again become the order of the day, there is little doubt that, however it may have been in the past, the healthy-minded would at present show themselves the less indulgent party of the two. In our own attitude, not yet abandoned, of impartial onlookers, what are we to say to this quarrel? It seems to me that we are bound to say that morbidmindedness ranges over the wider scale of experience, and that its survey is the one that overlaps.

Of course *An American Dream* isn't good or bad simply because it deals with aspects of life seldom treated with candor in serious literature, and even less frequently with Mailer's relish of detail. It is in fact an introspective novel, and in reading it — a very different activity from thinking afterward about those Terrible Things done by its hero — I was most often reminded, for comparison, of the recent poetry of Robert Lowell. Mailer and Lowell are alone, I think, in having created the *style* of contemporary introspection, at once violent, educated, and cool. Their language substantially extends the literary resources of English, and people will later turn to them in any effort to determine the shapes our consciousness has been taking.

Perhaps the reason for so many uncomprehending reviews is that Mailer put everyone on the wrong scent, especially those with the dubious advantage of having a nose for what a book is like even before the author is done with it. Mailer himself invited us to take the novel as yet another of his public displays. He vulgarly pushed himself, as would-be boxer, would-be mayor of New York, he trivialized the very images that are as often part of his nightmares, and he managed even to make his often bright talk about writing into a parody of Hemingway, which was parody enough to begin with. His antics are all, as related to this wondrously private book, simply worth forgetting. In this novel, and despite his big fuss about serializing it in *Esquire* (just like Dostoevski used to do in the magazine *Russky Vestnick!*), Mailer is not at all interested in advertising his or anyone else's private life. What most of the prose reveals instead is a nearly impersonal honesty about the tightest knots in himself and about the related, Gordian knots of contemporary history. This is our history as Hawthorne might have written it: just as private and nearly as melodramatic and allegorical.

When I refer, then, to Mailer's "self," it is not to the careerist who has sometimes resembled the hero of this novel, Stephen Rojack. It is rather to the writer who can be discovered at work in the language of this novel. He needs, for his purposes, a style that prevents anything like self-advertisement, that even resists translation into vocabularies that have some public authority, like those of psychoanalytic theory. In fact, not many contemporary writers have with such audacity treated the "findings" of psychoanalytical literature — of Freud, Reich, Norman O. Brown — as only another form of mythologizing. What the style registers is the war within Stephen Rojack of health and morbidity, creative sexuality and a destructive perversity, God and the Devil, the Devil's hideout being associated in the book with the anus and the discovery of it with buggery. Rojack's acts of self-degradation are referable less to any ascertainable neuroses within him than to the same public and political life that appeals to Mailer's own acts of self-debasement. And yet, quite marvelously, the result isn't a novel of displaced personal responsibility, as Bellow's *Herzog* often is: Rojack's perversities create in him a desire for health, associated here with the privacy, duty, difficulty of loving another, a desire that involves, implicitly and without cant, the acceptance of guilt for the nature of his own life and for the ruinous life around him.

Perversity is in many ways the subject and the villain of the book, or at least the evidence of villainy. One senses it most superficially in the great many disgusted and rather boyish allusions to homosexuality. Thus the kind of deception in which Rojack would have been involved had he remained (though privately obsessed with death) a public figure and politico is compared to that of male film star idols, adored publicly by women but "homosexual and private in their lives. They must live with insanity on every breath." Mailer is not much interested in homosexuality itself but only as one of the symptoms of other kinds of sickness within society, and the homosexual figures from his earlier novels who comes to mind are General Cummings in *The Naked and the Dead* or Leroy Hollingsworth in *Barbary Shore* — men in whom there is a direct connection between sexual deviation and the destructive assertions of public and private power — rather than Teddy Pope of *The Deer Park*. *An American Dream* reveals Mailer's increased revulsion from all kinds of sexuality that are, in the literal sense of the word, degenerate, that express what he takes to be the de-creative impulse, the turn toward death in American society. I cannot therefore recognize the novel described by most of the reviewers, especially the three already mentioned, claiming as they do that murder for Rojack is merely a sexual stimulant or that he isn't made to bear any responsibility for the death of his wife.

The moral problem of Rojack as a murderer unpunished by law and as a sexualist who finds murder exciting is confronted by Mailer in the opening pages, where any reader might also confront it who is able to see what is going on in the passages describing the hero's killing of four Germans in World War II. It is therefore scarcely understandable that Mr.

Rahv can wonder how Rojack *could* know before the strangulation of his wife that murder "is never asexual." The first of the four killings strikes a note that will resound through all the subsequent action, and does so in metaphors that shape the action here and throughout the novel. This early on, Mailer establishes the connections necessary to the impersonal and historical meanings of his work, between personal neuroses and neuroses so much at work in public affairs as to give, in the very plot of the book, a license for familial as well as national killings. What is most gruesomely comic about the novel — a really brilliant twist of plot that to Mr. Epstein is "a shamelessly shabby *deus ex machina*" — is that Rojack escapes prosecution for a personal crime, the murder of his wife, who is involved with spies, because, like his publicly awarded killing of Germans, the murder apparently fitted into the larger designs of international politics:

> Years later I read *Zen in the Art of Archery* and understood the book. Because I did not throw the grenades on that night on the hill under the moon, *it* threw them, and *it* did a near-perfect job. The grenades went off somewhere between five and ten yards over each machine gun, *blast, blast,* like a boxer's tattoo, one-two, and I was exploded in the butt from a piece of my own shrapnel, whacked with a delicious pain clean as a mistress's sharp teeth going "Yummy" in your rump, and then the barrel of my carbine swung around like a long fine antenna and pointed itself at the machine-gun hole on my right where a great bloody sweet German face, a healthy spoiled overspoiled young beauty of a face, mother-love all over its making, possessor of that overcurved mouth which only great fat sweet young faggots can have when their rectum is tuned and entertained from adolescence on, came crying, sliding, smiling up over the edge of the hole, "Hello death!" blood and mud like the herald of sodomy upon his chest, and I pulled the trigger as if I were squeezing the softest breast of the softest pigeon which ever flew, still a woman's breast takes me now and then to the pigeon on that trigger, and the shot cracked like a birth twig across

my palm, *whop!* and the round went in at the base of his nose and spread and I saw his face sucked in backward upon the gouge of the bullet, he looked suddenly like an old man, toothless, sly, reminiscent of lechery. Then he whimpered *"Mutter,"* one yelp from the first memory of the womb, and down he went into his own blood just in time, timed like the interval in a shooting gallery, for the next was up, his hole-mate, a hard avenging specter with a pistol in his hand and one arm off, blown off, rectitude like a stringer of saliva across the straight edge of his lip, the straightest lip I ever saw, German-Protestant rectitude.

On inspection of such a passage Miss Hardwick might want to rephrase her criticism of this novel as "poorly written" or of Mailer's style as "indolent." To get what these sentences have to offer, one must entirely put aside the assumption that Mailer is here writing out of any vulgarity of motive. He shows instead the most intense involvement in the words he uses and in the patterns of association among them. In that long middle sentence there is held in suspension, in a neutralizing balance, materials that would in shorter grammatical units — the kind familiar in popular literature of sexual crime — have a psychological luridness which Mailer is choosing here to avoid. Yes, he can remind us of James M. Cain, as Tom Wolfe was proud to observe in the New York *Book Week,** but only when he is on his way to other significances with which Mr. Wolfe's kind of blockbuster criticism is incapable of dealing.

Given the continuum of movement in that long, unbroken third sentence, none of the implications can be isolated; they are in an interdependent relation that is an image of Rojack's mind. And we are made to feel this even while the simple excitement of what is going on is itself sufficient warrant for the breathlessness of the narration. Perhaps Mailer planned this sentence, but I suspect it represents something better than

* Included in this collection. [Ed.]

planning, some saturation of the author's mind in what he wants to do that makes everything that spontaneously issues from it part of the life that the language has already produced. This fluidity of association is the most frightening aspect of the passage. Thus, though Rojack's dexterity of violence is first ascribed to a sort of magic, it is almost at once reassociated with the vanity of human skill in a sport, boxing, that has a strong component of homoeroticism. From this the mind of the hero quickly shifts to a heterosexual fantasy occasioned by his wound, the comparison being to a woman's affection for his rump, and from there his thoughts move more confidently to the German soldier-as-faggot, whose "rectum is tuned." At this point sodomy gets connected with blood and mud, with death and with something like bodily wastes, and then, from this extremity of explicitness, the drift is back again to a woman and her breast: the act of squeezing the trigger that kills the faggot is like squeezing a breast: the shot itself reminds him of childbirth (it feels like a "birth twig"), for Rojack the most creative and therefore worthy consequence of heterosexual intercourse. No wonder the cry of the German for "*Mutter*" seems dramatically powerful. And it is by the same token metaphorically relevant to the obsessive tension throughout the book between creative sexuality (the German's "one yelp" is from the first memory of the womb") and sex that is murderous, associated with blood, mud, feces, and buggery. While the allusion that follows, to the dead soldier's "hole-mate" (and to his "rectitude"), doesn't require explication, it has the remarkable quality, like everything else in the passage, of being so utterly right in an innocently descriptive way that its metaphoric implications seem natural rather than a result of contrivance. This is of course what the passage as a whole, the book as a whole, wants to express: that the world in which we ordinarily participate simply *is* a version of our most neurotic imaginings.

With such a passage at the opening, the novel nears its end in the Waldorf Towers with a proposition from Deborah's father (he is also her first seducer) to Rojack, and possibly also to Ruta, the German maid with whom Rojack committed an athletic combination of buggery and ordinary copulation immediately following his murder of Deborah: " 'Come on,' Kelly murmured, sitting on his throne, 'shall we get shitty?' " Though the perverse sexual desires that stir in Rojack and that he rejects are said to be "unfamiliar," they are, as we've just seen, hardly new, and Mailer at this point is coy and evasive. Nonetheless the scene, like other mad scenes in the book, has a credibility nearly astonishing, especially with accompanying evocations, always on the verge of being long-winded and ludicrous, of glamour excessive to the point of comedy, of unimaginable wealth, and of power so beyond the control of a single man as to be supernatural. The mad scenes are endowed with the ramifications they often have in Elizabethan drama, with significances reaching into governments, into organizations — the Mafia, the CIA — and beyond into the metaphysics of power. Kelly is a man who "has strings everywhere," and when he remarks that "there's nothing but magic at the top," he means that beyond the web of his influence is nothing but God and the Devil. His invitation to be "shitty" is one indication, within the metaphors of the book, of what might delicately be called the side he chooses to be on in the war of heaven and hell, and the effectively discreet hints of swishiness in his tone are another. From such "magic," such manifest power associated with de-creation — with sodomy and the odors of corruption that classically belong to the Devil — Rojack struggles to free himself. He doesn't wholly succeed, his hope of freedom being in his love for Cherry, who does not live to bear the child he wants to have given her. But partly because of her he has, by the end, had what James meant by a second birth, and we last see him alone in search of an environment in which he can be that second self, traveling in the car he and Cherry had hoped to take together across the continent.

Much of *An American Dream* is a grim saturnalia, under

the influence not so much of the moon as of the craters of the moon to which Rojack feels suicidally drawn. As a saturnalia, the book manages to create justifications not merely for extraordinary behavior but also for attitudes that, taken strictly as attitudes, would be offensively moral, even hysterically so. The attitudes toward sex, for example, are strangely puritanical, lacking any acknowledgment of the power not of sexual dexterity merely, but of sexual tenderness and of pleasures within the capacities of ordinarily able-bodied persons. Too much is required of sex by Mailer, so that both its perverse and its creative aspects are melodramatized. What saves the book is a commitment to creativity invested not in sexual acts but in acts of writing, and not even on every page, of course, but on many of them. The paragraph about killing the Germans is a paradigm in which a personal dream of creativity barely flickers within a publicly ordered nightmare of death. Necessarily this dream has no lasting embodiment in the story, not even in such a nucleus of a new society as Lawrence would have preserved in the marriage and isolation of lonely lovers, but the energy that derives from that dream gives velocity and life to the sentences in the book and the requisite courage for the exposure in the hero and in the author of all that is trying to kill it.

# The Interpretation of Dreams

## by Leo Bersani

An American Dream has been nearly as widely panned as it has been widely reviewed, but in how many cases has it really been read, or, to put the best construction on it, read in book form rather than in the *Esquire* installments? A dazzling performance, a recklessly generous yet disciplined exercise in self-exposure and self-invention, Mailer's latest novel has had the further distinction of provoking a quaint resurgence of neoclassical canons of taste. The strategy of attack has naturally been not entirely ineffective. It can't, after all, be denied that the novel sins continuously against the rules of propriety and verisimilitude, and the clarities of *bon sens*. So that by ignoring what Mailer has done, his attackers have been able to have quite a time of it showing what he should have done. Elizabeth Hardwick, in *Partisan*

This essay originally appeared in *Partisan Review* (Fall, 1965) and is reprinted here by permission of Leo Bersani and *Partisan Review*. Copyright © 1965 by *Partisan Review*.

*Review*, announced that *An American Dream* is "a very dirty book — dirty and extremely ugly." And if we look for something closer to a reasoned argument in her review, we find the curious logic that the story "is artless, unmysterious and so there is no pain in it, no triumphant cruelty or instructive evil." It's mysterious to *me* why mystery is necessary for pain, why cruelty should be triumphant (over what? exactly how?) or evil instructive (to make the reader a "better person"?), or indeed what relevance such ideas about the novel have in what purports to be an account of *this* novel. Tom Wolfe,* treating us once again to his special blend of *Wham-bang!* interjections and Comp. Lit. pedantry, thinks that Rojack is killed off with too much thinking in the first fourteen and a half pages of the novel, complains of "unreal dialogue," but finally concedes that Mailer may one day be able to "climb into the same ring as James M. Cain." For Joseph Epstein, *An American Dream*, "on any level one chooses to read it" (?), is "confused and silly," and (shades of English 223: Nineteenth-Century Realistic Fiction) he condemns Mailer for being "more interested in the novel as a spectacle than as a convincing representation of life, more concerned with projecting personal fantasies than creating verisimilitude."

Philip Rahv, writing in the *New York Review of Books*, manages both to capture Miss Hardwick's moralistic tone (he complains of Rojack's being freed, by plot manipulation, "from paying any sort of price for what he has done") and to echo Mr. Epstein's notions of what a novel is supposed to do (the story lacks "verisimilitude, even in the most literal sense"). Finally, in a plot summary apparently designed to show the uselessness of attempting a critical evaluation of this "dreadful novel," Stanley Edgar Hyman unwittingly demonstrates some of Mailer's marvelous humor and indifference to plot, and shows in addition his own inability to cope with the

* Both the Hardwick and Wolfe essays are included in this collection. [Ed.]

difficulty of Mailer's language and especially the exuberant inventiveness of his similes. Unfortunately, Mailer's defenders — with the notable exception of Richard Poirier in *Commentary**— seem as anxious as his detractors to get away from the book. John Aldrich, in an apocalyptic reading for *Life* which Mailer had printed in *Partisan Review* to offset Miss Hardwick's scolding comments, speaks of *An American Dream* as "a devil's encyclopedia of our secret visions and desires, an American dream or nightmare"; Mailer, we are told, has created "an image of our time which will undoubtedly stand as authoritative for this generation." And Conrad Knickerbocker, adopting that flattening perspective from which the *Times* reassures its readers that good books, good plays, and good movies are never special or particular but are always speaking to all of us about all our problems, praises Mailer for searching for something called "the mana, magics, submerged and hideous, that move the age."

But the seriousness of *An American Dream* involves a denial of certain kinds of novelistic seriousness, of social probability and relevance, as well as of so-called intellectual depth. It is an intensely private novel, and one key to what has offended or puzzled the reviewers is probably in the way Mailer allows his hero to treat himself, in that peculiar blend of self-concentration and self-deprecation which, in fact, largely accounts for the originality of his language. The expectations of a political novel which might be set up by the joke that begins the story are rapidly destroyed. Mailer in *An American Dream* is somewhat like Balzac in his attitudes toward social maneuvering and power: he seems just as naïvely melodramatic in his notion of what goes on at the top, and the images of political power in both novelists should be immediately recognizable as private mythologies expressing private obsessions and dreams of power ideally demonic. Both are impatient with the specific strategies

* Printed in this collection. [Ed.]

for gaining and keeping power, as distinct from the excitement of exercising it. Barney Kelly, like Vautrin, is a spooky
physical presence who overwhelms Rojack with a wild assortment of suffocating smells, just as Vautrin paralyzes Rastignac
and Lucien de Rubempré by shooting bulletlike particles of
his fantastic will through the air and into the soft soil of their
more passive minds. Mailer, like Balzac, is better at suggesting
some of the sexual impulses that perhaps account for the en-
joyment of power than at detailing the more prosaic and conscious calculations that pave the way to it. Kelly's success story
is brashly improbable (he possessed the stock market by
telepathy); what he really wants to talk about with Rojack is
the frightening thrill of incest with Bess and her daughter,
and later with Deborah, and the most impressive demonstration of his power is in the extraordinary passage where he
invites Rojack to "get shitty" with him and Ruta. In his wish
to have the three of them "pitch and tear and squat and kick,
swill and grovel on the Lucchese bed, fuck until our eyes were
out, bury the ghost of Deborah by gorging on her corpse," in
his brutal, simultaneous appeal to impulses of anality, homosexuality, necrophilia, and cannibalism, the magic of his
power is made marvelously concrete by the energy of his in-
dulgence in bodily fantasies, an energy so great that Rojack
begins to share the fantasies, to feel "unfamiliar desires."

It is power of this sort that both fascinates and terrifies
Rojack; the murder of Deborah and, perhaps more significantly, the story of that murder are his attempts to free himself
from it. If Rojack responds like an electric coil to multi-
tudinous "invasions" from the outside world, it is because he
is pathologically convinced that what he calls his "center" may
be stolen from him at any moment, at the same time that he
feeds on this sense of constant threat as a kind of substitute for
a sense of self. This fantasy provides what could be called the
psychological theme, or obsession, of the novel, and it may or
may not, incidentally, throw some light on what has often

seemed to be Mailer's facile talent for making himself obnoxious in public. When, for example, we read that Rojack, instead of feeling relief at being left alone for a few moments in the police station, yearns for Roberts's return, "much as if that merciless lack of charity which I had come to depend on in Deborah (as a keel to ballast the empty dread of my stomach) was now provided by the detective," we may at least wonder to what extent Mailer's own sense of himself has depended on his ability to provoke attack. *An American Dream*, at any rate, records a dramatic and exhilarating struggle with that "empty dread," an attempt to fight the vampire complex that makes Rojack both fear and need a world of devouring bitches, telepathic powers, and omnipotent smells. The novel, for all its apparently complacent acceptance of magic, is a continuous attack against magic, that is, an attack against fantasies of the self as both all-powerful and totally vulnerable.

The strategy of resistance is, inevitably, literary, and the power of *An American Dream* is in its demonstration of verbal tactics which finally make what I have called the psychological theme irrelevant. The "courage" which is made so much of in the novel, and which the reviewers have found lamentably banal as a moral philosophy, is much more of a brilliant and difficult trick than a virtue in the ordinary sense. While it is often merely the bravery born of a superstitious compulsion, as when Rojack forces himself to walk along the parapet of Kelly's terrace, it involves, more profoundly, a willingness to entertain the most extravagant fantasies and hallucinations in order to change their affective coefficient. By taking the risk of abandoning himself to the fantastic suggestiveness of every person, every object, every smell encountered during the thirty-two hours he writes about, Rojack discovers fantasy as a source of imaginative richness in himself instead of fearing it as an ominous signal from mysterious, external powers. He moves, in other words, from fantasy as a psychological illusion about the world to the use of fantasy as a somewhat self-conscious but exuberant display of his own inventive powers. Every menace becomes the occasion for a verbal performance, and his fluttering nervousness about being deprived of his "center" is rather humorously believed by the incredibly dense and diversified self which his language reveals and creates. Nothing in the book (not even Rojack's moving attempt to know love as something sane and decent with Cherry) except the virtuosity of the writing itself indicates a way out of the nightmare Rojack seems to be telling. The nightmare would be nothing more than a nasty story if Mailer, like his critics, had allowed it to separate itself from the virtuosity, from, especially, the metaphorical exuberance which is, I think, a way of mocking and outdoing the dangerous inventiveness of a magic-ridden world. This means, of course, that the *playfulness* of the novel is by no means a frivolous attitude toward "dirty" or "ugly" events, but rather the natural tone of a man for whom events have become strictly literary-novelistic situations to be freely exploited for the sake of a certain style and the self-enjoyment it perhaps unexpectedly provides.

It is, then, irrelevant to complain of improbable situations or unreal dialogue in *An American Dream*. Rojack's playfulness, his verbal exuberance is the sign of a confident use of power, and it involves an occasionally reckless indifference to the probability of his own experience. The telling of his story becomes *Rojack*'s invention as well as Mailer's once his life confronts him as choices to be made about language and novelistic form. The plot of *An American Dream* is, therefore, nothing more than a mode of Rojack's inventive exuberance, and, while it is perhaps understandable that the anecdotal aspect of fiction should trick us most easily into confusions between art and life, we should be admiring the power of extravagance in Rojack's tall story instead of upholding the faded banner of verisimilitude. Rojack's experience is largely a pretext for trying his hand at different ways of telling a story: making love to Ruta is a calculated allegory of good and evil, a parody of literary struggles between the Lord and the Devil, but the scene in the police station and Rojack's telephone calls are masterful exercises in the art of realistic dialogue and psychological detail. And much of the novel's humor is in the unexpected shifts from one kind of writing to another: the conversation with Dr. Tharchman moves from intricate, understated satire to an exaggerated display of *humour noir*, and some of the suspense of a spy story is brought in just long enough to make us feel the greater importance of what is more like a ghost story.

This free play of virtuosity in the narrative structure of *An American Dream* also characterizes Rojack's similes, which the reviewers have pounced on with a comical solemnity about stylistic propriety. Mr. Hyman, in his outraged enumeration of the similes he hates most, is only the most hilarious example of all those readers who have declared with absolute seriousness that they have never thought of a pigeon's breast when touching the trigger of a gun, or had an orgasm "fierce as a demon in the eyes of a bright golden child." Novelists themselves have, of course, been known to isolate their metaphors from their style, to test each one for its individual "rightness" or "objective" validity. Flaubert's maniacal search for a perfect equivalence between image and a preexistent "subject" (a fear of style disguised as an idolatry of style) probably accounts, to some degree, for his leaden metaphors and the clumsiness of his rhythms. But Mailer in *An American Dream*, unlike Flaubert, never uses metaphor for the purpose of arresting our attention, of making us stop to admire a tiny verbal island, an exquisite *trouvaille*. Rojack's similes *make* a self of enormous, even fantastic imaginative range, and their power lies in a kind of dialectical reference to, and denial of, characters and events in the novel. They change the story, as it is being told, into a challenge to the resources of fantasy; their complexity is not in their farfetched nature, but lies rather in the dramatic burden they carry of transforming oppressive experience into tokens of stylistic play. The plausibility of Rojack's similes is irrelevant; what matters is that he makes us feel his associations as spontaneous, irresistible fantasies and that we accept his most elaborate verbal constructions as illustrating the elaborateness of immediacy rather than of development toward an idea. For no intellectual strategy could explain the humor or justify the casual difficulty of Rojack's style. It is, in a sense, his very absence of thought (an absence deplored by Mr. Epstein and by Granville Hicks) which creates Rojack's "system" of defense, his refusal to conceptualize sensation and to be reasonable about the accumulation of metaphor which makes of his writing an act of total responsiveness.

*An American Dream* is an impressively original work, but it shouldn't be necessary to point out that Mailer is not the first novelist to prefer to the conventions of social probability in fiction a more direct form of self-display. The illusion of distinctness between the narrator and the social world he is presumably observing and reporting on is only weakly maintained in Proust and in James's later novels, where we already sense a certain impatience with the mediation of fantasy into "objective" characters and events. In both James and Proust, what seems to be a fascination with the suggestiveness and self-inventive possibilities of language leads to some carelessness about novelistic situations, a tendency to allegorize the world as a rather transparent (rather than hidden) projection of the self. But most of Mailer's critics surely know about all this, and if we are to dismiss the possibility of a deliberate ganging-up on him for past offenses, the irrelevance of what has been said about *An American Dream* must perhaps be explained by the shock and resentment produced by a work that would force us to admit the self-indulgence, the particularity, and even, in a certain sense, the irresponsibility of interesting art. Mailer's admirers are already hard at work making him responsible and relevant to all sorts of things, but to read *An American Dream* is, happily, to see the hopelessness of their good intentions. Nothing, after all, could be more typical of the marvelous lightness of imagination than to test, in the most scrupulous detail, the possibility of a grown-up love, built on tenderness and respect, with Cherry, and then to end the whole thing on the frivolous note of that charmingly nonsensical phone call to heaven.

# From Vietnam to Obscenity

## by John W. Aldridge

Late last summer, in a pious setting of green mountains, stone fences, unpolluted streams, and other reminders of our lost pastoral purity, two prominent writers made statements that were in fact outrageous attacks on the moral and emotional integrity of American life. The occasion was the Bread Loaf Writers' Conference in Vermont, and the writers were William J. Lederer and Norman Mailer. Lederer spoke with a full charge of anger about Vietnam, the organized draft and political corruption behind our activities there in this age of the Great Society. Mailer spoke like a bad boy in church about obscenity in literature, the necessary filthiness of language in this age of cancer, foiled feces, and pinched orgasm. Lederer's materials were facts and figures he had gathered at considerable personal risk from firsthand ob-

This essay originally appeared in *Harper's Magazine* (February 1968) and is reprinted here by permission of International Famous Agency, Inc., and John W. Aldridge. Copyright © 1968 by *Harper's Magazine*.

servation of the Vietnam scene. Mailer's were the radical intuitions of a mind almost pathologically sensitive to the psychic currents alive in the contemporary world. Yet one could not escape the feeling that in spite of their very different approaches, the two men were describing essentially the same phenomenon. There might be no literal connection between Vietnam and obscenity beyond the fact that both could be considered dirty words. But on some level beyond or beneath the literal, one sensed the possibility of connection, and for some time afterward was haunted by that possibility.

It therefore seemed something more than a nice coincidence when, a month or so later, Mailer published a new novel bearing the portentous title *Why Are We in Vietnam?* One was of course a bit baffled to discover that the book was not really about Vietnam at all but about an Alaskan bear hunt. Yet perverse whimsy could not have been Mailer's sole motive for using the title, although nothing else seemed to account for his decision to run two photographs of himself on the back of the jacket, one depicting a mean, sullen Max Baerish Mailer with an enormous black eye, the other showing a handsome, quite respectable face that smiled slightly in a manner almost enigmatic. Then one discovered, with some renewal of excitement, that the book was obscene — relentlessly, brilliantly, hilariously obscene, very probably the most obscene novel ever published in this country — and that, in view of Mailer's declarations at Bread Loaf, seemed far too pat for any coincidence.

There appeared to be good reason for supposing now that the book just might contain hidden depths and secrets, that if Mailer had two faces, so might the book — a verbal surface of grinning, foulmouthed inconoclasm and a concealed interior of diabolically subtle, even murderous intent. Little by little this suspicion grew stronger and one's reading of the book warier. Then suddenly the Jekyll and Hyde effect dissolved: the two faces became one face possessing features of remarkable coherence. Now for the first time the title seemed appropriate and the obscenity imperative. For it became clear that Mailer had indeed managed to bring Vietnam and obscenity together in a marvelous synthesis and that his book, properly read, could be seen as telling us something important not only about the obscenity of our situation in Vietnam, but far more crucially, about the possible power of obscenity to help alleviate that situation.

To appreciate the success with which the novel justifies these claims, it is first necessary to see that the action does not literally stand for the Vietnam war, but is rather a complex metaphorical statement of the moral and emotional sickness that may be responsible for the war. The book is not, in other words, merely a charade in which elements of the war are pantomimed, or in which the bear hunters represent generals, their weapons the Air Force, and the animals the poor napalmed women and children of Vietnam. Certain minor parallels of this kind may be suggested, and the book may finally become an outlandish comic parable of our national tragedy, a grotesque anatomy of our psychic melancholy, a nightmare map of LBJ's route to certain disaster. But it arrives at none of these incarnations all at once, nor do they exist simultaneously on the same plane of subtlety. Mailer has in the past cautioned his readers not to understand him too quickly, and in this case the warning is imperative. One moves toward something like full comprehension of what he is saying only by slow degrees and only after excavating down through levels of significance that grow progressively larger the more carefully one studies them.

On the simplest level, the story the novel tells is familiar to the point of cliché because almost every major American author from Melville to Faulkner has written his version of it. Two Texas adolescents, D. J. Jethroe and Tex Hyde, go to Alaska, in the company of D. J.'s father and two guides, to hunt grizzly bear. At a particularly dangerous moment of kill,

D. J. beats his father in courage and in so doing figuratively murders him and takes possession of his manhood. The boys are then freed to act independently of adult authority. They strike out alone into the mountains and climb far above the timberline. There in a state of complete isolation and as vulnerable as men can be to the elemental perils, they are able to put aside their fears and hatreds and come into some kind of mature engagement of their condition as human beings.

The story, in short, appears to be nothing more than a modernized and even rather banal retelling of the classic American mythic tale of quest, initiation and ultimate absolution. *Moby Dick, Huckleberry Finn,* and Faulkner's "The Bear" loom behind it and create both its historical precedent and its archetypal pattern: the escape from the repressive hypocrisies of civilized society; the search for reality in the wilderness which, symbolically, represents a return to the Great Mother womb of nature; the test of strength and courage; the achievement of moral rebirth in the renewal of harmonious relations between the self and the natural world. One may be intrigued to see how a writer of Mailer's radical imagination has turned to perhaps the most conventional and idealized of American literary modes for the structure of what is surely a subversive attack on the American character. But if that were all he had done, one would be justified in writing off his book as still another watery helping of instant ritual stew.

Yet just as the Puritan and frontier versions of this story had always their dark other side, a haunting intimation of violence and terror working just beneath the idyllic pastoral surfaces, so there is a demonic center to Mailer's book. The story may seem innocuous enough in its details. But the story is *told*, and it is told by D. J., and that makes a difference as powerfully sinister as Ahab's madness or the horrors that pursue Huck and Jim as they float on their raft down the tranquil

Mississippi. For D. J. is also mad in his way as well as very probably a genius, and he is a magnificent perversion of the ideal of wholesome, clean-cut American boyism which we sentimentally but erroneously associate with *Huckleberry Finn*. In fact, D. J. is a perversion of both the idealized Huck and the idealized Jim. In his white incarnation he is Ranald Jethroe Jellicoe Jethroe, handsome sixteen-year-old stud from Dallas, Big D, Texas, that Eden of assassinations. He is also Disk Jockey to the world and Doctor Jekyll to his pal, Tex Hyde, who happens to be the son of a necrophiliac undertaker. But when D. J. is high on pot, his relation to the universe becomes transistorized, and he imagines himself plugged into the brain of a bedridden genius Negro. White boy and black boy talk out of his mouth at the same time, and the result is the most brilliant babble of verbal ghastliness ever heard in literature. D. J. speaks by turns with the tongue of a Hell's Angel, a Harlem hippie, a small-town Southern deputy sheriff, a drunken tent-revivalist preacher, and the filthiest-minded top sergeant in the U. S. Army. But he is a militant moralist at heart, and his obscenity functions as the terrible swift sword of conscience that slices through the pretensions of everything he finds obscene in American society.

His most outrageous eloquence is directed against the pretensions of his father, Rutherford (Rusty) David Jethroe Jellicoe Jethroe, top executive of a firm engaged in manufacturing plastic cigarette filters called Pew Rapports — the filter with the purest porosity of purpose — which eventually cause cancer of the lip. D. J. fears and despises the corruption of his father's world, and from the moment the hunting party arrives in Alaska, we recognize that he and Tex are as much the hunted and victimized, and finally as desperately at bay, as the animals of the Brooks Range country — because both they and the animals are being exploited by the sick value system which has produced emotional casualties of men like Rusty Jethroe.

Here, briefly, the Vietnam parallel emerges at the level of charade, but the effect is one of shattering and altogether successful tour de force. The methods employed by the invading hunters from Rusty's world have so terrorized the animals that they have gone berserk. As the Indian guide, Big Ollie, says, "animal no wild no more, now crazy." They have been fired upon by gigantic Magnum rifles of near howitzer size. They have been badly maimed and left, out of their minds with pain, to die a little at a time, black murder eating their hearts. Helicopters have herded them together and held them paralyzed with fright so that the hunters could have an easy shot. As a result, they have been reduced to a state in which their actions are no longer predictable or in keeping with the laws of animal decorum, in which they may charge without warning or reason, attack from ambush, carry on their own instinctual form of guerrilla warfare. D.J. and Tex are also fighting guerrilla-fashion, using as weapons D.J.'s outrageous rhetoric and their combined defiance of adult authority, to escape a similar brutalization at the human level. Toward the end of the novel it appears that they do escape. But we come to understand long before this that the ovious symbolism of the heavy weaponry, helicopters, guerrilla tactics, and the terrible plight of the animals is finally important to Mailer not because it pertains to the boys or pantomimes Vietnam but because it dramatizes the plight of the hunters. Their sickness of soul is the issue that interests him above all else. Around it he builds his case study of the individual and national psychosis which, in its most virulent pathological extension, seems to him to have created the Vietnam war.

Rusty Jethroe stands in the book as the representative victim of this psychosis. The implication is that the forces that drive him to become a promiscuous slayer of animals are the same as those that have driven the nation into promiscuous military aggressiveness. In both cases the problem is creative energy subverted into a massive need to seek and exercise domination over others. At some point in Rusty's development his native pioneer impulses toward adventure and self-challenge, impulses which might once have found an outlet in the testing hazards of the frontier, have been blocked in him and become the poison of his psychic life. There are voids in his eyes and gleams of yellow fire, reflecting the rage burning in the wastes of his unconscious. Sometimes it seems to D.J. that there are fifty thousand miles of marble floor down those eyes, and you have to walk over them all to get to The Man. But it is questionable whether The Man is any longer there. For Rusty has never found the freedom to measure himself, to possess his courage, to develop his trust or his capacity for love. Hence, his existence has degenerated into a series of small, vicious, powerseeking conquests of the animal and business world. He achieves temporary relief from his frustrations in his sadistic version of the hunt, in the kind of compulsive trophyism in which the mounted heads of bear and deer symbolize not shooting skill but corporation status, in the humiliation of subordinates, whose obedience to him is measured, according to D. J., by the degree of instant sincerity they can put into their "gut yes" whenever Rusty wants them to confirm the truth of one of his boasts. But all his victories are won in a contest that never engages him at the level of his deepest needs. Rusty has brought death to animals, and he may, as Hemingway once confessed about himself, be forced to kill animals in order to keep from committing suicide. But he has never faced the fact of death in his own mind. He therefore has never discovered his potentialities for life. He knows only the experience of dread, the great contemporary fear of defeat, and it is very possible that he will finally fall victim to cancer, the great contemporary disease of those who dread. For cancer, in Mailer's view, is the revenge which the cells of the body take upon those who fail to discharge their aggressive impulses, and so cleanse themselves of dread, in emotionally healthy ways.

Within the terms of Mailer's almost medievally unitary vision of human life, the psychological character of a nation is indistinguishable from that of an individual. A nation too can embark on a cancer course when it finds itself balked in the effort to confront new challenges and move forward into new phases of creative growth. For America the most dangerous cancer symptom is Vietnam. We brutalize and slaughter the Vietnamese as Rusty brutalizes and slaughters animals because our aggressions are frozen in the traps of murder and we have lost the power to release them through other, less destructive means. There was a time, according to Mailer, when this country existed dynamically not only on the physical frontier of its westward expansion but on the psychological frontier of a free-ranging aliveness to the possibilities of romance, adventure, and imaginative self-discovery. For a moment in history we were energized by the dream of the potential heroism of every man. When the West was filled, that dream turned inward and became a fixture of our fantasy life. As Mailer observes in his essay, "The Existential Hero," it was once a vital proof of manhood and selfhood to be able to

> fight well, kill well (if always with honor), love well and love many, be cool, be daring, be dashing, be wild, be wily, be resourceful, be a brave gun. And this myth, that each of us was born to be free, to wander, to have adventure and to grow on the waves of the violent, the perfumed, and the unexpected, had a force which could not be tamed no matter how the nation's regulators . . . would brick-in the modern life with hygiene upon sanity, and middle-brow homily over platitudes . . . it was as if the message in the labyrinth of the genes would insist that violence was locked with creativity, and adventure was the secret of love.

Briefly, during the Second World War, life in America turned adventurous again. Some nerve in the national awareness came suddenly awake, and we lived for a while in repossession of our courage and once more on the fine edge of new possibilities for heroism. But the surprises, failures, and dangers of the war ended by sapping our resistance to insecurity, and in the bleak, dead years of Truman, Joe McCarthy, and Eisenhower, we retreated into conservatism and the ugly paranoia of the cold war. America's need at this time was, said Mailer, to "take an existential turn, to walk into the nightmare, to face into that terrible logic of history which demanded that the country and its people must become more extraordinary and more adventurous, or else perish."

To make this possible we needed a hero for a President, a man who could embody the fantasy of heroism, and so allow "each private mind the liberty to consider its fantasy and find a way to grow." In John Kennedy we had for a time such a President. When he was assassinated, the fantasy was forced underground, and in our frustration and rage we have quite simply gone berserk. We have become involved in a war whose end may be limitless, an obscene war which can "brutalize what is best in a nation and encourage every horror to rise from its sewer." But a war we have needed because we have needed action, "not brave action, but action; any kind of action; any move to get the motors going. A future death of the spirit lies close and heavy upon American life, a cancerous emptiness at the center which calls for a circus."

This cancerous emptiness is finally what *Why Are We in Vietnam?* is all about. The book thus provides its own answer to the question raised by the title. But far more importantly, it also proposes in its language a certain half-ludicrous, half-serious solution to the dilemma it describes. For if the language is obscenity of a particularly violent and imaginative sort, it is obscenity used with a clearly radical moral intention: to help alleviate the psychological pressures that have driven us to commit the atrocity of Vietnam.

There are two kinds of obscenity in the novel: scatological and fornicatory. Sometimes, in the mixed metaphors of evacuation and buggery, the two cohabit. But the scatological pre-dominates. D.J.'s talk is primarily lingual bowel movement, and this has its quirky appropriateness. For over the years Mailer has evolved a sort of eschatology of scatology, a highly idiosyncratic metaphysics of feces. Excrement represents to him the organic form of defeat and dread. It is linked in his mind to the work of the Devil, who is engaged in unremitting warfare with God to determine the ascendancy of death or life in the universe, a contest which on the human level becomes the individual's unremitting struggle against dread. Closely related to this is the concept of apocalyptic orgasm which Mailer first explored in his famous essay, "The White Negro." The apocalyptic orgasm so passionately sought after by the hipster is not merely the ultimate sexual spasm. It may be a physical consummation devoutly to be wished for, but it is above all else a psychomystical experience whereby new cir-cuits of energy are generated in the self, which in turn come into connection with circuits operating throughout the uni-verse. Finally, therefore, it is a means of attaining oneness with God. But for this to become possible, the Devil in us must first be vanquished. Hence, behind every apocalyptic orgasm is an apocalyptic defecation. From one exit we ejacu-late toward divinity. From the other we evacuate the Devil's work. The route to salvation is thus from anus to phallus, from organic excretion to orgasmic ecstasy. If there is in fact a Great Chain of Being, Mailer's advice would obviously be to pull it.

At the literary level scatological obscenity is a means of clearing the psychic bowels of defeat and dread. It is a way of ridding ourselves of the blocked aggressions, the spiritual con-stipations, which goad us to violence even as they inhibit our powers of creative self-rejuvenation. In the broad sociological terms suggested by Mailer in his Bread Loaf lecture and again in a recent *Esquire* article, the literary use of obscenity may also be a means of renewing vital contact between those portions of the population who habitually and at grave peril to themselves repress their aggressive impulses, and those to whom obscenity is part of the accepted vernacular language and thus constitutes a natural and healthy mode of release for those impulses. Ideally, the function of obscenity would be to mediate between the superego and the id elements of American society, releasing the buried fears and hatreds of the WASP Establishment classes to something like the emotional freedom of the Negro and hipster.

"We live," says Mailer, "in an American society which can remind you of nothing so much as two lobes of a brain, two hemispheres of communication themselves intact but surgically severed from one another . . . the Establishment will not begin to come its half of the distance through the national gap until its knowledge of the real social life of that other isolated and . . . deprived world is accurate rather than liberal, condescending, and overprogrammatic. Yet for this to happen, every real and subterranean language must first have its hearing, even if taste will be in the process as outraged as a vegetarian forced to watch the flushing of entrails in a stockyards. . . .

". . . if the world is thus turned a shift more barbarous, it is also a click less insane. Each year, civilization gives its delineated promise of being further coterminous with schizophrenia. Good taste . . . may be ultimately the jailer. . . . The aim of a robust art still remains: that it be hearty, that it be savage, that it serve to feed audiences with the marrow of its honest presence. In the end robust art . . . gives . . . light and definition and blasts of fresh air to the corners of the world, it is a firm presence in the world, and so helps to protect the world from its dissolution in compromise, lack of focus, and entropy, entropy, that disease of progressive formlessness, that smog, last and most poisonous exhaust of the Devil's foul mouth. Yeah, and yes! Obscenity is where God and Devil meet, and so is another of the avatars in which art ferments and man distills. . . ."

The savage, robust art of Mailer's novel not only proposes through its obscenity a purgative treatment for some of the major illnesses of the age. It ends in an act of purgation and in the achievement of precisely the kind of psychic renewal which Mailer believes should be the logical result of such an act. In a long closing passage containing some of the finest descriptive writing Mailer or anyone else has ever done, D.J. and Tex leave behind Rusty's "mixed shit" world and climb high into the snow-covered peaks of the Brooks Range mountains. There, alone and, like Ike McCaslin in "The Bear," sacramentally weaponless, they discover an animal paradise not yet corrupted or brutalized by men. The animals are therefore still living in a state of telepathic communication with one another and with the electromagnetic currents of the universe, which seem to D. J. to be most heavily concentrated in the polar regions. But he and Tex are also telepathically connected with the animals. They find that by sending out intense psychic voltages of murder they can frighten away a white wolf which threatens them, and a moment later they observe the destructive effect their message has had on his courage when he ineffectually fights off an attacking eagle. The boys too achieve harmony with the elemental forces of life, and during a long night while they lie awake under the electric blaze of the aurora borealis, they pass through the locks of homosexually homocidal impulses toward each other. They have hung together on the edge of a conflict between sexually possessing each other and killing each other. But "as the hour went by and the lights shifted, something in the radiance of the north went into them, and owned their fear, some communion of telepathies and new powers, and they were twins, never to be near as lovers again."

It may be an irony that on the last page of the novel D. J. reveals that he and Tex are on their way to the Army and Vietnam. But the point, one suspects, is that by now they have conquered the impulse to Vietnam in themselves. They do not *need* Vietnam as an outlet for their hostilities, and so it is certain that they will be as derisively antagonistic to the war as they have been to the sick pretensions of Rusty's world. For both have learned from their experience in the mountains how to live a bit closer to the centers of their moral and emotional aliveness. Both can now conduct themselves with some fidelity to a vision of their possible freedom. Both are ever so slightly nearer to a condition of sainthood, even if it be the sainthood of the social outlaw and the obscene genius madman. Yet Mailer may be saying that it is precisely to this kind of sainthood that we must look to be saved. For in these plague years of Vietnam to be outlaw is to be a champion of humanity, to be obscene is to be morally purified and to evacuate the dread and defeat of the world out of the world, so that we can recapture our courage and reopen the channels of adventure in ourselves.

# The Aesthetics of Norman Mailer

**by Jack Richardson**

There have been times when writing was considered an act of grace, a form of almost supernatural intervention in the ordinary affairs of the human imagination. The modern masters, however, have made it clear that the merely inspired soon perish and that the writer and his book are best, if not entirely, sustained by an act of will. James, Flaubert, Joyce, Mann — their testament can be seen as much in the persistent struggle to create a disciplined and meaningful language as in the worlds and characters that they left us. One need not be acquainted with their biographies to understand that a long battle of attrition once took place to ferret out of the rough matter of inspiration a strong, polished, personal idiom. Indeed, again and again readers have discovered that, at its best, the modern novel often deals with

This essay originally appeared in *The New York Review of Books* (May 8, 1969) and is reprinted with permission from *The New York Review of Books*. Copyright © 1969 by The New York Review.

the adventure of its own making and that, while celebrating itself, it more than insinuates that its real hero is its creator, whose passion and agony we, for convenience, simply call his "style."

To many, Norman Mailer may seem far removed from these aesthetic preoccupations, but he is in fact one of the very few writers in the last decade or so who has really understood the hard lesson that the modern masters have taught. He has certainly grasped the act of will — the style — necessary to the writer-as-protagonist, and he has insisted stubbornly on exercising it again and again for its own sake as well as for the periodic re-creation of himself as a writer. He has done this, of course, without the aid of the faith in aesthetic form which sustained his predecessors; nor does he conceal his literary strategy and self-awareness by using an ironic and formal mode of expression. Rather he spreads everything out for us so that we may see to the bone and muscle of the writer's determination to survive. For all his pose as an activist and his well-advertised involvement in public life, Mailer's response to the controversy in which he is so much engaged is almost completely stylistic, and one soon realizes that his literary manner is in itself a dramatic dialectic. Mailer seems to be intellectually exhilarated by language, and I honestly believe he would much rather narrate for us the way he has tracked down the proper, self-revealing adverb than give us sagas of how wars are won or analyses of the tactics of political revolution.

Many of his critics have misunderstood the purely literary quality of Mailer's work, its unabashed, almost precious, obsession with itself. They have taken part of the author's public style as a clue to his intentions and have been pleased or exasperated accordingly. But no matter how diligently Mailer insists on creating a persona in the thick of political and social joustings, a persona part demagogue, part clown, part visionary, one cannot help feeling that his forays into the community are little more than intentionally self-lacerating experiences meant to sharpen the nuance and the tone of what he knows will finally be their literary reenactment.

His last novel, for example, *Why Are We in Vietnam?*, clearly displays Mailer's method of digesting experience. Taken as a collection of social insights into Corporate America, it is an outlandish caricature; taken as a narrative of the American spirit coming upon its pagan god at the end of a man's hunting trip, it is simple and familiar stuff; but, considered as the re-creation by means of language of the notions Mailer has about America, it is brilliant. The monologues of the narrator, D.J., are as superbly monstrous as tortured with vernacular fustian as are the forms of our national existence which he both comments on and embodies. The novel, to be sure, is an indictment, "J'accuse," but it is, in every way, the "J'accuse" of a writer obsessed with language — the "J'accuse," finally of a belletrist. The oblique title of the novel has its purpose: it is as if Mailer has said, "These words are my politics. Think of this semantic *Walpurgisnacht* the next time the Secretary of State speaks statistically about our war."

The ability to make convincing resolutions almost entirely through literary style is Mailer's major gift. However, finding occasions for the exercise of this gift seems always to have been a problem for him. Though he is what many consider an almost too personal writer, he has produced very little about small, isolated experiences. Everything he writes seems at first glance to be occasional to be encased in some prevalent mood, some new philosophy, some general current phenomenon. Again, his critics have seen him as always ready to attach himself and his prose style to any event that is fashionable and guarantees a certain amount of public attention. Indeed, it is true that Mailer's work often seems propped up by the styles of the times. Beat literature, pot, the Black Rebellion, urban planning, sexual freedom — one can wonder if there has been any cult in the last twenty years that he has not used as fuel.

Anti-Mailer moralists see this as a sinister form of exploitation, and even his fans talk about the novel he could and should be writing, as though there were some special excellence attached to this particular literary form. Mailer himself admits, in the swaggering boxing metaphors he occasionally uses, to being a counterpuncher, and it appears that only when he is struck by something on the scale of a social movement is he moved to hit back, to draw on the literary energy he apparently keeps ready for all occasions he considers to be in his weight class.

Still, no matter how grand the subject he decided to challenge, it often seemed that his literary sensibility was too well-trained and dazzling to give it a fair fight. One would watch fascinated as Mailer transformed a public event into private expression, but, while grateful for his suprising reflections, one somehow missed the old, recognizable outlines of that event once he was through with it. The aspic of Mailer's prose often covered over events a bit too easily, turning them into grotesque and fascinating semi-philosophical bursts of rhetoric.

Yet so pugnacious a literary will as Mailer's seemed always to be searching for the tougher adversaries he deserved; and in his frequent restive appearances in print he was like some Jacob in extreme need of an angel to wrestle with. Now the 1968 Republican and Democratic conventions hardly suggest angels, but they, along with the Pentagon Peace March of the previous year, have proven to be for Mailer the agents for the action he understands best, the adventure of literary art in the world. He had often before matched himself against a historic moment, but this time history, while not exactly forcing an accommodation, at least succeeded in winning the right of coexistence.

The result is a tense balance between social and literary observation which often reads like a good old-fashioned novel in which suspense, character, plot revelations, and pungently describable action abound. Indeed, I am certain that one of the main reasons *The Armies of the Night* and *Miami and the Siege of Chicago* have been so widely praised is that they permit the well-worn, comfortable habits of reading. Here, after all, the writer-as-hero has come out from behind his aesthetic camouflage and placed himself and the gestation of his work into an arena nicely suited to his battle between public and private style, an arena where no architectual details get in the way of an open, entertaining view. As he proved by his earlier study of the nomination of Barry Goldwater, Mailer has few equals at describing the national rituals of American life; and these last two works demonstrate that he has no equal at all when it comes to matching one's personality against these rituals.

These virtues have been duly celebrated, and certainly Mailer has an eye for and on the souls of his compatriots. He can pin down the immaculate WASP, in town from Iowa to give his polite, Christian consent to Richard Nixon, as well as, with a certain reserved affection, the Yippie who consents to nothing but the halfhearted practice of Japanese riot techniques. Mailer is also an extraordinary synthesizer, a reporter who can sense moods and the subtler vibrations of political performance, and who can turn often tedious and random happenings into interesting, cohesive speculation. Finally, one must mention his ego and his honesty, a combination which permits him to confront events and personages as their antagonist and their equal, certain that it will be *he* who will illuminate *them*.

Still, it is not simply the extraordinary personal journalism that is most impressive about *The Armies of the Night* and *Miami and the Siege of Chicago*. The peculiar power of these books comes not from the fact that Mailer offers us better writing than that to which we are generally accustomed in politics, but, rather, from the uncanny way in which he has managed to maintain in these works the stylistic play and form of the most complex literary fiction. One should never forget the allegiance Mailer feels to fictional truth and judge these two books as showing an elementary split between confessional data on the one hand and public facts on the other.

Consider, for example, the first part of *The Armies of the Night,* the section which is entitled "History as a Novel: The Steps of the Pentagon." Here we have Mailer as character observing himself perform, preparing those observations for the Mailer who is relating to us as we read what he has observed about those observations. And, too, at most times, there is yet another watchful instrument, a television camera, on hand to effect one more layer of awareness. The whole sequence is an elaborate orchestration in which tones merge and blend in a manner which forces one to listen very carefully for the truth of things shaded by style, moments caught in an expressive reality which Mailer sets against the banalties of a *Time* reporter. Mailer has used here the apperceptive techniques of the modern novel, and used them to make a heavy literary assault on the common notions about history. It is not simply a question of the oddities of a single personality brought to bear on a subject that is generally dealt with "objectively." Rather, what Mailer does is to tinker consciously with the ways through which we are used to receiving information and reflection about certain areas of national experience. In short, for three quarters of *The Armies of the Night* Mailer is a literary modernist, juggling forms and experimenting with the narrative voice, teasing our sensibility which insists on getting quickly to the heart of the matter, forcing it to put up with dissertations on rhetoric, and surreal and pedestrian asides, until we admit that we are in a special terrain and must proceed with caution.

However, as I have said, history has made its own demands on Mailer's style, and these have kept him from being too much a formalist, from being a self-indulgent verbal speculator. The historic voice has its own traditions, and these have impressed themselves on Mailer and kept him finally within the boundaries of readability. Taken together, *The Armies of the Night* and *Miami and the Siege of Chicago* form a stylistic argosy from one form of awareness which is antic and novelistic to another which, with some melancholy, admits the strength of a simpler and more brutal actuality. In his reports on the conventions, Mailer seems at times completely overwhelmed by the deep ruptures he senses in America and by the final incapacity of even the most disciplined artistic will to force an adhesion. He becomes less and less concerned with maintaining a literary center to the second work, and allows the sequences from Miami to Chicago to unfold for the most part unchallenged by his imagination.

Whereas in *The Armies of the Night* he was in every sense a participant, in its sequel he is more detached, more wary, as tentative in his verbal manner as he is in his role of Old Guard Revolutionary. Between the quiet inexorability of Miami and the porcine hysteria of Chicago, there seemed less and less room for aesthetic sportiveness, and, as the pressure of these events increased, one felt Mailer's constriction of spirit, a slow sentence-by-sentence admission that there are forces of obliteration uncowed by even the most intricate artifice.

*Miami and the Siege of Chicago* is like the second part of an artistic *Bildungsroman* in which the hero finally allows the social order its right to a reality of its own. As the book slips into a glum catalogue of events, such as trips to a Hugh Hefner party and missed opportunities to be on hand when the police charged the formidable band of McCarthy supporters, it is as though the end of some passion were being described in a purposefully flat and muted way, as though history and art had worn themselves out in a magnificently equal encounter.

The last few years have produced much talk about the new "creative journalism" and the use of novelistic techniques in reporting. Whatever these phrases meant before — and it is my impression that they meant very little — they have now acquired a definition after the vent of these two books. Mailer has created a fresh entente between the personal mode and the public record, and, at a time when it is badly needed, he has reaffirmed the rights of the individualistic idiom to move in any social sphere. Simply, he has enlarged the territories of language, something the very best writers have always done for us.

# PART THREE:
# The Argument Ad Hominem

# by Dwight Macdonald
# Massachusetts
# vs.
# Mailer

It began as just another D. & D. case
— Drunk & Disorderly. It won't be found in the lawbooks —
there wasn't even a court stenographer — but it's already part
of the folklore of Provincetown, also known as Eighth Street
by the Sea. Every summer, this Cape Cod seashore town becomes what the sociologists would call a focus of conflicting
cultures. The *Kulturkampf* is waged between the natives —
mostly either Protestant New Englanders or Portuguese-de-
scended Catholic fishermen, two breeds not notable for the
breadth of their morality — and the summer people, whose
morals are latitudinarian, and who are a rich mixture of
artists, writers, beats, hipsters, homosexuals, and other estival
hedonists. The police force is definitely on the side of the
native culture.

This essay first appeared in *The New Yorker* (October 8, 1960) and is
reprinted here by permission. Copyright © 1960 by The New Yorker
Magazine, Inc.

The case of the Commonwealth of Massachusetts vs. Norman Mailer began on Commercial Street, in Provincetown, at about 1:10 on the morning of June 9 last. The bars close at one in Provincetown, and Mailer and his pretty brunette wife, Adele, who was acting at the Provincetown Playhouse this summer, were walking home after some pub-crawling. They were making for the Hawthorne House, a big place on a hill and one of the town's landmarks, which was built by the turn-of-the-century painter Charles Hawthorne; they had rented it for the season for themselves and their two small children. A police car came nosing along the deserted street in that unsettling way police cars have, like Melville's pale shark slipping ominously through tropical waters.

"Taxi! Taxi!" Mailer called out, mocking the tribal enemy.

"Be quiet, you damn fool!" said Mrs. Mailer, in a wifely fashion.

"TAXI!" he insisted, in satisfactory defiance of both police and wife.

The car glided shakily on, went around the block and came back — this is the moment in the nightmare at which you wake up if you're lucky — and pulled around a corner in front of the Mailers just as they were about to cross the street. Two cops got out.

"Did you yell 'Taxi'?"

"Yes."

"Does this car look to you like a taxi?"

"Well, you know — that thing on top."

"All right, move on!"

"I'll move on when you get out of my way."

At this point, the cops grabbed Mailer and pushed him into the car. With considerable presence of mind, he called out as he disappeared, "Adele! You're my witness. I'm not resisting arrest." The car drove off, leaving Adele on the street, as alone as Ariadne. Provincetown cops have been known to drop the wife at her home in such late arrests, but the present acting police chief, Francis H. (Cheyney) Marshall, has put a stop to such gallantry.

During the ride to the jail — both sides agree — no one said anything. When they arrived, the cops got out. They were Patrolman George St. Amand and Special Patrolman — that is, on the summer force only — William Sylvia, known throughout town as Cobra. Still without a word, Cobra reached in and pulled Mailer out of the car. What happened next was described by the victim in a letter written several weeks later to the New York *Post*. The letter is a good specimen of Basic Mailerese.

The rumble was a touch copacetic. It began when we got out of the police car outside the station house, and they would not let me walk in, but endeavored to assist me in. The scrimmage started because I did not want their hands on me. Yet all the way through, I was afraid of a flip, afraid I would begin to hit a uniform. I had the sustained image of a summer or a year in cellular, and so I did no more; let us say I was reduced by this caution to no more than ducking, spinning, slipping, blocking, and sidestepping. At one point one of the policemen tripped and fell, but I was on my feet all the way, a point to take no vast pride in because the cops were smaller than me, and did not know how to fight. And maybe I was yellow not to hit them back. A difficult point. When I was hit with something heavier than his fist . . . it was from behind and I kept standing but I think it took a bit away from my pride to resist because the form my thoughts next took were liberal rather than radical: Give up a little or they'll beat your head in. So I relinquished the defense of an arm, and let one of the cops manage to apply the grip he had been trying to apply for the last minute — he was proud when he got it — and then he bent me over the trunk of a parked car, and liquid started falling in dark half-dollar drops on the polish of the automobile, and I said, "Okay, you happy now, I'm bleeding," and that seemed to cool them a little, and in we went, into the jailhouse which was safe.

The clubbing resulted in a thirteen-stitch cut on the back of Mailer's head. After permitting him to make a telephone call to his wife, the cops put him in a bare cell, without bed or toilet. He improvised an antiphonal barrage of antipolice insults with a young boy in the next cell, another D. & D. case. Officer St. Amand came around and explained to Mailer that he had cut his head on a car bumper.

"Are you a Catholic?" asked Mailer.

"Yes."

"You'll go to Hell for lying!"

Chief Marshall soon showed up. He and Mailer got into an exchange of insults, like Homeric heroes before battle.

"I could beat up those two toy cops of yours, and you know it, kid."

"Listen, boy, I could take you with one hand."

"Maybe you could and maybe you couldn't, but you picked the wrong pigeon this time. You cops are used to dealing with people who can't defend themselves. Well, I'm a writer and I know how to use words, and, boy, I'm going to use them."

At three-thirty, Mrs. Mailer arrived, bringing fifty dollars bail, but Mailer had to wait till the bondsman appeared, two hours later, for release. Although her husband had warned her on the phone that he had been clubbed, when Mrs. Mailer saw his bandaged head she was furious. "Look what you've done to my husband. You'll wish you'd never begun this!" It is not known precisely when the cops realized that they had beaten up not an anonymous beatnik but a writer of reputation, and that both the writer and the writer's wife were not going to be good sports about it.

I went up to Provincetown to cover the trial. Upon my arrival — on July 22nd, the day before the trial — Mailer told me that he had decided to undertake his own defense, because he felt that an out-of-town lawyer would be resented and a local lawyer, while he might win the case, would be inclined not to attack the police. That night, the Mailers and I spent several hours drinking with the local beatniks in the Old Colony Bar, at the east end of town. (The homosexuals' turf is the other end.) Mailer was a kind of big brother to them, both a leader and a confidant; he clearly enjoyed not only talking to them but also listening to them. I heard a lot about the police: that the former chief, now ill with heart trouble, was relatively mild but that Cheyney Marshall, who had been acting chief for the past three months, had been cracking down on the summer latitudinarians; that the slightest public exuberance after the bars close might land one in jail suddenly; that Franz Kline, the painter, was arrested, without warning, for playing records in his home late at night; that homosexual bars and night clubs were being closed down by legalistic hokeypokey about licenses; that the police tried to get restaurant and nightclub proprietors to fire homosexual employees; that one officious young cop diverted himself by stopping people who looked odd to his untraveled eyes and demanding that they "identify" themselves — this from a young Negro artist, who thought it was his paint-stained trousers, and from a white artist, who thought it was his beard.

The next morning, I joined the Mailers for breakfast. Over coffee, Mailer revealed to his wife that he was going to put her on the stand, explaining that he had said nothing about it earlier, lest she get tensed up. She showed signs of alarm.

"All you have to do is tell the truth and look the judge in the eye and don't get angry," he said.

"Yes, I know, but —"

"Don't worry, baby. I'll take care of you. It'll be all right."

Mailer decided that he and his wife should both dress in sober black for the occasion. The three of us were about to set off for the trial, in the Mailers' car — he had decided, for tactical reasons, to use the ancient family sedan instead of an English sports roadster, something low and dashing called a Triumph TR-3, he has recently acquired — when he noticed that she was not wearing stockings. He sent her back for stockings.

The courtroom, done in the usual police-court light oak, with the usual flags, was packed. Chief Marshall and his two cops sat along one wall, in civilian clothes, and so did various local dignitaries, including S. Osborn Ball, landlord, realtor, lawyer, and the town's leading offbeat eminence.

"Hey, Norman!" Mr. Ball called across the room. "I'll visit you in state's prison!"

"OK, Ozzie, don't forget," Mailer called back, grinning.

The judge entered, and everybody stood up. He was the Honorable Gershom Hall, a circuit judge from Harwichport, up the Cape. He was long and lean and composed, with an impassive New England expression and a voice that was low but audible, and slightly chilling.

Two short cases first — a bored young man in dungarees who pleaded guilty to dangerous operation of a motor scooter, and a red-eyed, unshaven workingman who pleaded guilty to Drunk & Disorderly, and clowned around a bit, scoring once. The Judge asked him, "Why do you drink?" and he replied, "I like it."

Then the main event. Mailer began by asking to have not only his wife sworn as a witness but also me. I scrambled up and raised my hand, my notes tumbling about my feet; he hadn't alerted *me* at breakfast. Can one report a trial in which one is a witness? I wondered uneasily. Always willing to try anything once, Mailer had thought I could testify that he had had more drinks the night before than on the night of the arrest and yet had shown no signs of being drunk. True. But the Judge pointed out that since I hadn't been there on June 9th, my testimony was irrelevant. I sat down, and began taking notes again.

Chief Marshall, who was doubling as prosecuting attorney, took the stand as a witness — a well-set-up man with a big brown face, hot of eye and jutting of jaw. When he got to the jail, he testified, he had found the defendant drunk and abusive. "I detected a strong odor of liquor on his breath," he said. The defendant had called up Mr. Ball and asked him to come down and get him out; when Mr. Ball had demurred, because of the lateness of the hour, the defendant had shouted angrily into the phone, "You're a lawyer, aren't you? Why don't you get down here?" When Dr. Daniel Hiebert, summoned from his bed, had wanted to shave the defendant's head, the latter had indignantly refused to let him, saying he was going to a dance the next night; he had made many loud and uncomplimentary remarks to the doctor (though he had finally let him bandage his head). "Why don't you sober up?" Dr. Hiebert had said as he left.

Mailer rose to cross-examine Chief Marshall. He walked up with a slight swagger — something between the new gun in town and Perry Mason — and his first questions were delivered in a sinister Texas drawl; throughout the hearing, he shifted gears between this accent and his normal one (Brooklyn-Harvard), according to the dramatic voltage he felt was required.

"Why did you come to the jail at two in the morning?" Mailer began.

This drew a blank. The chief had been called out to look into a possible case of drowning — he had the record sheet to back him up — and had dropped in at the jail as a matter of routine.

Mailer opened up a second front. "Before I dismiss you" — the chief's large jaw tightened — "I want to ask one thing: Do you insist I was going to a *dance* the next night? Actually, I was going to the Robinson-Pender fight in Boston. I haven't been to a dance in years."

"You said a dance."

"Have you ever been wrong?"

"Yes, I suppose so."

"Mr. Marshall, you are not an electronic machine. You might be in error."

The chief admitted that he was not an electronic machine.

The nonbelligerent cop, Patrolman St. Amand, next took the stand — pale, puffy, eyeglassed, somewhat bald, more like a bookkeeper than a policeman. He seemed uneasy, and stared at his shoes as he was testifying. He went through the story, stating that when the police cruiser arrived at the station, the defendant had jumped out swinging at Officer Sylvia; that there was "a little mealie" (melee); that all three of them fell down; and that when the defendant got up, "I noticed his head was lacerated and bleeding; I don't know how it happened." He had apparently given up the car-bumper theory.

"Did you find it offensive that I called the police car a taxi?" asked Mailer, cross-examining. "Is driving a taxi a contemptible occupation?"

"No."

"Then why did you circle back around the block?"

"We didn't. We completed our regular tour as far as the Ace of Spades and then came back."

There followed some virtuoso questioning in which Mailer got the witness to place him on the street the first time the car passed and then the second. Mailer pointed out that these two spots were less than two hundred feet apart, and then drew his conclusion: The police car could not have gone to the Ace of Spades, a night spot a half mile away, in the interval. (Point unimportant, except to show that the police did resent being called taxi drivers, and that their testimony was not to be relied upon.)

"Did you put me into a bare cell?" asked Mailer.

"Yes."

"This cell had no bed to lie on. No toilet, not even a pail. I had a bad cut, which was still bleeding. Is it possible you were being vindictive?"

"No. I just put you in the first handy cell."

"Mr. St. Amand, how long have you worked for the police force?"

"Five years."

"How many cells are there in that wing?"

"Four."

"In five years you haven't been able to learn the separate characteristics of those four cells?"

"Well, there was no other one open."

"Are you certain? At the time I was brought in, there were only two other men in the cells."

"The fourth cell is the women's cell."

"I was transferred to that hours later. It had no bed, but it had raised planks on which you could lie down. It also had a pail. Is that the women's cell?"

"I guess it isn't."

"So you had a choice of putting me in a cell where I could lie down, or one where I couldn't, and you put me in the bare cell."

Patrolman St. Amand found his shoes more and more fascinating.

MAILER: When we arrived at the station, did Cobra reach in and —

CHIEF MARSHALL: I object.

JUDGE: Mr. Mailer, the officer's name is Sylvia, not Cobra.

MAILER: Your Honor, I have heard this man called nothing but Cobra since I've been in town. I will try to call him Sylvia, but if I slip I wish to assure Your Honor it will not be an intentional trick. (*To witness*) Did Officer Sylvia pull me out of the car?

ST. AMAND: He did assist you from the cruiser, yes. (*Laughter in court*)

JUDGE: If there are any more demonstrations, I will clear the court. (*To witness*) You stated the defendant came out of the car swinging. Did you see him throw any punches?

ST. AMAND: He was fighting and aggressive and —

JUDGE: *Did you see him throw a punch?*

ST. AMAND: I did not actually see him swing at Officer Sylvia.

Special Officer William Sylvia took the stand — small, stocky, sharp-featured, hard-eyed. As he was rehearsing the tale again — with that wooden-faced impassivity cops assume in court — the Judge interrupted. "You back there, you with the cigarette, come up here!"

A callow young beatnik, with whom I had drunk the evening before, made his way forward. One could fairly hear the Judge ticking, like a grenade. It was an awful moment.

"Were you *smoking?*"

"Yes. I'm sorry."

"Don't you know I could send you to jail for contempt? This is not a circus." To the officer of the court: "Officer, get this man out at once. Get him out of the building."

Officer Sylvia resumed. When he had finished, the Judge asked him, "Did he refuse to get out of the car?"

"No."

"Do you know how he got the cut on his head?"

"No."

Mailer had planned to cross-examine Officer Sylvia along psychiatric lines (he had written the questions out in advance on cards): "Are you aware that your nickname in this town is Cobra?" "Do you know what Cobra means? Webster defines it as 'any of several very venomous Asiatic and African snakes.'" He had also written down such questions for Police Chief Marshall as "Are you aware that people in the town believe they have a bullying and brutal police force?" and "Do you know that the nickname for the police here is the Gestapo?" Judge Hall, however, had made it clear almost immediately that such questions, interesting as they were, did not fall within his concept of cross-examination, and Mailer had forgone them. But he found it difficult to abstain from interpretation. As the trial progressed, the Judge gave the defendant-cum-attorney-for-the-defense an elementary course in courtroom procedure. "You have no right to comment on proceedings at this point," he kept repeating as Mailer kept inserting conclusions into his questions. "Mr. Mailer is not a lawyer," the Judge usually added. "We'll give him a little leeway."

It was the legal versus the novelistic mind, and the latter always gave way politely — and temporarily. For, as a writer, Mailer had done a rough draft before he entered the courtroom, and, also as a writer, he couldn't bear to have this draft wholly wasted; he worked it in wherever he saw an opening, like a beaver instinctively using what comes at hand.

MAILER: You grabbed my arms from behind — isn't that right, Cobra?

CHIEF MARSHALL: Objection!

MAILER: I'm very sorry, Your Honor. I forgot. I should have said "Mr. Sylvia."

SYLVIA: Yes.

MAILER: Have you been in this sort of trouble before, Mr. Sylvia? I mean, have there been violent episodes in your past?

JUDGE: We're not interested in the past. Only in what happened on June 9.

MAILER: Yes, Your Honor. . . . Now, have you no fear of getting out of control?

SYLVIA: No.

MAILER: Do you ever have bad dreams about violence?

CHIEF MARSHALL: *I object!*

JUDGE: That is not a proper question, Mr. Mailer.

MAILER: I'm sorry, Your Honor.

The prosecution rested, and the defense called Mrs. Mailer. She took the stand, looking very pretty and nervous and unprofessional — a pleasant contrast to the three wooden-faced cops.

"What did we have for supper on the night of June 9th?" Mailer asked her, sensing her nervousness.

"Steak," she replied triumphantly.

"And where did we go after supper?"

"To the Ace of Spades."

Mailer looked a little dashed. "But didn't we go somewhere else first? To a drive-in movie, for instance?"

"Oh, yes, that's right."

"And after that to the Atlantic House, where we had one drink each?"

"Yes, we did."

At this point, the Judge said something about leading the witness. Mailer said earnestly that he had no such intention, adding, "Your Honor, I think it is clear that the testimony of this witness has not been rehearsed."

Mrs. Mailer then fixed the number of further drinks that evening at one for her, three for him, all at the Ace of Spades, and identified them as gin-and-tonic.

"Could you be in error?" Mailer asked ruminatively. "Was it not possibly gin-and-tonic for you and gin-on-the-rocks for me?"

Mrs. Mailer agreed that it might indeed have been so.

After this display of candor, her testimony went along smoothly enough, except that the Judge had to ask her to address herself to him rather than to the spectators. The important point came at the end, when she testified that her husband had called out to her as the cops hustled him into the squad car, "You're my witness. I'm not resisting arrest."

Mailer now took the stand as his own witness and told, in more conversational terms, the story of the "rumble" already given above in his letter. He admitted he had been "a little coy" with the cops, but explained that his aggressiveness was due to the lack of tobacco rather than the presence of alcohol. "I was a little high but I don't get drunk on four drinks," he said. "That night, I was irritable, because I had stopped smoking two days earlier. I was worried about myself when they began hitting me. I have a bad temper. They may have thought I was a dangerous beatnik; maybe they look at television too much." He admitted he had insulted Dr. Hiebert. "I'm very sorry about that — I was angry and he seemed to me at that moment just a representative of the police and I hated the police. I was cocky, sassy, arrogant — call it what you will. When they took me into the station, I was in a state of great anger and I remained angry for hours. Shaving my head I thought was the last indignity."

Chief Marshall's cross-examination centered on the call to Mr. Ball, which he cited as an example of drunken belligerence, and on Mailer's rudeness to the doctor (ditto).

Mailer then called S. Osborn Ball to the stand and asked him if he concluded from their phone talk that he (Mailer) was drunk.

After a rather dramatic pause, Mr. Ball replied, "You showed no signs of drunkenness."

"Was I offensive when I asked you if you were a lawyer?"

"No. You had dealt with me only as a tenant. And some have had doubts about the matter anyway."

"Mr. Ball, you have upstaged me forever," said Mailer.

"Don't put me into your next novel, that's all I ask," said Mr. Ball, getting in the last word. Mr. Ball just happened to be in court, on another case; neither side had thought of subpoenaing him. For all his advance preparation, Mailer forgot to include in his testimony that it took thirteen stitches to sew up the cut on his head. At the postmortem after the trial, over a pitcher of beer at the Old Colony, someone asked why he hadn't mentioned this. "Didn't I?" he said. "Damn!" It was that kind of trial — sort of free-form. The police forgot to subpoena Dr. Hiebert — an omission that the Judge commented on unfavorably, as he also did on the failure of the police witnesses either to report or deny Mailer's parting words to his wife about not resisting arrest. Nothing-up-his-sleeve Mailer *had* asked Dr. Hiebert's wife, informally, the evening before, to ask him to appear, but he didn't.

Mailer summed up his case: "A middle ground may apply here. A man has had a few drinks and is sassy, but I question whether this is a cause for arrest. . . . I don't want to be flowery. I've been coming here ten times in the last fifteen years. I like Provincetown, and there's no reason it can't have a police force that is as good as the rest of the town."

Chief Marshall's summary was long on rhetoric: "This man is an intelligent man. He did not ask for a drunk test. Is this the action of a normal person? Is this the action of a sober man? He presents himself here clean as the new-fallen snow. But we have seen he behaved in a rude and disorderly manner."

JUDGE: Was it rude and disorderly to call your men hack drivers?

CHIEF MARSHALL: Police officers are called many things.

JUDGE: Rightly so.

Chief Marshall then finished his speech.

After a short recess, Judge Hall pronounced his decision: "I'm going to say pretty frankly what I think about the whole business. I think the defendant had enough to drink to act like a fool. On the other hand"— turning to the cops —"you police officers were too thin-skinned. You have to deal with many summer visitors here, and you can't manhandle a man because he says something you don't like. If any more cases like this come before me, there will be some action taken. I say that in this case the police went too far. . . . I find you"— turning to Mailer —"guilty of drunkenness, and I advise you in future to show more respect to the police. The verdict will be filed" — i.e., no fine or sentence; nothing on the record, unless it happens again. "I find you not guilty of disorderly conduct."

Finis. Subdued jubilation in the audience. Reporters from

the local and Boston papers leave to write their stories. Attorney Ball congratulates Mailer on his handling of the case. Much handshaking and backslapping, centering on Mailer, who finally slips off to retrieve his fifty dollars bail from the clerk of the court. General *détente*, and *exeunt omnes* with a sense of having been in on a bit of legal and literary history in the making.

# The Black Boy Looks at the White Boy

## by James Baldwin

*I walked and I walked*
*Till I wore out my shoes.*
*I can't walk so far, but*
*Yonder come the blues.*

—Ma Rainey

I first met Norman Mailer about five years ago, in Paris, at the home of Jean Malaquais. Let me bring in at once the theme that will repeat itself over and over throughout this love letter: I was then (and I have not changed much) a very tight, tense, lean, abnormally ambitious, abnormally intelligent, and hungry black cat. It is important that I admit that, at the time I met Norman, I was extremely worried about my career; and a writer who is worried about his career is also fighting for his life. I was approaching the end of a love affair, and I was not taking it very well. Norman and I are alike in this, that we both tend to suspect others of putting us down, and we strike before we're struck. Only, our styles are very different: I am a black boy from the Harlem streets, and Norman is a middle-class Jew. I am not dragging my personal history into this gratuitously, and I hope I do not need to say that no sneer is implied in the above description of Norman. But these are the facts and in my own relationship to Norman they are crucial facts.

Also, I have no right to talk about Norman without risking a distinctly chilling self-exposure. I take him very seriously, he is very dear to me. And I think I know something about his journey from my black boy's point of view because my own journey is not really so very different, and also because I have spent most of my life, after all, watching white people and outwitting them, so that I might survive. I think that I know something about the American masculinity which most men of my generation do not know because they have not been menaced by it in the way that I have been. It is still true, alas, that to be an American Negro male is also to be a kind of walking phallic symbol: which means that one pays, in one's own personality, for the sexual insecurity of others. The relationship, therefore, of a black boy to a white boy is a very complex thing.

There is a difference, though, between Norman and myself in that I think he still imagines that he has something to save, whereas I have never had anything to lose. Or, perhaps I ought to put it another way: the thing that most white people imagine that they can salvage from the storm of life is really, in sum, their innocence. It was this commodity precisely which I had to get rid of at once, literally, on pain of death. I am afraid that most of the white people I have ever known impressed me as being in the grip of a weird nostalgia, dreaming of a vanished state of security and order, against which dream, unfailingly and unconsciously, they tested and very often lost their lives. It is a terrible thing to say, but I am afraid that for a very long time the troubles of white people failed to impress me as being real trouble. They put me in mind of children crying because the breast has been taken away. Time and love have modified my tough-boy lack of charity, but the attitude sketched above was my first attitude and I am sure that there is a great deal of it left.

To proceed: two lean cats, one white and one black, met in a French living room. I had heard of him, he had heard of me. And here we were, suddenly, circling around each other. We liked each other at once, but each was frightened that the other would pull rank. He could have pulled rank on me because he was more famous and had more money and also because he was white; but I could have pulled rank on him precisely because I was black and knew more about that periphery he so helplessly maligns in "The White Negro" than he could ever hope to know. Already, you see, we were trapped in our roles and our attitudes: the toughest kid on the block was meeting the toughest kid on the block. I think that both of us were pretty weary of this grueling and thankless role, I know that I am; but the roles that we construct are constructed because we feel that they will help us to survive and also, of course, because they fulfill something in our personalities; and one does not, therefore, cease playing a role simply because one has begun to understand it. All roles are dangerous. The world tends to trap and immobilize you in the role you play; and it is not always easy — in fact, it is always extremely hard — to maintain a kind of watchful, mocking distance between oneself as one appears to be and oneself as one actually is.

I think that Norman was working on *The Deer Park* at that time, or had just finished it, and Malaquais, who had translated *The Naked and the Dead* into French, did not like *The Deer Park*. I had not then read the book; if I had, I would have been astonished that Norman could have expected Malaquais to like it. What Norman was trying to do in *The*

*Deer Park*, and quite apart, now, from whether or not he succeeded, could only — it seems to me — baffle and annoy a French intellectual who seemed to me essentially rationalistic. Norman has many qualities and faults, but I have never heard anyone accuse him of possessing this particular one. But Malaquais's opinion seemed to mean a great deal to him — this astonished me, too; and there was a running, good-natured but astringent argument between them, with Malaquais playing the role of the old lion and Norman playing the role of the powerful but clumsy cub. And, I must say, I think that each of them got a great deal of pleasure out of the other's performance. The night we met, we stayed up very late, and did a great deal of drinking and shouting. But beneath all the shouting and the posing and the mutual showing off, something very wonderful was happening. I was aware of a new and warm presence in my life, for I had met someone I wanted to know, who wanted to know me.

Norman and his wife, Adele, along with a Negro jazz musician friend, and myself, met fairly often during the few weeks that found us all in the same city. I think that Norman had come in from Spain, and he was shortly to return to the States; and it was not long after Norman's departure that I left Paris for Corsica. My memory of that time is both blurred and sharp, and, oddly enough, is principally of Norman — confident, boastful, exuberant, and loving — striding through the soft Paris nights like a gladiator. And I think, alas, that I envied him: his success, and his youth, and his love. And this meant that though Norman really wanted to know me, and though I really wanted to know him, I hung back, held fire, danced, and lied. I was not going to come crawling out of my ruined house, all bloody, no, baby, sing no sad songs for *me*. And the great gap between Norman's state and my own had a terrible effect on our relationship, for it inevitably connected, not to say collided, with that myth of the sexuality of Negroes which Norman, like so many others, refuses to give up. The sexual battleground, if I may call it that, is really the same for everyone; and I, at this point, was just about to be carried off the battleground on my shield, if anyone could find it; so how could I play, in any way whatever, the noble savage?

At the same time, my temperament and my experience in this country had led me to expect very little from most American whites, especially, horribly enough, my friends: so it did not seem worthwhile to challenge, in any real way, Norman's views of life on the periphery, or to put him down for them. I was weary, to tell the truth. I had tried, in the States, to convey something of what it felt like to be a Negro and no one had been able to listen: they wanted their romance. And, anyway, the really ghastly thing about trying to convey to a white man the reality of the Negro experience has nothing whatever to do with the fact of color, but has to do with this man's relationship to his own life. He will face in your life only what he is willing to face in his. Well, this means that one finds oneself tampering with the insides of a stranger, to no purpose, which one probably has no right to do, and I chickened out. And matters were not helped at all by the fact that the Negro jazz musicians, among whom we sometimes found ourselves, who really liked Norman, did not for an instant consider him as being even remotely "hip" and Norman did not know this and I could not tell him. He never broke through to them, at least not as far as I know; and they were far too "hip," if that is the word I want, even to consider breaking through to him. They thought he was a real sweet ofay cat, but a little frantic.

But we were far more cheerful than anything I've said might indicate, and none of the above seemed to matter very much at the time. Other things mattered, like walking and talking and drinking and eating, and the way Adele laughed, and the way Norman argued. He argued like a young man, he argued to win: and while I found him charming, he may have found me exasperating, for I kept moving back before that short, prodding forefinger. I couldn't submit my arguments, or my real questions, for I had too much to hide. Or so it seemed to me then. I submit, though I may be wrong, that I was then at the beginning of a terrifying adventure, not too unlike the conundrum which seems to menace Norman now:

"I had done a few things and earned a few pence"; but the things I had written were behind me, could not be written again, could not be repeated. I was also realizing that all that the world could give me as an artist, it had, in effect, already given. In the years that stretched before me, all that I could look forward to, in that way, were a few more prizes, or a lot more, and a little more, or a lot more money. And my private life had failed — had failed, had failed. One of the reasons I had fought so hard, after all, was to wrest from the world fame and money and love. And here I was, at thirty-two, finding my notoriety hard to bear, since its principal effect was to make me more lonely; money, it turned out, was exactly like sex, you thought of nothing else if you didn't have it and thought of other things if you did; and love, as far as I could see, was over. Love seemed to be over not merely because an affair was ending; it would have seemed to be over under any circumstances; for it was the dream of love which was ending. I was beginning to realize, most unwillingly, all the things love could not do. It could not make me over, for example. It could not undo the journey which had made of me such a strange man and brought me to such a strange place.

But at that time it seemed only too clear that love had gone out of the world, and not, as I had thought once, because I was poor and ugly and obscure, but precisely because I was no longer any of these things. What point, then, was there in working if the best I could hope for was the Nobel Prize? And *how*, indeed, would I be able to keep on working if I could never be released from the prison of my egocentricity? By what act could I escape this horror? For horror it was, let us make no mistake about that.

And, beneath all this, which simplified nothing, was that sense, that suspicion — which is the glory and torment of every writer — that what was happening to me might be turned to good account, that I was trembling on the edge of great revelations, was being prepared for a very long journey, and might now begin, having survived my apprenticeship (but had I survived?), a great work. I might really become a great writer. But in order to do this I would have to sit down at the typewriter again, alone — I would have to accept my despair: and I could not do it. It really does not help to be a strong-willed person or, anyway, I think it is a great error to misunderstand the nature of the will. In the most important areas of anybody's life, the will usually operates as a traitor. My own will was busily pointing out to me the most fantastically unreal alternatives to my pain, all of which I tried, all of which — luckily — failed. When, late in the evening or early in the morning, Norman and Adele returned to their hotel on the Quai Voltaire, I wandered through Paris, the underside of Paris, drinking, screwing, fighting — it's a wonder I wasn't killed. And then it was morning, I would somehow be home — usually, anyway — and the typewriter would be there, staring at me; and the manuscript of the new novel, which it seemed I would never be able to achieve, and from which clearly I was never going to be released, was scattered all over the floor.

That's the way it is. I think it is the most dangerous point in the life of any artist, his longest, most hideous turning; and especially for a man, an American man, whose principle is action and whose jewel is optimism, who must now accept what certainly then seems to be a gray passivity and an endless despair. It is the point at which many artists lose their minds, or commit suicide, or throw themselves into good works, or try to enter politics. For all of this is happening not only in the wilderness of the soul, but in the real world which accomplishes its seductions not by offering you opportunities to be wicked but by offering opportunities to be good, to be active and effective, to be admired and central and apparently loved.

Norman came on to America, and I went to Corsica. We wrote each other a few times. I confided to Norman that I was very apprehensive about the reception of *Giovanni's Room,* and he was good enough to write some very encouraging things about it when it came out. The critics had jumped on him with both their left feet when he published *The Deer Park* — which I still had not read — and this created a kind of bond, or strengthened the bond already existing between us. About a year and several overflowing wastebaskets later, I, too, returned to America, not vastly improved by having been out of it, but not knowing where else to go; and one day, while I was sitting dully in my house, Norman called me from Connecticut. A few people were going to be there — for the weekend — and he wanted me to come, too. We had not seen each other since Paris.

Well, I wanted to go, that is, I wanted to see Norman; but I did not want to see any people, and so the tone of my acceptance was not very enthusiastic. I realized that he felt this, but I did not know what to do about it. He gave me train schedules and hung up.

Getting to Connecticut would have been no hassle if I could have pulled myself together to get to the train. And I was sorry, as I meandered around my house and time flew and trains left, that I had not been more honest with Norman and told him exactly how I felt. But I had not known how to do this, or it had not really occurred to me to do it, especially not over the phone.

So there was another phone call, I forget who called whom, which went something like this:

N: Don't feel you have to. I'm not trying to bug you.

J: It's not that. It's just —

N: You don't really want to come, do you?

J: I don't really feel up to it.

N: I understand. I guess you just don't like the Connecticut gentry.

J: Well — don't you ever come to the city?

N: Sure. We'll see each other.

J: I hope so. I'd like to see you.

N: OK, till then.

And he hung up. I thought, I ought to write him a letter, but of course I did nothing of the sort. It was around this time I went south, I think; anyway, we did not see each other for a long time.

But I thought about him a great deal. The grapevine keeps all of us advised of the others' movements, so I knew when Norman left Connecticut for New York, heard that he had been present at this or that party and what he had said: usually something rude, often something penetrating, sometimes something so hilariously silly that it was difficult to believe he had been serious. (This was my reaction when I first heard his famous running-for-President remark. I dismissed it. I was wrong.) Or he had been seen in this or that Village spot, in which unfailingly there would be someone — out of spite, idleness, envy, exasperation, out of the bottomless, eerie, aimless hostility which characterizes almost every bar in New York, to speak only of bars — to put him down. I heard of a couple of fistfights, and, of course, I was always encountering people who hated his guts. These people always mildly surprised me, and so did the news of his fights: it was hard for me to imagine that anyone could really dislike Norman, anyone that is, who had encountered him personally. I knew of one fight he had had, forced on him, apparently, by a blowhard Village type whom I considered rather pathetic. I didn't blame Norman for this fight, but I couldn't help wondering why he bothered to rise to such a shapeless challenge. It seemed simpler, as I was always telling myself, just to stay out of Village bars.

And people talked about Norman with a kind of avid glee, which I found very ugly. Pleasure made their saliva flow, they sprayed and all but drooled, and their eyes shone with that bloodlust which is the only real tribute the mediocre are capable of bringing to the extraordinary. Many of the people who claimed to be seeing Norman all the time impressed me as being, to tell the truth, pitifully far beneath him. But this is also true, alas, of much of my own entourage. The people who are in one's life or merely continually in one's presence reveal a great deal about one's needs and terrors. Also, one's hopes.

I was not, however, on the scene. I was on the road — not quite, I trust, in the sense that Kerouac's boys are; but I presented, certainly, a moving target. And I was reading Norman Mailer. Before I had met him, I had only read *The Naked and the Dead,* "The White Negro," and *Barbary Shore* — I think this is right, though it may be that I only read "The White Negro" later and confuse my reading of that piece with some of my discussions with Norman. Anyway, I could not, with the best will in the world, make any sense out of "The White Negro," and, in fact, it was hard for me to imagine that this essay had been written by the same man who wrote the novels. Both *The Naked and the Dead* and (for the most part) *Barbary Shore* are written in a lean, spare, muscular prose which accomplishes almost exactly what it sets out to do. Even *Barbary Shore*, which loses itself in its last half (and which deserves, by the way, far more serious treatment than it has received), never becomes as downright impenetrable as "The White Negro" does.

Now, much of this, I told myself, had to do with my resistance to the title, and with a kind of fury that so antique a vision of the blacks should, at this late hour, and in so many borrowed heirlooms, be stepping off the A train. But I was also baffled by the passion with which Norman appeared to be imitating so many people inferior to himself, i.e., Kerouac, and all the other Suzuki rhythm boys. From them, indeed, I expected nothing more than their pablum-clogged cries of

*Kicks!* and *Holy!* It seemed very clear to me that their glorification of the orgasm was but a way of avoiding all of the terrors of life and love. But Norman knew better, had to know better. *The Naked and the Dead, Barbary Shore,* and *The Deer Park* proved it. In each of these novels, there is a toughness and subtlety of conception, and a sense of the danger and complexity of human relationships which one will search for in vain, not only in the work produced by the aforementioned coterie, but in most of the novels produced by Norman's contemporaries. What in the world, then, was he doing, slumming so outrageously, in such a dreary crowd?

For, exactly because he knew better, and in exactly the same way that no one can become more lewdly vicious than an imitation libertine, Norman felt compelled to carry their mystique further than they had, to be more "hip," or more "beat," to dominate, in fact, their dreaming field; and since this mystique depended on a total rejection of life, and insisted on the fulfillment of an infantile dream of love, the mystique could only be extended into violence. No one is more dangerous than he who imagines himself pure in heart: for his purity, by definition, is unassailable.

But *why* should it be necessary to borrow the Depression language of deprived Negroes, which eventually evolved into jive and bop talk, in order to justify such a grim system of delusions? Why malign the sorely menaced sexuality of Negroes in order to justify the white man's own sexual panic? Especially as, in Norman's case, and as indicated by his work, he has a very real sense of sexual responsibility, and, even, odd as it may sound to some, of sexual morality, and a genuine commitment to life. None of his people, I beg you to notice, spend their lives on the road. They really become entangled with each other, and with life. They really suffer, they spill real blood, they have real lives to lose. This is no small achievement; in fact, it is absolutely rare. No matter how uneven one judges Norman's work to be, all of it is genuine work. No matter how harshly one judges it, it is the work of a genuine novelist, and an absolutely first-rate talent.

Which makes the questions I have tried to raise — or, rather, the questions which Norman Mailer irresistibly represents — all the more troubling and terrible. I certainly do not know the answers, and even if I did, this is probably not the place to state them.

But I have a few ideas. Here is Kerouac, ruminating on what I take to be the loss of the garden of Eden:

> At lilac evening I walked with every muscle aching among the lights of 27th and Welton in the Denver colored section, wishing I were a Negro, feeling that the best the white world had offered was not enough ecstasy for me, not enough life, joy, kicks, darkness, music, not enough night. I wished I were a Denver Mexican, or even a poor overworked Jap, anything but what I so drearily was, a "white man" disillusioned. All my life I'd had white ambitions. . . .
> I passed the dark porches of Mexican and Negro homes; soft voices were there, occasionally the dusky knee of some mysterious sensuous gal; and dark faces of the men behind rose arbors. Little children sat like sages in ancient rocking chairs.

Now, this is absolute nonsense, of course, objectively considered, and offensive nonsense at that: I would hate to be in Kerouac's shoes if he should ever be mad enough to read this aloud from the stage of Harlem's Apollo Theater.

And yet there is real pain in it, and real loss, however thin; and it *is* thin, like soup too long diluted; thin because it does not refer to reality, but to a dream. Compare it, at random, with any old blues:

> *Backwater blues done caused me*
> *To pack my things and go.*
> *'Cause my house fell down*
> *And I can't live there no mo'.*

"Man," said a Negro musician to me once, talking about Norman, "the only trouble with that cat is that he's white." This does not mean exactly what it says — or, rather, it *does* mean exactly what it says, and not what it might be taken to mean — and it is a very shrewd observation. What my friend meant was that to become a Negro man, let alone a Negro artist, one had to make oneself up as one went along. This had to be done in the not-at-all-metaphorical teeth of the world's determination to destroy you. The world had prepared no place for you, and if the world had its way, no place would ever exist. Now, this is true for everyone, but, in the case of a Negro, this truth is absolutely naked: if he deludes himself about it, he will die. This is not the way this truth presents itself to white men, who believe the world is theirs and who, albeit unconsciously, expect the world to help them in the achievement of their identity. But the world does not do this — for anyone; the world is not interested in anyone's identity. And, therefore, the anguish which can overtake a white man comes in the middle of his life, when he must make the almost inconceivable effort to divest himself of everything he has ever expected or believed, when he must take himself apart and put himself together again, walking out of the world, into limbo, or into what certainly looks like limbo. This cannot yet happen to any Negro of Norman's age, for the reason that his delusions and defenses are either absolutely impenetrable by this time, or he has failed to survive them. "I want to know how power works," Norman once said to me, "how it really works, in detail." Well, I know how power works, it has worked on me, and if I didn't know how power worked, I would be dead. And it goes without saying, perhaps, that I have simply never been able to afford myself any illusions concerning the manipulation of that power. My revenge, I decided very early, would be to achieve a power which outlasts kingdoms.

## 2

When I saw Norman again, I was beginning to suspect daylight at the end of my long tunnel, it was a summer day. I was on my way back to Paris, and I was very cheerful. We were at an afternoon party, Norman was standing in the kitchen, a drink in his hand, holding forth for the benefit of a small group of people. There seemed something different about him, it was the belligerence of his stance, and the really rather pontifical tone of his voice. I had only seen him, remember, in Malaquais's living room, which Malaquais indefatigably dominates, and on various terraces and in various dives in Paris. I do not mean that there was anything unfriendly about him. On the contrary, he was smiling and having a ball. And yet — he was leaning against the refrigerator, rather as though he had his back to the wall, ready to take on all comers.

Norman has a trick, at least with me, of watching, somewhat ironically, as you stand on the edge of the crowd around him, waiting for his attention. I suppose this ought to be exasperating, but in fact I find it rather endearing, because it is so transparent and because he gets such a bang out of being the center of attention. So do I, of course, at least some of the time.

We talked, bantered, a little tensely, made the usual, doomed effort to bring each other up to date on what we had been doing. I did not want to talk about my novel, which was only just beginning to seem to take shape, and, therefore, did not dare ask him if he were working on a novel. He seemed very pleased to see me, and I was pleased to see him, but I also had the feeling that he had made up his mind about me, adversely, in some way. It was as though he were saying, OK, so now I know who *you* are, baby.

I was taking a boat in a few days, and I asked him to call me.

"Oh, no," he said, grinning, and thrusting that forefinger at me, "*you* call me."

"That's fair enough," I said, and I left the party and went on back to Paris. While I was out of the country, Norman published *Advertisements for Myself*, which presently crossed the ocean to the apartment of James Jones. Bill Styron was also in Paris at that time, and one evening the three of us sat in Jim's living room, reading aloud, in a kind of drunken, masochistic fascination, Norman's judgment of our personalities and our work. Actually, I came off best, I suppose; there was less about me, and it was less venomous. But the condescension infuriated me; also, to tell the truth, my feelings were hurt. I felt that if that was the way Norman felt about me, he should have told me so. He had said that I was incapable of saying "F—— you" to the reader. My first temptation was to send him a cablegram which would disabuse him of that notion, at least insofar as one reader was concerned. But then I thought, No, I would be cool about it, and fail to react as he so clearly wanted me to. Also, I must say, his judgment of myself seemed so wide of the mark and so childish that it was hard to stay angry. I wondered what in the world was going on in his mind. Did he really suppose that he had now become the builder and destroyer of reputations,

And of *my* reputation?

We met in the Actors' Studio one afternoon, after a performance of *The Deer Park* — which I deliberately arrived too late to see, since I really did not know how I was going to react to Norman, and didn't want to betray myself by clobbering his play. When the discussion ended, I stood, again on the edge of the crowd around him, waiting. Over someone's shoulder, our eyes met, and Norman smiled.

"We've got something to talk about," I told him.

"I figured that," he said, smiling.

We went to a bar, and sat opposite each other. I was relieved to discover that I was not angry, not even (as far as I could tell) at the bottom of my heart. But, "Why did you write those things about me?"

"Well, I'll tell you about that," he said — Norman has several accents, and I think this was his Texas one —"I sort of figured you had it coming to you."

"Why?"

"Well, I think there's some truth in it."

"Well, if you felt that way, why didn't you ever say so — to me?"

"Well, I figured if this was going to break up our friendship, something else would come along to break it up just as fast."

I couldn't disagree with that.

"You're the only one I kind of regret hitting so hard," he said, with a grin. "I think I — probably — wouldn't say it quite that way now."

With this, I had to be content. We sat for perhaps an hour, talking of other things, and, again, I was struck by his stance: leaning on the table, shoulders hunched, seeming, really, to roll like a boxer's, and his hands moving as though he were dealing with a sparring partner. And we were talking of physical courage, and the necessity of never letting another guy get the better of you.

I laughed. "Norman, I can't go through the world the way you do because I haven't got your shoulders."

He grinned, as though I were his pupil. "But you're a pretty tough little mother, too," he said, and referred to one of the grimmer of my Village misadventures, a misadventure which certainly proved that I had a dangerously sharp tongue, but which didn't really prove anything about my courage. Which, anyway, I had long ago given up trying to prove.

I did not see Norman again until Provincetown, just after his celebrated brush with the police there, which resulted, according to Norman, in making the climate of Provincetown as "mellow as Jello." The climate didn't seem very different to me — dull natives, dull tourists, malevolent policemen; I certainly, in any case, would never have dreamed of testing Norman's sanguine conclusion. But we had a great time, lying around the beach, and driving about, and we began to be closer than we had been for a long time.

It was during this Provincetown visit that I realized, for the first time, during a long exchange Norman and I had, in a kitchen, at someone else's party, that Norman was really fascinated by the nature of political power. But, though he said so, I did not really believe that he was fascinated by it as a possibility for himself. He was then doing the great piece on the Democratic convention which was published in *Esquire,* and I put his fascination down to that. I tend not to worry about writers as long as they are working — which is not as romantic as it may sound — and he seemed quite happy with his wife, his family, himself. I declined, naturally, to rise at dawn, as he apparently often did, to go running or swimming or boxing, but Norman seemed to get a great charge out of these admirable pursuits and didn't put me down too hard for my comparative decadence.

He and Adele and the two children took me to the plane one afternoon, the tiny plane which shuttles from Provincetown to Boston. It was a great day, clear and sunny, and that was the way I felt: for it seemed to me that we had all, at last, reestablished our old connection.

And then I heard that Norman was running for mayor, which I dismissed as a joke and refused to believe until it became hideously clear that it was not a joke at all. I was furious. I thought, You son of a bitch, you're copping out. You're one of the very few writers around who might really become a great writer, who might help to excavate the buried consciousness of this country, and you want to settle for being the lousy mayor of New York. *It's not your job.* And I don't at all mean to suggest that writers are not responsible to and for — in any case, always for — the social order. I don't, for that matter, even mean to suggest that Norman would have made a particularly bad mayor, though I confess that I simply cannot see him in this role. And there is probably some truth in the suggestion, put forward by Norman and others, that the shock value of having such a man in such an office, or merely running for such an office, would have had a salutary effect on the life of this city — particularly, I must say, as relates to our young people, who are certainly in desperate need of adults who love them and take them seriously, and whom they can respect. (Serious citizens may not respect Norman, but young people do, and do not respect the serious citizens; and their instincts are quite sound.)

But I do not feel that a writer's responsibility can be discharged in this way. I do not think, if one is a writer, that one escapes it by trying to become something else. One does *not* become something else: one becomes nothing. And what is crucial here is that the writer, however unwillingly, always, somewhere, knows this. There is no structure he can build strong enough to keep out this self-knowledge. What *has* happened, however, time and time again, is that the fantasy structure the writer builds in order to escape his central responsibility operates not as his fortress, but his prison, and he perishes within it. Or: the structure he has built becomes so stifling, so lonely, so false, and acquires such a violent and dangerous life of its own, that he can break out of it only by bringing the entire structure down. With a great crash, inevitably, and on his own head, and on the heads of those closest to him. It is like smashing the windows one second before one asphyxiates; it is like burning down the house in order, at last, to be free of it. And this, I think, really, to touch upon it lightly, is the key to the events at that monstrous, baffling, and so publicized party.* Nearly everyone in the world — or nearly everyone, at least, in this extraordinary

* In the fall of 1960, after a party given on the eve of announcing his candidacy for mayor of New York, Mailer was arrested and charged with assaulting his wife. After a brief period of examination in Bellevue Hospital he was released and not prosecuted. [Ed.]

city — was there: policemen, Mafia types, the people whom we quaintly refer to as "beatniks," writers, actors, editors, politicians, and gossip columnists. It must be admitted that it was a considerable achievement to have brought so many unlikely types together under one roof; and, in spite of everything, I can't help wishing that I had been there to witness the mutual bewilderment. But the point is that no politician would have dreamed of giving such a party in order to launch his mayoralty campaign. Such an imaginative route is not usually an attribute of politicians. In addition, the price one pays for pursuing any profession, or calling, is an intimate knowledge of its ugly side. It is scarcely worth observing that political activity is often, to put it mildly, pungent, and I think that Norman, perhaps for the first time, really doubted his ability to deal with such a world, and blindly struck his way out of it. We do not, in this country now, have much taste for, or any real sense of, the extremes human beings can reach; time will improve us in this regard; but in the meantime the general fear of experience is one of the reasons that the American writer has so peculiarly difficult and dangerous a time.

One can never really see into the heart, the mind, the soul of another. Norman is my very good friend, but perhaps I do not really understand him at all, and perhaps everything I have tried to suggest in the foregoing is false. I do not think so, but it may be. One thing, however, I am certain is *not* false, and that is simply the fact of his being a writer, and the incalculable potential he as a writer contains. His work, after all, is all that will be left when the newspapers are yellowed, all the gossip columnists silenced, and all the cocktail parties over, and when Norman and you and I are dead. I know that this point of view is not terribly fashionable these days, but I think we *do* have a responsibility, not only to ourselves and to our own time, but to those who are coming after us. (I refuse to believe that no one is coming after us.) And I suppose that this responsibility can only be discharged by dealing as truthfully as we know how with our present fortunes, these present days. So that my concern with Norman, finally, has to do with how deeply he has understood these last sad and stormy events. If he has understood them, then he is richer and we are richer, too; if he has not understood them, we are all much poorer. For, though it clearly needs to be brought into focus, he has a real vision of ourselves as we are, and it cannot be too often repeated in this country now, that, where there is no vision, the people perish.

# The Way It Isn't Done:

## by Calder Willingham

Notes on the Distress of
Norman Mailer

Every person who has published books
is familiar with the question: "How does one become a
writer?" The question is not totally unanswerable; many sensible suggestions are possible. For example, "Write" is a good
suggestion, and "Read" is another. But such positive advice
does not reveal the pitfalls of a writing career and it cannot
explain the fate of those horrifying literary skeletons strewn
by the wayside. Let us take a negative approach and ask:
"How does one *not* become a writer?"

First of all, it is helpful to feel a bitter competitiveness
toward other writers. Secondly, a continuous exercise of the
critical faculty will tend to reduce to a soggy self-consciousness
whatever creative power one might have. Thirdly, an ideological dependence is much to be preferred over a personal vision

of the world based on one's own experience. Fourthly, an adolescent public rebelliousness combined with a search for notoriety will effectively distract the would-be writer from his real problems. Fifthly, the basics of good fiction — i.e., character, narrative, a concern for moral truth — must be subordinated at all times to literary technique. And, finally, the would-be writer must not permit himself feelings of sympathy toward other human beings; rather, he must carefully cultivate the nasty hostility and offensive egotism of a spoiled brat. These practices and attitudes, and perhaps a few others akin to them or derived from them, will go far in helping one not become a writer.

It seems to me that Norman Mailer reveals *all* these practices and attitudes in his career on the whole, and most of them with an especial repulsiveness in his essay, "Some Children of the Goddess" (*Esquire*, July [1963]).* I cannot imagine a more truly splendid example of how not to be a writer than that provided by Mailer in this murky, disorganized, and downright incoherent essay; even the relatively comprehensible parts of it reek with the odor of an acute literary illness. Other productions of Mailer's feverish typewriter cannot match it, a thing I would have thought hard to believe, since for some time now Norman Mailer has been one of the wildest essayists in the world. While he tosses and turns in his painful literary distress, let's step up to the foot of his bed and take a look at his chart.

(1) A bitter, narrow, unconstrained competitiveness toward other writers can only reflect an undue preoccupation with status. There can never be a surplus of great writing, and real writers are not in competition with each other. Genius is singular and inspiration unique. An artificial competition between writers results from the manipulations and politics of the literary world; this competition is subtly but firmly based

* The essay evaluating the recent work of nine writers, in Mailer's 1966 collection, *Cannibals and Christians*. [Ed.]

on vested financial interests, and it is concerned wholly with immediate status. Such status is more dangerous than rewarding, since vanity is a weakness of most men. The primary goal of a real writer must be the fulfillment of his gifts, however great or small those gifts might be. Literary status not only inflames a writer's vanity, it also fails to satisfy the deeper needs of his nature. Those needs are satisfied only by work. The writer obsessed with prestige cannot dare subordinate his vanity to his true gifts, because true gifts by their very nature have the singularity of genius; true gifts are original gifts and original gifts very seldom win immediate praise. The desire for status is not a friend, but an enemy the writer must conquer; it saps the strength and courage required to be true to oneself. If status comes first, then honest emotion must come second. The status-grubbing writer is inevitably a derivative writer, an imitator. It is only natural that such a man would be jealous of every other writer on earth. The gibbering terror and malevolent competitiveness of Mailer's essay reveal an obsession with status.

(2) It is no accident that few creative writers (and none of the first rank) have ever been concerned to exercise continuously the critical faculty. Great critics are not great writers. A critic is a picky and measuring man, self-conscious and deficient in vital power; he has little spontaneity and less inspiration. The creative faculty and the critical faculty fight each other within him, and the stronger loses. The most gifted writers have a critical faculty, but they use it seldom and rarely. The self-consciousness of a critic is totally fatal to a work of art. A good writer knows this, but a bad writer does not. Every good book has emotional power first and intellectual interest second. The irony is that the "critic" writer's books aren't even interesting intellectually — which takes us nicely to the next notation on this grim hospital chart.

(3) Ideological dependence, rather than an independent struggle with experience, is a very common mark of the liter-

ary pretender. Books based on the moral definitions of the Popular Front, on the metaphors of Freudian psychology, on the teachings of Zen Buddhism, and on any formal value system cannot project a personal vision of life, thus they cannot have emotional power or original meaning. Norman Mailer began his literary career with a sophomoric, grandiose work crudely based on the moral definitions of the Popular Front and the stylistic mannerisms of John Dos Passos. He then abandoned elementary Marxism for Leon Trotsky and the anarchistic idealism of Jean Malaquais, and wrote a book based on a new set of moral definitions. Then, as the currents of our time drifted and swirled, he turned to neo-Freudian psychology for still other moral definitions. After that, the beatnik "movement" for stylistic guidance and a bastardized Zen Buddhism for still another set of moral definitions. How can such slavish obeisance to passing fashion lead to the production of significant literature? Where in such arid schemes is the breath of life? Where, indeed? True, there are countless logrolling academic idiots in the literary world and many of them become book reviewers, but it's a hopeless proposition. The philosophical "leaner," who cannot write in the honest terms of his own experience, must tend to produce lifeless books filled with lifeless characters, because art can never be subordinate to any formal ideology.

(4) Public rebelliousness and notority-at-any-price conform to a naïve American view of the writer as a screwball, but this has nothing to do with the process of writing and little relationship to the problems of a serious writer. The discipline of writing is too severe and demanding to allow either time or energy for the hunting of the snark. Movie stars spend much of their time seeking publicity, but a real writer is too busy. It is true that if a writer constantly screams and howls "Me! Me! Me!" some naïve souls will conclude perhaps he really has something. All that egotistical caterwauling: Could it be a total bluff? The answer is yes, it could be, and in Norman

Mailer's case that's exactly what it is. In the long run, noto-riety-at-any-price must backfire. The unfortunate thing is that sooner or later the impressionable public will conclude the man who constantly shouts "Me! Me! Me!" does not really have anything to say.

(5) And neither is "style" a path to glory, which brings us to the Law of the Perpetually Repeating Literary Lie. All *poor* writers (if they are familiar with the literary world at all) can be spotted instantly by a tendency to substitute style for content. Of all the attributes of literature, style is the most evanescent, but the most noticeable — to those dilettantes who know virtually nothing about the real difficulties of writing. It is not by accident that the two greatest novelists of all time (Tolstoi and Dostoevski) were considered inferior stylists in their day. Style is that thing which is fashionable at the mo-ment and great writers are *never* fashionable. The basics of good fiction are beyond the reach of the mediocrities who forever infest the literary world. Thus, "informed" critical opinion in every age must declare the surface aspects of litera-ture to be the essence of it. The Law of the Perpetually Re-peating Literary Lie is so derived. Noman Mailer understands this law perfectly. Living characters?— that is square; lifeless symbols are better. A genuine narrative?— that is squarer; a static mess is really cool. Moral truth?— God no; self-pitying skepticism is what us cats blow. The most apparent aspect of literary technique is the manner of handling language, al-though other technique is incomparably more difficult. It was ever the same: the emphasis of a poor writer is on technique that is noticed, in particular a verbal facility — words, words, words, and the more startling a combination of them the bet-ter. To be a nimble verbalizer is not only enough, that's the whole show. The outlandish adjective, the deliberately inept metaphor, the wild and murky tangle of dependent clauses — this superficially impressive verbosity is substituted for real ideas and real feelings. The most striking thing about Mailer's essay on his fellow writers, aside from its meanness of spirit, is

the painful and endless effort to bowl over the reader with language. Fancy-sounding phrases are stuck in the thing like plums — but not real plums, phony plums made of dust and pretension; the fancy phrases, in reality, have no meaning whatsoever. Whom does it fool? What price glory? If a few gullible and ignorant nitwits think one is a clever writer, does that provide a fulfillment of gifts bestowed by God? The hallmark of a bad writer is an unawareness of his obligation to be honest with himself; he is willing and able to fake it with words.

(6) The basis of all significant literature is the capacity of the writer for sympathetic emotion toward other human beings. If the writer boils and burns with hatred, then nevertheless he must also weep with compassion, because from this conflict all art originates. The writer incapable of sympathy is no writer at all. How could such a person possibly write with real feeling, and how could his work have any broad human meaning? The theory of genius derived from the devil is a concoction of small and jealous minds, a rationalization of untalented neurotics; a true artist is more than hostile and alienated, he is also a man who cares about other people. Mailer's essay on his fellow writers is so full of hostility and egotism one wonders how such a thing could be written at all. Surely, one thinks, somewhere there must be a trace of generosity or a touch of fellow feeling — after all, these men have labored long and hard in an effort to give something to the world. How can a man who has endured the pains of writing talk in such a way about other writers? There is something profoundly disgusting about Mailer's performance, and perhaps the most loathsome thing about it is the transparent trick of praising a little in order to damn all the more. One is bound to conclude that Norman Mailer's human sympathies are either temporarily suppressed or atrophied altogether. But a cold, vain, and icy heart does not a writer make — that isn't the way it's done.

Styron, Jones, Baldwin, Bellow, Heller, Updike, Burroughs,

Salinger, and Roth don't need to be defended from an asinine attack, and to defend them has not been the purpose of these remarks, which despite all outrage are eleemosynary rather than polemical. Perhaps even at this late date Mailer himself might wake up and return to the honest two-dimensional storytelling of which he is capable; he might abandon this hopeless dream of a literary glory wholly beyond him.

But if not, then at least others might learn a little bit about the way it isn't done. The path of Norman Mailer does not lead to the bitch goddess of literature, but to a moldy witch of his own imagination, a spectral hag conjured up from vanity and anger. There is no "bitch goddess" in the first place and no question of "getting a piece of her"—this predatory whimsy is as pitiful as it's absurd. When Leo Tolstoi gave the world *Anna Karenina*, did he roll in the hay with a slut? Perhaps it is too much to expect Norman Mailer to respect the giants of the past and the masterpieces they have left behind. Whatever estimate is made of the current literary scene, the truth in the human heart, illuminated by the creative power of genius, is not a bitch but a beautiful lady, remote and far-removed from the grubbing hands of would-be seducers.

And yet, something remains to be said, and it is sad. The real victim of Mailer's attempted assassination of his fellow writers is Mailer himself. A compulsion to win glory and fame is a dreadful curse. No matter how outrageous the conduct of Norman Mailer, no matter how often he has asked and even begged for the truth, in the last analysis one must pity him in his distress.

# Norman Mailer at Graduate School

## by Norman Martien

### or, One Man's Effort

Norman Mailer looks like my uncle. I hadn't expected it, but when I saw Mailer I knew I should have. It seemed one of those odd conjunctions of separate worlds, a coincidence with some location of the mind. Because there it was, in his eyes. Not the color, because my uncle's are brown and dark, and Mailer's are, you have to say, steely gray-blue. It was around the eyes, really. In the exaggerated fold and droop of the face there — lived out, rich, dirty, hilarious — so that you knew my uncle would say kiddo and talk about Felix the Cat and devils and other things no one talked about anymore. You can see in the creases around Mailer's eyes that he will talk that way. Words are stored there in the way he squints his eyes, pieces of vision glance and dazzle as he looks sideways. And you knew before either man

This essay was originally published in *New American Review I* (September 1967) and is reprinted by permission of the author. Copyright © 1967 by Norman Martien.

spoke that the words would be a tall tale of seeing what the eyes had seen. The eyes spill over a dozen false and funny accents, and they all say Son, they say, Son, they ain't nothing in this whole damn world I ain't seen . . . and done, too.

But nobody thought Mailer was going to say much about Felix the Cat, not to graduate students in English. That was not what worried them. Because The Mailer was coming and anything could happen. The English Department was groping for a tone: stories, gossip, jokes, questions, slander, and a lot of excitement that was admiration, curiosity, or maybe just anxious awe. It was Norman Mailer vs. The Graduate School, and he had them running. But they trained bravely and sweated at night. In groups they sparred, lots of dodging, now a feinting *interrogatio*, a deadly *contra* to some vulnerable point. It was nasty: Norm, baby, how's your wife? It was clumsy: Do you feel there is any literary value in the Vietnam war? It was funny: Don't bend over, Mailer the nailer is coming. It was a gently hysterical week. Who was invited and who not and why. What would he say and not say and why. We so rarely encounter so nearly the embodiment of our myths.

He was Deerslayer and Joe Palooka, John Wayne and Captain Marvel, the Good Angel and the Bad-Ass Mothah, the Great Sage and the Big Daddy. So that there was some anxiety about tone. Norman Mailer was going to talk to us, and one hardly knew what that might mean.

A house across town had been chosen for the event. It was old and institutionally neat, tightly wallpapered and elegant. Behind the house there were trees, and from the porch rolled out an acre or two of lawn. My uncle would have liked it, without knowing why. We all stood on the porch or in front of it or on the steps: talking quietly, smiling, and laughing a little. But everyone was watching, everyone stood with necks bent a little stiffly, with eyes squinting into the bright sky where a kite flew above the grass and trees. It hovered and bucked and coaxed its string and the person far out on the grass watched it and shifted his feet and looked uncomfortable. Do you have a question, someone asked, and of course I did have a question. Everyone did. The porch was almost lifting off the house with questions and wonderings. No, I said, I didn't have a question. You know he's not going to talk, don't you?— just answer questions. No, I didn't know that. Maybe I did have a question.

But then Mailer did talk: for more than an hour he talked beautifully, awkwardly, kindly; he read, he laughed, he kicked up old metaphors, he surprised us all, he surprised himself. We were seated around him where he sat in an armchair with his back to the fireplace. There was no fire, but it was a warm enough day, and it was not going to be a fireside chat. The room was large enough and windowed, and one was finally discovered to open. Even folding chairs did not spoil the rightness of the scene. It was for the moment as a house of fiction, and Lyndon Johnson had never seemed farther away.

Norman Mailer had come to speak to us of style, and there it was, made all around us and before us. Style, he said, is manners, meant to keep out all intrusion from what we want to say to each other, so in a few words you will tell all that need be known of the thing you want to talk about — of taking a horse over a jump, say, how it was done, what it was like. But then he warned us that a style could exclude too much, that no one in Henry James, say, could take off his hat and you'd see a smashed egg on top of his head. That was funny, and everyone laughed. But as I watched Mailer — the way he leaned forward, moved his body quickly, almost before I saw it starting at the edges of his eyes — as I watched him I could see that Mailer was a skilled smasher of eggs. I hadn't expected that either, not quite that. But again I should have. I might have seen it in the novels and in the characters, all dripping of egg in the face. Heroically, even, like Croft. As

247

though Ahab had stood, not with an ivory leg, but with an egg in the face, chucked at him by Ishmael. It made you wonder about the violent and comic possibilities of egg smashing, about egg smashing as a style. And it made you recall James's profiled portrait, his wonderful big high hat, which might (but you would never know) conceal a thousand broken eggs.

Of course Mailer hadn't worn a hat; probably any of us would have refused to wear one. But the mention of James suggested that some grace was lost by the refusal. For in all the freedom of Mailer's conversation, his standing up and sitting down, his looking for a page that he would not have looked up beforehand, in the gesture of reading and smiling in redis- covery, even in all this there was a strange tightness and con- striction of the mind, seeming always to lead one place and not another, not ever another. He read first the introductory paragraph of *Advertisements*. He asked us to think of it as the opening of a novel, the voice of a character in a novel, and of course there was hardly another way we could have thought of it.

> . . . I have been running for President these last ten years. . . . I contain within myself the bitter exhaustions of an old man, and the cocky arguments of a bright boy. . . . I am imprisoned with a perception which will settle for nothing less than making a revolution in the consciousness of our time. . . . I would go so far as to think it is my present and future work which will have the deepest influence on any work being done by an American novelist in these years. I could be wrong, and if I am, then I'm the fool who will pay the bill.

He talked about the internal sources of this style, but you weren't thinking then of where it came from. *"My present and future work . . . I'm the fool who will pay the bill."* That was what he had come to talk about, and perhaps it was the absurd contradiction of it that recalled something, almost asked us to forget what was said, to look someplace else; but out the window above the grass there was only the kite still bouncing away from its string, poking around at the evening sky.

After a while, graduate students all around, watching, listening, he began to talk to us of *An American Dream*. He told us now of the external necessities of his style, but still the question I wanted to ask was about something else. I wanted to ask about the style of his downcast boyish grin when he told us how he had written the novel in need of money. Call it, he said, paying for the past. Because you would have thought by the way he sort of boastfully ducked his head, grinned, that Her Old Man had maybe asked, Boy, was it you knocked up my gal? Well, maybe it was. He invited you to think so, that God's own plenty of shotguns would be nothing to the lucky fool who'd pay the bill. Hell yes, paying would be easier than slipping it to her, and it might even be more fun. Summer nights out back in the swing; hard days up along the road. Internal and external styles. Finally, I didn't know quite what he meant: Posture and Action, Wharton and Dreiser the Artist and the Man, Fuck 'em and Forget 'em?— any number of things probably. As I listened my mind wandered about, half opening doors, standing among them, undecided and even a little discouraged.

It was only later, when Mailer was reading from his novel, that I could begin to see what the questions might be, though not the questions any of us had come with, or probably would even want to ask him. It was when he was reading, describing, bringing out the characters of the scene: an Italian judge with two tarts, a pair of detectives, one light-skinned plump young Negro with a mandarin's goatee, some old woman. . . . But it wasn't the list that told us so much, it was how those people had got into the room, how he brought them there from the novel: the Italian judge — and as the left hand held the novel the right pulled slowly back in a fist, just a few inches, and came down ("judge") and punched him out at us; the two tarts — and again a slow short swing; the detectives, the Negro, the old woman, a prize fighter — Plumpf, plumpf, plumpf, quietly and tensely he plugged them into the waiting solidity of the room, insisted on them, made them right.

He read on, of Rojack's magic bullets and arrows, of exhaustion and imaginings: he almost sang, "If you want to buy my wares, follow me and climb the stairs. Lu, uh, ove, love for sale. . . ." But it was as if my mind had already made its stairs, or had lost itself somewhere else, for those gestures had seemed to open a door outward. His movements had recalled something, had found again, in an old forgotten hatbox, a photograph of thirty years ago. It was a photo of my uncle, taken, I suppose, on a day off from a WPA or CCC project; but tinted brown and brittle-looking, it seemed much older than it was. They were building a road, I think, up along some part of the Sierra Nevada. Probably no one needed a road there. Down one side is the San Joaquin River and its valley, and down the other is the desert floor stretching in the blank sun. But the photograph leads the eye upward, where an empty sky hangs over the whole scene, a tinted, faded brown sky as if it were just a covering of old rags or parchment. In the center of the photo is my uncle, standing a few yards off, and behind him, between him and the brown sky, there are pine trees. They are much darker than anything else, they stand straight — pointing upward, thick and heavy-branched, and they seem impenetrable. There must have been a ring or at least a platform nearby, but it is not visible. My uncle stands there in the cleared earth of the foreground, and he wears boxing trunks and large heavy gloves. There is no one else.

Everyone has an old photo like that, but there is something in this one that Mailer knew about, or seemed to, when he read from his novel. It is something seen only after looking at it for a long while, something in the way my uncle stands there, crouched slightly, the left glove forward, the right held back and close. But the posture is not stable, the left glove is too far forward, the right foot only lightly touches the ground. There is no blur in the photo, but it describes an action, as if it had caught a gesture just a moment since completed. He seems to be moving forward, or to have moved forward, to have just come out from the trees behind him — as if ridiculously, heroically, he had punched his way through the landscape, had just that moment before jabbed through its surface, and brought himself out from the thick screen of trunk and branches, out from the rough-slapping boughs, the clinging sap, and stinging needles. Wham-bam: one man's effort. And there he was, not a scratch, as though newly born, right out in the mountain sunlight, under the brown sky. There he was, grinning a little at one side of his face, and not a mark on him anywhere. It was only later, long after the photo was taken, when I saw him after he had been many years in prison, that I began to see what it might have cost him to force that separation from the landscape. And maybe even then what I saw in his eyes was not the cost of that first gesture of discovery, but the too great willingness to pay its price, to revive the debt and to repay it, for many years with the work of every day and the life of every night.

It may be, after all, it was worth the price, left him the clear, clean love of the good fight, made the past something sharp and new as the smell of pine branch. Or, as Pound would have it:

> *What thou lovest well remains,*
> *the rest is dross*
> *What thou lovest well shall not be reft from thee*
> *What thou lovest well is thy true heritage*
> *Whose world, or mine or theirs*
> *or is it of none?*

But you had to wonder what it cost to do so much clearing away, to break out a hard stone and to fashion of it a cameo of the past. Thy true heritage, Pound, in how many cantos. And Gaudier-Brzeska's chisel, Floyd Patterson's left hand, are they to be the same after all? Well, it was on my mind that afternoon. One wanted at least the choice put before him; one wished some view of consequences as the novelist's talk went on of strategy and tactics, of boxing, the Presidency. And as he talked, the shoulders once in a while made a quick feinting gesture. All of Hemingway's games, with a few neat twists but maybe not different after all. Thy true heritage: how long to live off that, how long deliciously to pay the price for having been tough enough and large enough to discover and thus create it? Perhaps the questions are only of myth, but they were real enough that afternoon. They were present in the reading that was taking place for me on another afternoon as well, in the imitation of that improbable and recurring gesture of discovery — as if the reading were a reenactment of the dreamy violence of some faded landscape.

There was an incoherent period of questions and answers, an ominous difference of vocabularies, clumsy jousting upon creaking hobbyhorses. Then we all dismounted and walked into the next room for drinks. When the room had settled half an hour later, Mailer was standing firmly braced against the table where the drinks were served, and he was politely surrounded. The talk went round and round the room. Wasn't he nice; he really was nice; I was surprised how nice he was. . . . His physical presence, I mean his body; he was physically so . . . What did he say? What *did* he say; I don't know, what did he say. . . . As an advertisement it seemed to have been a beautiful success. He had come to talk to us of style and everyone was full of it, up to the ears in all kinds of manners, modes, and means; the room blossomed smiles, bourbon, questions, all lovely and meaningful. It was difficult to ask Mailer a question, there were so many around him, and I kept thinking it would be like arm wrestling, so I listened for a while to his imitation of Johnson (Lyndon) and kept watching the way he watched people just at that moment when they had finished speaking or listening to him. It was just a glance, but it measured meanings and response in a way that let the eyes give away not a thing. The smile or the tiredness, the generosity or the selfishness, these and innumerable wonderful promises, or tough disappointments — whatever it was that reminded me of my uncle — made me want to talk to him. I knew he would want to listen; but I stayed just out of reach because maybe he would smash an egg on my head. So I went to make a phone call, found a phone, dialed several times, and got no answer. I waited and heard ringing at the other end. It was dark now and the person with the kite had gone. Still I got no answer, so I gave it up and went back to the party. Someone said I had been ringing the next room.

Mailer was still there and for some reason this surprised me. But he was so nice, everyone had said, and so after all I did ask him a question. I had been reading Mailer's essays and I had been reading Fenimore Cooper's letters; their complaints and expectations of American life seemed to me enough alike that the question was more like an argument. But it came to a moment's talk of Cooper's ideal solution of American difficulties — what Mailer called "The Wilds." I suppose he meant that Cooper's solution was no longer useful, but perhaps not; what he said was, The Wilds are now twelve thousand miles away. Yes, I agreed, good wilds is hard to find. But that is not what I wish I had said, because I hoped that he did not believe that. He laughed when he said it, took a drink, measured appreciation, but there was a quantity of seriousness in the way he so quickly located The Wilds; he knew where they were, or where he thought they were, and what they were called. It would have been easy enough to say to him, "Ah, but Mr. Mailer, the wilds are within us." Or something like that. One might have said that to Conrad, if Conrad had needed to ask about it. But it was not what Mailer had meant.

What he seemed to mean, if he meant anything at all, was that The Wilds are the place where books are made truly, as though a novel were a place where the writer had lived, a good thing he had done. Like Whitman telling you he went to the shore to write the poems that were there; like my uncle banging his whole past and future out of the mountain landscape.

My uncle always talked about The Wilds. I don't remember what he called them, but they were a place he wanted to get to, I could tell that; almost as if he would meet himself there coming out of the wild land, as if he would recover an old grace that he had paid for as though it were his all along. He could do many things well, my uncle. He was no Sergius O'Shaugnessy, but he could build a house, hunt, plant beans, whittle, paint a car, weld a beam, fight, swear — anything at all. He knew what he had done and he knew what he was doing, but it always seemed to last just a day or two, then another place, maybe another job, maybe jail or a woman or nothing at all. All of these, it seems to me now, were advertisements, and if they were not concretely available later, but showed only in the manners of his face, perhaps that was for the best. Because even without them visibly there, I knew he kept living with his best moments, the times when he had done something well, among others, the things he kept looking for in some impossible vision of himself among The Wilds. Whatever was in that old photograph, it was as if he had come to believe in its action as a graspable moment of self-creation. He was somehow imprisoned in that belief and that past gesture.

It may have been, after all, only an odd correspondence of momentary surfaces that made him seem like Mailer. Perhaps a glance of that imagination of The Wilds, the only place where he could be as good all the time as he had been once — the time he painted that '37 Ford sedan a fine glossy black, the times he drank so well, the afternoon at a WPA camp when he knocked down his cousin three times. But the life with that moment and with those times was hard, the cost maybe more than he thought, and it made him old. So there was bitter drinking, weeks at a time lost, and finally someone killed. And even after this, there was a place, a ranch way down in Mexico, and maybe that was The Wilds, finally, or maybe only the last of many fictions. But we only took him as far as the border; he never got there, and I never saw him again. It was the way he looked then, the way Mailer looked when I first saw him, that made me recall my uncle: the tone of the face about the eyes, the vision there, the weary pride and the fun, the way he looked as we drove south that night toward Mexico.

# PART FOUR:

# The
# Last
# Word

# Playboy Interview

## by Paul Carroll

The first of two long sessions with
*Playboy* interviewer Paul Carroll took place in Mailer's
Heights duplex apartment, which has become something of
a celebrity itself: nautical items abound, from the brass ship's
clock over the kitchen and the dismantled engine-room tele-
graph beside the big bookcases to the glass-and-wood gable
forecastle, which Mailer built above the kitchen and bed-
rooms and which can be reached only by climbing ropes,
trapezes, or deck ladders. Dressed in his work clothes — dungarees and Army-surplus shirt — Mailer sat at the dining-room
table, occasionally glancing out of the large bay window at
the panorama of tugboats, ocean liners, and merchant ships
dotting the East River, and beyond to the skyline of lower
Manhattan. As Mailer spoke, he frequently leaned forward to

emphasize a point by jabbing his fist in the air; at other times, he'd pause for a long while, his thoughts sinking deep into the the topic at hand, before he'd give an answer. What was most apparent about him during the interviewing sessions was not only the energy, intelligence, wit, and gravity with which Mailer probed the subjects but also the bristling, tough honesty of the man. We began by asking about his alleged aversion to the interview form itself.

PLAYBOY: How do you feel about being interviewed?

MAILER: I start with a general sense of woe.

PLAYBOY: Why?

MAILER: The interviewer serves up 1 percent of himself in the questions and the man who answers has to give back 99 percent. I feel exploited the moment I step into an interview. Of course, once in a while there is such a thing as a good interview; but even then, the tape recorder eats up half the mood. It isn't the interview I really dislike so much as the tape recorder.

PLAYBOY: What do you think is the best way to conduct an interview?

MAILER: There's no good way. It's just a matter of hard, professional technique. In professional football, a quarterback has to contemplate the problem that every third or fourth play he's probably got to gain some yards through the center of the line; and when he's got four very tough linemen opposing him, there's not much he can do that's surprising, so it's just a matter of grinding through — that's all.

PLAYBOY: If you feel so negative about being interviewed, why did you consent to this one?

MAILER: About every two or three years, I feel I have to have a psychic housecleaning, go through my ideas in general, even brutal form — the brutal form of the interview — just to see about where I stand. Because most of the time, I spend my time thinking privately. Without this kind of psychic housecleaning, I might get too infatuated with some ideas. It's a way, I suppose, of exposing ideas that are weak. After that, you can either discard them or think about them a little harder.

PLAYBOY: As you talk about housecleaning your ideas — disregarding, changing, or improving them — we're reminded of your sentence in *The Deer Park* about growth: "There was that law of life, so cruel and so just, that one must grow or else pay more for remaining the same." Yet you've been charged by many critics with dissipating the potential growth of a major talent in American fiction by wearing so many hats. They point out that there's Mailer the politician, who once seriously considered running for mayor of New York City; there's Mailer the journalist, who writes about the maladies in American life and about the political brutalities; there's Mailer the celebrity, who grabs headlines by booze brawls and other acts of public violence. How do you answer that criticism?

MAILER: Moving from one activity to another makes sense if you do it with a hint of wit or a touch of grace — which I don't say I've always done; far from it — but I think moving from one activity to another can give momentum. If you do it well, you can increase the energy you bring to the next piece of work. Growth, in some curious way, I expect, depends on being always in motion just a little bit, one way or another. Growth is not simply going forward; it's going forward until you have to make a delicate decision either to continue in a difficult situation or to retreat and look for another way to go forward. The pattern that this creates — no, pattern is a poor word — the *line* of the movement reveals the nature of form. A breast is beautiful because it decides to go down until that point where it decides to go up, and after it decides to go up, it decides to go down again and then decides to go up again, and you have the beginning of the nipple. The nipple goes through its own particular curve, which consists of going out to the heavens as far as it can, then dropping down toward hell, and then returning to the body — all within the space of a quarter of an inch. But there's an extraordinary difference between a beautiful nipple and a dull one.

More to the point, I've been accused of having frittered many talents away, of having taken on too many activities, of having worked too self-consciously at being a celebrity, of having performed at the edges and, indeed, at the center of my own public legend. And, of course, like any criminal in the dock, I can sing a pretty tune; I can defend myself; I'm my own best lawyer; the day when I'm not will be a sad day. The defense I'll enter today depends on my favorite notion: that an expert, by definition, is opposed to growth. Why? Because an expert is a man who works forward in one direction until he reaches that point where he has to use all his energy to maintain his advance; he cannot allow himself to look in other directions. In other words, he's become nearsighted. Now, I, as a man who's been nearsighted almost all of his life, know that anyone who's born nearsighted or becomes nearsighted early is a man become an expert prematurely. That's why kids with glasses are usually disliked by kids who don't wear glasses. The kids with good eyesight sense that the boy with glasses is an expert who's going to run the world. The first chronic personal shame I suppose I ever felt was having to wear glasses. And I don't wear them today, even though I'm so nearsighted I don't recognize old friends from ten feet away. Having been a premature expert myself, I think I may have reacted against it with a sense that expertise was the trap for me, that to get particularly good at any one thing would leave me a top-heavy expert.

PLAYBOY: Is all this related to *The Naked and the Dead* and the celebrity that followed in its wake?

MAILER: Yes. Being well known at twenty-five created a chain of legend for everything I did. If I left a party early, it wasn't because I might have been sleepy; it was because I had put down the party. This immediately created champions for me: "That Mailer's too much — put down the hostess when he left the party." Others would say, "Dreadful — no manners; a barbarian." People expected me to grab the hostess of a party, sound her, yank her, pump her, and if I didn't like her, throw her out the window, then turn to my host, say, "Up your buns, guns," and walk over to sock the nearest guy in the eye. So when I went into a place and didn't behave like that, the other guests would say: "Why, he has such nice manners." Every little thing I did was exaggerated. Lo! There was a feedback that had little to do with me. It was as if — if you will — every one of my actions was tuned to an amplifier.

PLAYBOY: Is this what you meant when you once remarked that your success at twenty-five was "like a lobotomy"?

MAILER: It cut me off from my past. I felt like someone who had been dropped onto Mars.

PLAYBOY: Did you dig your sudden fame?

MAILER: Of course I dug it. I had to dig it. I mean, to be brutally frank for all our swell *Playboy* readers out there: it enabled me to get girls I would not otherwise have gotten.

PLAYBOY: You make a distinction between the legendary Mailer in the spotlight whose acts were scrutinized and gossiped about and the Mailer who wanted to grow in his own sweet time. Could you contrast the two Mailers a bit more?

MAILER: Well, contrasting two Mailers might have value in a novel, but to talk about it would end up being tiresome. This is the point I want to make: I had some instinctive sense — right or wrong — that the best way to grow was not to write one novel after another but to move from activity to activity, a notion that began with Renaissance man; it's not my idea, after all. My personal celebrity was an obstacle to any natural ability to move quickly and easily. For years, it was a tremendous obstacle; and I ended up having a very dull, dogged personality that sought to wrestle with the legend, and that tried to say, "Look, fellows, I'm really simple, honest, hardworking; I'm as close to Abe Lincoln as Arthur Miller is."

The hoarseness of this confession is not to enlist sympathy but to prepare the ground for my boast: I learned how to accept and live with my legend. The legend becomes your friend, the beard, a front man, a pimp, a procurer of new situations. You live with a ghost who is more real to people than yourself; every single action you take with another person is part of a triangle. Every girl you talk to is not only in love with you or disappointed in you but also is in love with or hating your legend — who, incidentally, is more real to her than you. There are times, therefore, when you beef up your legend, perform some action to support it; times when you draw credit back from your legend, like cashing in the desire of somebody else to do something nice for you. Either way, you don't pretend — as I did for years — that the legend ain't there; it *is*. By the same token, when you're dealing with a man, there are now two of you against him; you're two linemen having to take out one other guy.

PLAYBOY: In other words, if you got drunk and got into a scrap at a party, there'd be three men fighting instead of two?

MAILER: Yeah. Of course, that doesn't always work to your advantage, because sometimes a guy who is fighting two guys is braver than when he's fighting one. I've gotten licked by guys who I think might not have licked me if I hadn't had my twin, the legend, on my side, too.

PLAYBOY: One of your celebrated experiments with growth was your experience with drugs. You were on marijuana, Benzedrine, and sleeping pills for a few years and were addicted to Seconal. Later, you said that a man on drugs will pay for it by "a gutted and burned-out nervous system." How do you feel about that topic today?"

MAILER: Drugs are a spiritual form of gambling. This is a poetic equation that can be carried right down to the end of its metaphor, because on drugs you're even bucking the house percentage — which for a drug like marijuana is probably something like 30 or 40 percent.

PLAYBOY: Would you expand this?

MAILER: Marijuana does something with the sense of time: it accelerates you; it opens you to your unconscious. But it's as if you're calling on the reserves of the next three days. All the sweets, all the crystals, all the little decisions, all the unconscious work of the next three days — or, if the experience is deep, part of the next thirty days, or the next thirty years — is called forward. For a half hour or two hours — whatever is the high of the pot — you're *better* than you are normally and you get into situations you wouldn't get into normally, and generally more happens to you. You make love better, you talk better, you think better, you dig people better. The point is, you've got to get in pretty far, because you're using up three days in an hour — or whatever the particular ratio is for any particular person. So unless you come back with — let us say — seventy-two hours in one hour, you lose. Because you have to spend the next three or four days recovering. You might ask: What happens to the guy who smokes pot all the time? I don't know. But I do know something is being mortgaged; something is being drawn out of the future. If his own future has already been used up in one or another mysterious or sinister sense, then maybe the pot is drawing it out of the very substance of what I may as well confess I call God. I suspect God feeds drug addicts the way a healthy body feeds parasites.

PLAYBOY: How do you mean?

MAILER: Well, if God has great compassion, He may not be willing to cut the drug addict off from Him. During the time the addict has some of his most intense and divine experiences, it is because he is literally imbibing the very marrow and nutrient of existence. But since I do not believe that God is necessarily inexhaustible, the drug addict may end up by bleeding Him.

PLAYBOY: Do you think this happens on LSD?

MAILER: I don't think you have a mystical experience on chemicals without taking the risk of exploiting something in the creation. If you haven't paid the real wages of love or courage or abstention or discipline or sacrifice or wit in the eye of danger, then taking a psychedelic drug is living the life of a parasite; it's drawing on sweets you have not earned. Please do not say, by the way, that LBJ is the biggest cornball in America; with the above, I have just presented my credentials.

PLAYBOY: What is the danger of this parasitical self-exploitation on LSD?

MAILER: I'm not going to say that LSD is bad in every way for everyone, but I'm convinced it's bad if you keep taking it. Any drug is bad finally in the same way that being a confirmed gambler is bad. A confirmed gambler ends up losing all his friends because he blows their money and blows their trust. A gambler will tell any lie to get back into the action. By the same token, if you stay on any drug for too long, then you have a habit; you're a victim; to anticipate something, you're a totalitarian.

Let me put it this way: LSD is marvelous for experts to take when they get too frozen in their expertise. Let's suppose they've driven deep into something impenetrable, some obstacle that was bound to trap them because of the shortsighted nature of their expertise. Although they work and work manfully as experts, at this point they're similar to soldiers who have pushed far into enemy territory but are now up against a resistance they cannot get through. Their only action is to retreat, but they don't know how to, because they have no habits of retreat. They're experts; they know only how to move forward to amass more knowledge and put more concentration upon a point. When this concentration does not succeed in poking through the resistance of the problem, the expert is psychically in great trouble. He begins to live in increasing depression; he has to retreat and doesn't know how: he wasn't built to retreat.

My guess is: On LSD, you begin to die a little. That's why you get this extraordinary, even divine sense of revelation. Perhaps you taste the door and essence of your own death in the trip; in excess, it's a deadly poison, after all. Therefore, what's given to the expert is a broader vision: dying a little, he begins to retreat from his expertise and begins to rejoin his backward brothers. Hallelujah! So that LSD taken a few times could be very good, I would imagine. But before very long, if the expert keeps taking LSD, he can become nothing but an expert on LSD.

PLAYBOY: What do you think of Timothy Leary?

MAILER: Well, I wonder who we were just talking about.

PLAYBOY: More of an answer, please.

MAILER: I never met him. Perhaps I'd like him if I did. Many of my friends like him. But I have heard him speak, and he is then nought but simple shit.

PLAYBOY: Alcohol seems to be another way by which you've tried to grow or "move forward." One of the characters in your stage version of *The Deer Park* declares: "A man must drink until he locates the truth." How does alcohol help a man do that?

MAILER: I'm going to offer the hardworking magazine readers of America one fundamental equation: A man who drinks is attempting to dissolve an obsession.

PLAYBOY: What's the obsession?

MAILER: Talk first about what *an* obsession is. I've thought about obsession a great deal, but I'm not sure I know the answer. Everybody talks about obsessions; nobody's ever really explained them. We can define them, but we don't really know what we're talking about. An obsession, I'd like to suggest, is not unlike a pole of magnetism, a psychic field of force. An obsession is created, I think, in the wake of some event that has altered our life profoundly, or perhaps we have passed through some relation with someone else that has altered our life drastically, yet we don't know whether we were changed for good or for bad; it's the most fundamental sort of event or relation. It has marked us, yet it's morally ambiguous.

PLAYBOY: What kind of event?

MAILER: Suppose a marriage breaks up. You don't know if it was finally your fault or your wife's fault or God's fault or the Devil's fault — four uncertainties. Let's reduce them to two: a man or his wife. Put it this way: People move forward into the future out of the way they comprehend the past. When we don't understand something in our past, we are therefore crippled. Use the metaphor of the Army here: If you move forward to attack a town and the center of this attack depends upon a road that will feed your attack, and this road passes through a town, yet you don't know if your people hold that town or someone else holds it, then, obviously, if you were a general, you'd be pretty obsessive about that town. You'd keep asking, "Will you please find out who owns that town?" You'd send out reconnaissance parties to locate the town, enter it, patrol it. If all sorts of mysterious things occurred — if, for example, your reconnaissance platoon didn't return — you'd feel so uncertain you might not move forward to attack. The obsession is a search for a useful reality. What finally did occur? What is real?

PLAYBOY: You haven't told us yet how drink helps dissolve an obsession.

MAILER: Well, if a man's drink takes him back to an earlier, younger state of sensitivity, it is then taking him to a place back of the place where he originally got into the impasse that created the obsession. If you can return to a state just preceding the one you were in when these various ambiguous events occurred, you can say to yourself, "Now, I'm approaching the event again. What really did happen? Who was right? Who was wrong? Let me not miss it this time." A man must drink until he locates the truth. I think that's why it's so hard for people to give up booze. There's an artwork going on with most serious drinkers. Usually, it's a failed artwork. Once again, one's playing against the house percentage: one drinks, one wrecks one's liver, dims one's vision, burns out one's memory. Drinking is a serious activity — a serious moral and spiritual activity. We consume ourselves in order to search for a truth. It's no accident that a part of small-town common sense insists: "I don't trust a man who never takes a drink," because that man either has no obsessions and so has never lived through a bad and tricky time or has obsessions so prevalent that he has buried them and live bodies are screaming under the ground. Whereas, in contrast, the small town will put up with a lot from a drinker, because anyone who takes a frequent nip has had revelations on drink. Drink is the active man's drug addiction. Madison Avenue, please copy.

Note: You take a drug lying on your back, whereas the way to drink is standing up.

PLAYBOY: Do you feel that you've experienced moments of truth through drink?

MAILER: Extraordinary moments of truth. The thing that had me ready to bawl was that I was close to the truth but too drunk to do anything about it.

PLAYBOY: What sort of thing did you discover?

MAILER: Whatever the truth was. The kind of truths you find in moments like that. Discovering that somebody you thought loved you hated you, or vice versa. All I'm underlining is that sense of certainty we all know when past moments of ambiguity are resolved. The ambiguity sinks into the earth; a crystal remains; you say, "Yes, there's the truth. Yes, this is what did happen." A relationship alters in one's memory from a morass to a crystal of recollection.

PLAYBOY: In terms of your concept of growth, you've made in *An American Dream* and other writings a brilliant, dazzling, and rather puzzling remark concerning the possibility that God Himself may be involved in a process of growth. You've said that you have an "obsession with how God exists," and you've argued for the possibility that He may be a God whose final nature is not yet comprehended, even by Himself. Could you comment on this?

MAILER: I think I decided some time ago that if there is a

269

God and He's all-powerful, then His relation to us is absurd. All we can see in our human condition are thundering, monumental disproportions, injustices of such dimension that even the conservative notion of existence — which might postulate that man is here on earth not to complain but to receive his just deserts and that the man who acts piggishly on earth will be repaid in hell, regardless of whether he was rich or poor — yes, even this conservative vision depends on a God who is able to run a world of reasonable proportions. If the only world we have is one of abysmal, idiotic disproportions, then it becomes too difficult to conceive of an all-powerful God who is all good. It is far easier to conceive of a God who died or who is dying or who is an imperfect God. But once I think of an imperfect God, I can begin to imagine a Being greater than ourselves, who nonetheless shares His instinctive logic with us: we as men seek to grow, so He seeks to grow; even as we each have a conception of being — my conception of being, my idea of how we should live, may triumph over yours, or yours over mine — so, in parallel, this God may be engaged in a similar war in the universe with other gods. We may even be the embodiment, the partial expression of His vision. If we fail, He fails, too. He is imperfect in the way we are imperfect. He is not always as brave or extraordinary or as graceful as He might care to be. This is my notion of God and growth. The thing about it that gives me sustenance is that it enables me to love God, if you will bear these words, rather than hate Him, because I can see Him as someone who is like other men and myself, except more noble, more tortured, more desirous of a good that He wishes to receive and give to others — a torturous ethical activity at which He may fail. Man's condition is, then, by this logic, epic or tragic — for the outcome is unknown. It is not written.

PLAYBOY: Could you talk a bit more about the relationship between a man and this God who is still involved in discovering His own nature?

MAILER: In capsule: There are times when He has to exploit us; there are times when we have to exploit Him; there are times when He has to drive us beyond our own natural depth because He needs us — those of us, at least, who are working for Him: We have yet to talk of the Devil. But a man who talks about his religion is not to be trusted. Who knows—I may be working for the Devil. In fact, I sometimes suspect every novelist is a Devil's helper. The ability to put an eye on your own heart is icy.

PLAYBOY: You said recently that maybe the Devil is God in exile. What did you mean?

MAILER: I don't know. What I mean is, I don't know if the Devil is finally an evil principle of God — a fallen angel, a prince of darkness, Lucifer — a creature of the first dimension engaged in a tragic, monumental war with God, or whether the Devil is a species of nonexistence, like plastic. By which I mean every single pervasive substance in the technological world that comes from artificial synthesis rather than from nature. Plastic surfaces have no resonance — no echo of nature. I don't know if plastic is a second principle of evil just as much opposed to the Devil as it is opposed to God — a visitor from a small planet, if you will. So when I talk about the Devil these days, I don't really know whether I'm talking about a corrupter of the soul or a deadening influence. I don't know who or where the enemy is. In fact, I don't have the remotest notion of who or what I'm working for. Sometimes I think I'm unemployed. That's despair, son.

PLAYBOY: Let's get into something that may have a tangential relation to this despair. You've written extensively about John F. Kennedy and his impact on our times. In your essay "Superman Comes to the Supermarket," published during the 1960 Presidential campaign, you suggested that Kennedy was an "existential politician." Existential is a term that crops up frequently in your writing: existential God, existential politician. Exactly what do you mean by it?

MAILER: Existential — no precedents, no traditions, no disciplines, no books, no guides sufficiently familiar with the situation to take you through.

PLAYBOY: In what way was Kennedy an existential politician?

MAILER: Kennedy was a man who could define himself — or, in other words, comprehend himself — only by his actions. He had such extraordinary ambition that if he had not succeeded in being President, he might have ended up a bad piece of work. There is such a thing as a man starting as a bad piece of work because he has a nature that is extraordinarily disharmonious; he lives with unendurable disproportions and ambitions. If he succeeds in what the psychoanalysts call "acting it out" — with some scorn they say "acting out" — the fact remains that he also has to have huge courage, high wit, and vast imagination. Kennedy succeeded in getting to play the one role that could allow him to realize himself: the President of the United States. When I call him an existential politician, I mean that Kennedy had no nature other than the particular nature he discovered in himself by the act of living. If he had tried to live a more conventional life, he would have sealed his psyche in a vault and probably would have died young and schizophrenic.

PLAYBOY: Do you have any theory about who killed Kennedy?

MAILER: I have no special insight into that. What I'm more ready to speculate is on the events after the assassination. There must have been one incredible moment for every secret-police agency in the world when they first heard that Oswald had been in the Soviet Union and had come back here to America. Every intelligence operation everywhere must have known the odds were great that Oswald was an agent for several quite separate espionage services, because you don't let men and boys like Oswald in and out of cold war countries without making them pay a little price: They've got to become a little agent — not a big agent, just a little agent, a pawn. As for most of these guys in secret services — I won't say they're clowns; some are able, but they don't have a great deal of personnel to work with, when you get down to it. Their best material is found in one another's agents. So they play games with one another's agents. They develop the same attraction toward one another's agents that buddies work up for the same girl. Two guys in love with the same girl get great play back and forth. So, yes, once in a while, a poor guy like Oswald gets caught in a situation — becomes an agent for two countries, and two or three other secret services or espionage services will get in on it. It's possible Oswald may have been an agent or on the working list of a dozen different secret services throughout the world.

When the assassination occurred, I think a tremendous panic erupted. An enormous effort was made to begin destroying all evidence in sight — in every possible way. To top that, you had the Dallas Police Department — which I don't know anything about — but, give or take a few points, it has to be as corrupt as the next big-city police force. Moreover, a cop under a searchlight is not the most resourceful of creatures; he tends to stampede — he's not called a bull for nothing.

PLAYBOY: How did you feel when you heard Kennedy had been shot?

MAILER: Horrible. Horrible. At first, in some cockeyed way, I thought it was a gag — like, he wasn't really hurt that bad. For some reason or other, I was bitter about him in those days and I made a sardonic remark I've been ashamed of since: I said, "That son of a bitch, he's got hard Irish smarts; he's probably lying there with that flesh wound in his arm, saying, 'Let America sweat for an hour thinking I'm about to die. They'll realize how much they need me.' " Of course, when I realized he was indeed dead, I came to the conclusion that my on-the-spot divination of events was not particularly incisive, tasty, or superb.

PLAYBOY: If Kennedy had been only wounded and then had recovered and resumed his responsibilities as President, what do you think America would be like today?

MAILER: It might still be in serious trouble. Kennedy was a fine man, maybe even a magical man, and he changed the style of America; he opened it up. Something racy came back into American life. The country was saltier; it swung more. Still, you would have had technicological society eroding most of his efforts; in addition, terrible problems with Congress and civil rights. I have a hunch, however, that Kennedy wouldn't have been such a fool as to get us into Vietnam the way Lyndon Johnson got us in; I think Kennedy would have kept the war going about the way it was going, and he might have looked for a way to write it off. Kennedy might even have come to pay attention to an idea that doesn't have enough attention paid to it — that the way to fight Communism is not by warring against it but by letting Communists fight one another. There's something in the nature of Communism that makes it attack itself. Communism is profoundly cannibalistic.

PLAYBOY: Isn't that why you said we should get out of Vietnam — in the controversial talk you delivered on Vietnam Day at the University of California at Berkeley two and a half years ago?

MAILER: Yes. Except it's next to impossible for us to get out of Vietnam. Psychologically impossible. Militarily, of course, the war is next to meaningless. But America, more than any other country on earth, has an image of herself as a fighting nation. Americans really *want* to fight; they really want a war. It's good for them, healthy for them. Fine. Have war games every year. I offered this suggestion in a satirical piece, but I've since become a little more serious about it. Buy some place — some desert or jungle — and invite any countries we have eyes for to come to fight. If they don't accept, they're conceivably too yellow to show up. Or, at least, so we can tell the world. But if they do, they have 50,000 men, we have

50,000 men; we get 200 or 400 airplanes — name it — they get the same; all ordnance similar in category, the same count of weapons. Then you have the biggest professional war game in the history of the world. Let it go on for two or three months, or to a conclusion, covered by color television, radio, interviews with some of the stars who come out of this engagement. Some will call it musical comedy, barbaric; but, in point of fact, the one difference between this war game and Vietnam is that we won't be burning kids in any number or smashing property that belongs to others. Americans will just be doing what they want to be doing: some shooting, some war.

Many men love to be in battle. They are better men at the end of it if they are engaged in a war that has some modicum of purpose. If you're engaged in a purposeless war, you can end up healthy, but you're still a pig with a distorted mentality, because you have to justify the act of killing as being a patriotic act when, in fact, all you want to do is kill. If I wish to blast somebody and I say, "Yeah, that's what I want to do," then I'm existentially tuned; I know what I am. I am obeying the first dictate of ethics: Know thyself. But if I want to kill somebody and I say, "I'm doing it for my country and for freedom," then I'm a bad piece of work. I'm psychically disoriented.

PLAYBOY: In the Berkeley talk, you also argued that the reasons given by the Johnson Administration for America's involvement in Vietnam are patently phony. In particular, you rejected the claim that we're there because we're battling Communism. Why do you think we entered the war?

MAILER: Because we had to. America was profoundly afraid of the Negro Revolution. In the secret councils of our sleep, we were ready to do anything to stop it. War in Vietnam was the quickest way to slow it down. Another reason: The potential for violence in American life was accelerating every year, the social fabric was beginning to break down. I think in some deep instinctive way, Johnson reasoned that a war would enable him to control the country better. America was getting out of his control; nothing inspires profound anxiety in a man like Johnson more than losing control over every last little button. Vietnam was an instrument Johnson could use to manipulate public opinion, to apply leverage to the economy, to stand up against the civil rights movement. I think he saw Vietnam that way. It was *the* fatal error of his life. This talented, wily, seasoned politician made an error of Shakespearean proportions when he decided to embark on that war in Vietnam. The smartest President in America's history had just become the stupidest. Because Vietnam will yet prove to be the war in which America lost control of its ability to control a large part of the world and Johnson lost his power to lead the American people on an ideological leash.

PLAYBOY: Do you think Johnson stands a chance for reelection in 1968?

MAILER: If Richard Nixon runs, Johnson has a chance.

PLAYBOY: Of all the major political figures about whom you've written extensively, you've hardly ever paid serious attention to Nixon. Why?

MAILER: One reason is that Nixon was written about very well all through the fifties. He became a natural target for every good political writer on the left, so it felt like kicking the cat to go to work on Nixon. I'm not fond of the man, but I didn't see any reason to duplicate a job done so many times. If he gives signs of becoming powerful again, that'll be another matter. That *will* be serious. I don't know anyone who has ever heard Richard Nixon say anything interesting in all the years he's invaded our life. Nixon is resolute in his refusal to become more interesting. It's a remarkable power — this passionate embrace of monotony.

PLAYBOY: Do you see any politician on the scene today who might be an existential politician in the way of JFK?

MAILER: I think Bobby Kennedy might be. You can't begin to know what direction the man will take. I don't mean his directions are cheap or contradictory, but he has a nature that finally is resistant to analysis — so at least he gives you a ride for your money. Bill Buckley, replete with all his vices and virtues, is certainly an existential politician.

PLAYBOY: What do you think of the other Republican Presidential potentials, Romney, Percy, Reagan, and Rockefeller?

MAILER: They are the tragedy of the Republican party. They are the embodiment, the present-day focus of the mediocrity of — nay, let us say they are the *tragedy* of — the Republican party.

PLAYBOY: In *Cannibals and Christians,* you said that Bobby Kennedy has made a pilgrim's progress since the murder of his brother. What did you mean?

MAILER: He's become more interesting than he used to be; that's a pilgrim's progress. How many people can that be said about?

PLAYBOY: What do you think his chances are in 1968?

MAILER: I don't have any idea. My approach to politics is from outside. I don't like being filled with inside stories. There was a period in my life when I knew people who knew every inside story. It took me a while to find out they knew nothing. For instance, they knew in 1963 that Bill Scranton was going to be the Republican candidate in 1964.

PLAYBOY: A while ago, you praised John Kennedy for changing the style of America by opening it up and making it "saltier." What would the nation be like under a Robert Kennedy administration?

MAILER: It would depend on what kind of country he might inherit in this election or in 1972 or whenever. It might be a country damaged irreparably by the horrors, pusillanimities, and hypocrisies of the Johnson Administration, the Vietnam war — which may have done more damage to America than anything in our history — and the "Great Society."

PLAYBOY: How do you feel about Johnson's Great Society?

MAILER: It's a comedy. The Great Society is not only not

277

going to come into being but it shouldn't. It's artificial. The only growth with meaning is organic growth that does not become separated from the root of its origin. Any time you find a great society developed from the top, what you've got, in effect, is a test-tube baby — artificial insemination of the worst sort. Let's say the Great Society is drug addiction on a huge political scale. It's similar to shooting $B_{12}$ complex into your butt. The patient may feel healthier for a while, but the fact of the matter is that a part of his ass has been violated in a way that bears no relation to his life — at least not as his own flesh can feel it. In other words, your flesh is visited abruptly by a tubular needle that punctures skin, rips delicate strands of muscle, and cuts holes in a vein wall. To what end? The body doesn't understand. If you're in a fight and get hit, your body can usually understand that: it was probably mobilized for action. But what action are you mobilized for when a needle goes into your flesh? The same thing happens, I think, with economic growth. Take the first idea of the poverty program — making jobs. What pleasure can a man take in a job that has been made for him?

PLAYBOY: Doesn't that statement place you in league with the right wing?

MAILER: I don't mean we have to go all the way back to nineteenth-century conservatism. Instead, take Harlem as an example of what I'm talking about. Right now, part of the New York City police force works in Harlem. It's a hopeless job for any white policeman. He doesn't have a prayer of being a good cop; he's too hated because of all the bad white cops who've been there and also because of all the bad Negro cops who've worked in Harlem. He's hated because he comes from outside and is a symbol of oppression. Suppose the existential fact were recognized that Harlem is more separated from New York City than East Berlin from West Berlin; it is a separate principality, a kingdom in and of itself. Suppose, then, that Harlem had its own police force and was offered its

278

fair share of the funds that run the New York Police Department. Suppose they even used part of that money for other purposes and had a volunteer police force, just like the Hasidic Jews in Crown Heights, Brooklyn, a couple of years ago. Anything that functions on the basis of volunteer effort by people who have come to feel they have to do this particular job in order to feel respect for themselves will work better than obliging a professional to do a job in some place where he's miserable professionally. The advantage of having an all-Negro professional and volunteer police force in Harlem is that every time something ugly happened, the Negroes would have to recognize one particular complexity in life, which is that not only can their own people be bad but that police brutality might be something that comes out of being a policeman. And they'd have to face the fact that Whitey ain't the only devil in town. That might be good.

Take schooling in Harlem. All these educational programs that come from the outside are absurd. I've never met a stupid Negro in my life; I've met many Negroes I couldn't talk to, but I never had the feeling of a stupid man behind the face. I have met stupid whites. The point is: The Negro has a life experience that prevents him from being stupid. As a result, he has a culture that is thus different from our own, and his school education should begin with *his* culture before he is asked to move over to ours. So, again, let the city allocate board-of-education funds to let the Negro administer his own schools and evolve his own curriculum. There might be chaos for a time. Could it be any worse than the daily chaos in Harlem schools now? Why should Negroes be forced to learn to read by methods devised by Midwestern WASPs? Totally different kinds of people — as different as Japanese and Georgians.

Concerning housing projects, I see no reason to come in with these tremendous urban-renewal jobs that are unspeakably ugly and tear up neighborhoods; they are like metal plates put in your head or plastic tubes stuck in your gut. These projects disrupt a neighborhood. Instead, some of these tenements could be saved. You could have a scheme where a man could start by being given one hundred dollars' worth of materials — I use the figure arbitrarily — and a little professional labor, and he could set out to improve his apartment: plaster a wall, this or that; say his wife will be in on it. He's working for his own apartment. If he goes out and drinks up the money, all right, he drank it up and presumably he won't get anymore. His neighbors might lean on him. Not lean on him hard, probably, because if he's the guy who drank it up, he's possibly the meanest guy in the house. Still, what you get this way is a house interested in itself; whereas the other way, housing projects, poverty programs, Great Society — any Negro who doesn't set out to exploit the white man who is giving him money is nothing but a fool. With such handouts, honor for the Negro becomes his ability to lie, cheat, and exploit the white man. Whereas a few thousand dollars given bit by bit to a man working very hard on his own apartment over a few years would obviously do much more for that apartment than twenty thousand dollars spent to renovate it by outside methods.

PLAYBOY: Prior to the riots in Newark and Detroit, you said that civil war would erupt soon in this country. Did you see it as happening between Negroes and whites?

MAILER: I think there's a tendency toward civil war — not a war in the sense of people shooting it out over the hills and on battle lines; but certain kinds of functions might cease to exist in this society — technological functions. It may be that people will lose the habit of depending on the subway to get to work, or people might lose the real possibility of driving into certain cities at certain hours of the day or night. What might happen would be scattered outbreaks of violence: people, for example, who've gotten fed up with the Long Island Expressway and so start overturning cars in traffic jams.

All sorts of things — products getting worse and worse, shoddiness at the center of production, breakdowns, fissures.

PLAYBOY: How much of this will be the result of what you've often and passionately condemned as our technological society?

MAILER: Oh, much of it. Most of it, perhaps. Another great part of the tendency toward violence might derive from our guilt of the past: we've never paid for the crimes of the past; now we're trying to bury them. That's one reason the technological society advances at such a great rate: it frees people from having to look back into the horrors of the past. Western man has never faced up to the slave trade, the concentration camps, the colonization of the world, the imperialization of the world — the list could go on as long as one's knowledge of history.

PLAYBOY: In *Cannibals and Christians*, you described the cold war as useless, brutal, and enervating. You said we should stop it and get on with the destiny of Western man. What is that destiny?

MAILER: A huge phrase —"the destiny of Western man." I suppose I meant that the West is built ultimately on one final assumption — that life is heroic. It's a Faustian notion. Of course, one immediately rushes to say that the West is also Christian, but there's always been a contradiction at the heart. Christianity, the gentlest of religious professions, is the most militant and warlike of religions, the most successful and Faustian of religions. Indeed, it conquered the world. In that limited sense, Christianity is the most heroic. The alternative to this heroic notion of man is that passive acceptance of the universe that characterizes Hindu or Oriental philosophy and religion.

One of the ironies of our century is that the technological society creates an atmosphere of such passivity in people that they are now prepared to entertain Oriental notions precisely because they have lost much of the real power to shape their own lives. The citizens of a technological society are as existentially powerless as an Oriental peasant. Their living standard may be vastly superior, but their essential social impotence is similar: they command less and less; they are manipulated more and more. They may think they are picking their channel, but TV channels them.

Note: The more we wage a religious war against Communism, the more we create the real social equivalent of Communism in America — which will be the total technological society. You can look forward into a future where Communism's technological society grows nearly identical with ours; the differences will be of the mildest local color. For the natural tendency of the technological society is to try to clean up all sorts of social excesses and to root out random oppression because these activities are illogical; they interfere with the smooth working of the machine. You never want a piston to drive with more force than is necessary to direct the action of the machine; you never put a part in the machine that is heavier than it needs to be. So the natural desire of the technological society is to create a smooth totalitarian society free from the ranker forms of injustice. Its long-term tendency in Russia is to make a totalitarian environment that is relatively civilized and pleasant. Both countries may well end by serving up a life to their citizens about as anonymous and vitiated and pill-ridden and dull as some of our new office buildings.

PLAYBOY: Then why does America fight Communism?

MAILER: Because we're Faustian. We believe we have to grapple with the universe; we have the secret faith that we are inspired by a national genius that enables us to take on anything and do anything. The tragic irony is that in fighting Communism, we are creating the absolute equivalent of Communism in this country. And we will destroy our own Faustian dream in the act of fighting Communism, for the technological society looks to destroy any idea of the heroic because such ideas seem irrational and unscientific to the technician.

On the other hand, each time Communism has captured some small part of the West, it has been shaken by Western complexities that open huge rents in the Russian Communist ideology. A backward country like Yugoslavia did more to halt Stalinism than fifty military adventures dreamed up by John Foster Dulles. Yugoslavia introduced a complex notion into the center of Communism: the idea that there could be two kinds of Communism, each equally devout and heroic in itself, each more or less oppressive. This made the Communist bureaucrat begin to contemplate the nature of his own system and therefore to doubt his faith and so look for ways to ameliorate the oppressiveness of it.

Communism is cannibalistic, as I said earlier. Any ideology that attempts to dominate all of existence has to split into sects and segments, because the moment disagreement exists between members, it cannot be adjudicated or compromised without losing the primitive force of the ideology. Compromise impossible, splits occur. What you get then is two ideologies equally monotonous, equally total, soon equally at war with each other.

PLAYBOY: Opposed to this, then, is what you call the heroic destiny of the West?

MAILER: Let's say, an *exploration* into the heroic.

PLAYBOY: Is existential politics an exploration into the heroic?

MAILER: To a degree. Existential politics can be understood only by talking practically, specifically, about what you are going to do here in this particular place and time. After you talk about, say, twenty such situations, you get some notion of existential politics. The basic principle is that you do not separate the act from the receiver. Existential politics depends on a certain intimacy between the law and the people upon whom the law is enacted. For example, the most paradoxical notion of existential politics is not that there should be no capital punishment but that if someone is going to get killed by the state, then make a spectacle of the event. Let people watch while a professional executioner and the condemned man fight hand to hand in an arena. Since the executioner is professional, he wins practically every time; but he doesn't win to a certainty; that gives the prisoner some last chance to fight for his own existence. It gives him the right of any man to fight for existence under extraordinary circumstances. Such a spectacle also opens the public to the real nature of execution. Let them see that blood on the sand. They may then decide if they still want capital punishment. If they do, more power to them. They like blood. But at least one profound hypocrisy — our quarantine of the execution from the eyes of the public that decrees the act — won't be able to exist anymore.

PLAYBOY: In terms of the possibility of your becoming an existential political figure yourself, you once planned to run for mayor of New York City, although recently you said that you've decided to devote your time to writing instead of political activities. Do you still feel that way?

MAILER: I disqualified myself from being in political office; you can't stab your wife and get away with it. It's as simple as that.

PLAYBOY: Yourself apart, do you have any prognostications about the American political and social scene in general?

MAILER: I'm gloomy. I won't say I don't think we're going to make it; but I am gloomy because, quite beyond politics and any related or unrelated discussions of courage, honor, love, beauty, and so forth, rests this technological society that sits upon us like an incubus. It's impossible, for instance, to have any contact with anything in your existence that is not incapsulated by this technological society. I can't take a pat of butter at breakfast that doesn't have some chemical additive to deaden the taste of the butter just a bit, and therefore my taste buds, and therefore deaden me, as well as line my stomach cells with a new if minuscule addition of the chemical. If you could eat a fresh piece of butter for breakfast, certain sensory messages might be able to reach down deep into the secret needs of your nerves — enough to enrich you. You might live a hint better. The technological society gets between us and existence in everything we do, the air we breathe, the buildings we live in with their abstract monotonous forms, the synthetic fibers we wear; ever notice how a rash from a synthetic fiber is more disagreeable than one from cotton or wool? The list is endless. I've written about little else for years.

PLAYBOY: What can be done about it?

MAILER: I don't know. My feeling is that there is going to be some extraordinary holocaust. Who knows? We may all die off in mysterious fashion. For instance, about the time we discover some cure for cancer, a new disease even worse will probably be spawned by the cure — just as new viruses were spawned in relation to penicillin. Modern disease and modern technology are inseparably connected.

PLAYBOY: You've often connected this, which you call "the plague," with the modern technological society. How did the plague begin?

MAILER: I think it began somewhat back with primitive man, when the first mediocrity discovered he could get power over men stronger than himself by employing magic for control over others rather than using magic for communion with his existence. Jacques Ellul, in his book *The Technological Society*, suggests that the beginning of all scientific technique came from a perversion of primitive magic.

PLAYBOY: You've written that one aspect of totalitarianism is fear of orgasm, particularly by the liberal mentality, because the orgasm, you claim, is "the existential moment. Every lie we have told, every fear we have indulged, every aggression we have tamed," you say, "arises again at that instant to constrict the turns and possibilities of our becoming." Could you tell us more about that?

MAILER: Orgasm is the moment when you can't cheat life. If the orgasm was no good, something in you — or in your mate, but probably in you — was no good. In an existential moment, something bad can happen to you, because you can't control it; you don't know how it's going to turn out. Anybody who's ever been in an automobile accident experiences such a moment — three or four or five fragments of time that seem endless — and you're into something that is brand-new.

But the American liberal is programmatic about sex. Yesterday he believed in sex hygiene. Today he believes in promiscuity. He thinks it's good. I think that's innocent. Promiscuity is good at given times. Other times, dreadful. When sex becomes programmatic, in walks the totalitarian. Because a program does not permit of surprises. Sometimes, existence can reveal itself only by its surprises.

PLAYBOY: Do you think the abundance of sex manuals available today contributes to the programming of sex?

MAILER: Taking them at their best, the psychological sex manuals, I'd still say I'm not a champion of Albert Ellis's opinions. Although there's one thing in Ellis's ideas that isn't so bad: the notion he has of sex as will. For instance, I remember he once told me a story about one of his patients who was terribly timid and nervous about women. After they'd worked for a while in the analytical relationship, Ellis finally said one day to his patient: "Look, you like this girl; you find her attractive. Neck with her tonight; take her to the movies and neck with her." Ellis said the patient went to the movies with the girl and suffered and sweated and died but finally made a pass; he did neck with her. Ellis said the real reason was that the patient was more afraid of Ellis than he was of the girl. There's something in that. A healthier reflex can sometimes be initiated by an act of will.

PLAYBOY: Is that an example of existential sex?

MAILER: Yes: it's leaping a gap. But, you know, I distrust this talk. The older I get and the more I learn about sex, the more I know I don't know anything at all. Sex is more mysterious today than it was the day I started.

PLAYBOY: In what sense?

MAILER: I find it harder to come up with value judgments that can be used from one day to the next. I prefer it this way — having fewer and fewer answers about sex as the years go by.

PLAYBOY: In that case, do you still believe, as you wrote several years ago, that birth control is evil — that it's a kind of murder of what may have been a man's best son?

MAILER: Yes. In fact, not too long ago, I was reading a very generous review of *Cannibals and Christians* in a Catholic magazine called *The Critic*; and at one point the critic said, Of course, Mailer's ideas are almost absurdly sentimental about birth control. I am now to the right of the Catholic Church.

PLAYBOY: Indeed, the Catholic Church is presently struggling with its birth-control position, in order to square it with the problems of the world population explosion and the individual moral problems raised by families that are too large.

MAILER: Regardless of what the Church finally decides, the problem of birth control is the same as all of the other problems in our technological society. They're all part of the same damn problem; something is insulating us away from our existence. My guess is that in primitive times it was much more difficult to conceive and — as a result — more natural. In a just existence, the best things are always the most difficult. Since primitive man lived in a relation to his life that was more biological — which is to say, he felt everything around him with his own body — he was therefore more intelligent *physically* than he is today, even though he might have been smaller. Each man was more an animal; his senses told him more. We notice that many animals don't conceive all that easily. I would judge the problems of breeding are considerable with animals because they don't conceive unless they really want it to take.

In our modern life, on the other hand, the body is so deadened at its sexual center by contraceptives and pills that we no longer can afford to be as selective as we used to be. This adds desperation. Because people are less sensitive to conceiving, they have to make damn sure they conceive. So men put a child into many a woman they would not choose in the real calling of their blood; and many a woman accepts the seed of a man she would normally despise or half despise. There's an adulteration of distinctions, a losing of the intimacies of form, in the sense that a fine key for a fine lock is intimate. I repeat: People now conceive too easily because they're afraid if they don't, they won't conceive at all.

PLAYBOY: What would happen if there were no birth control?

MAILER: It's possible that it might then become much more difficult to conceive, because there would be more real terror of conceiving for too little.

PLAYBOY: Isn't it also possible that the social consequences would be calamitous — if your theory didn't work?

MAILER: Perhaps — but one thing you can be sure of: People would start making love a lot less; they'd make it only when they really wanted to make it; they'd have to be carried away more. On a flood of passion, yeah. How many people ride on a flood today? One thing I've learned in all these years is not to make love when you really don't feel it; there's probably nothing worse you can do to yourself than that.

PLAYBOY: Why?

MAILER: Well, it's like taking your vitals, putting them on a stone block, and pounding away with a hammer. It's bad for the back — that I know.

PLAYBOY: Do you think it's possible for a couple to have an enduring sexual relationship?

MAILER: Yes, I do. Even after you've been married awhile, it can still be the thing you go through the day for.

PLAYBOY: You don't believe, then, in the old cliché that the early days of marriage are the great times and after that the sexual scene gets less interesting?

MAILER: I think a marriage should get better all the time. By the time they're eighty, a couple should die fucking. But I don't think that happens, because none of us have the guts for that; none of us are clean enough; all of us are yellower than we ought to be. Cowardice kills love.

PLAYBOY: Cowardice in what sense?

MAILER: It centers around possession. A curious thing: If you gamble with your possession and gamble foolishly and you're not possessive enough, that's fatal. There's something in a woman that is profoundly outraged if you don't want to make her all your own; women will never forgive you for that. Permissiveness to a woman is permissive shit. They hate it. Everything primitive rebels in a woman if a man does not want her absolutely for himself. At the same time, once you claim a woman, you start killing everything in her. Nothing in love or sex is ever simple, because you're always walking between two paradoxes.

PLAYBOY: What are they?

MAILER: They go by many names: possession versus liberty; protection versus spontaneity; novelty versus tradition.

PLAYBOY: You've been married four times—

MAILER: Heroines, every one.

PLAYBOY: How do you feel about marriage?

MAILER: I love marriage, but I don't think I'd love it unless I were a novelist. I love it because it's a curious relationship. It's artificial and yet, on the other hand, it has such primitive roots and territorial rights. A novelist can become absolutely obsessed with marriage. I've never written much about it, but I think it's a gold mine: to write about marriage, to really write about marriage and what *really* goes on between a man and a woman — the way they kill each other and keep each other alive.

PLAYBOY: Do you think you may write about it someday?

MAILER: I don't know; I don't know. It's difficult. After all, the marriage you're usually thinking about at the moment is your present marriage, and you can't start writing about that.

PLAYBOY: Many of your critics accuse you of harboring a

good deal of hostility to women. They point to the classic scene in your story "The Time of Her Time" when the protagonist calls his penis the "avenger" and rapes a girl anally.

MAILER: Let's get something hotsy-totsy. Let's say: takes carnal possession of her posterior territories.

PLAYBOY: All right. Critics also point to the well-known scene in *An American Dream* when Rojack deprives a German maid of her orgasm by insisting at the last second on having his orgasm in her rectum instead of her vagina. Critics say that here again is an example of Mailer's deep hostility toward and distrust of women. What do you say about it?

MAILER: I think I've got as much anger against women as anyone I know, but I'm perfectly willing to let the defense rest right here — I don't give a damn — and, you know, I sometimes have as much hostility against women as I've got against men. The reason I wrote about those things twice deliberately was something writers will understand but no critic ever will; it was just to say to the critic: "Fuck you. I wrote about it once; I'll write about it again. What are you going to do about it? Say I'm anally oriented? O.K. Say I'm anally oriented. I'll say I'm Cassius Clay. Fuck you."

PLAYBOY: Some of the same critics have taken you to task for a poem in your *Deaths for the Ladies (and other disasters)*:

*So long*
*as*
*you*
*use*
*a knife,*
*there's*
*some*
*love*
*left.*

They say this boastfully exploits the episode when you stabbed your second wife. How do you feel about this charge?

MAILER: I don't want to talk about the stabbing anymore.

Not anymore. Say the word eighteen times and it loses its force. I'll just say — this could be hard to believe — that I was not really thinking about the act or myself at the moment I wrote the poem; I was really thinking about a long conversation I had with a man who stabbed his brother. He had been telling me about it and he had such complexity of feeling for his brother that the poem came: "So long as you use a knife. . . ." My feeling about writing such things is simple: If you're not ruthless about your work, you can't be an artist of interest. Once something crystallizes, you have to be ruthless about presenting it; it doesn't matter who gets hurt, starting with yourself. Your message in the ear of the reader is going to be worth the damage that's done. You've got to be impersonal; you can't look back. If, on the other hand, you go in the other direction and start thinking, "Will writing about this experience hurt me?" — well, then, you're a bad writer, the kind who spends his life humping for *The New Yorker*. You spend your life hurting other people — not yourself.

PLAYBOY: Why?

MAILER: A sadist can't bear pain, self-examination, anything injurious to the ego. His ego, after all, has to give him sanction to do harm to others.

PLAYBOY: In *Cannibals and Christians*, you spoke of the dangers of the womanization of America. Could you expand on that point?

MAILER: The gist of what I said is that women are getting more power because men want them to. Today, a man wants a wife who is a military assistant, a woman who can go out into the world with her husband and help him climb those hills of status.

PLAYBOY: Do you feel that a woman's place is in the home?

MAILER: That takes us right back into the technological society. When a woman is in the home today, she's miserable. Our technological society has transformed her home into a minor-league factory with all sorts of plastic and electric serv-

ices and appliances that keep breaking down constantly — at
a far greater rate, be it said, then the clumsiest machines of the
nineteenth century. That's part of the mystery of our technological society: nothing really works well. I, of course, put
the blame on plastic. The machine bears some umbilical relation to metal, just as a house does to stone or wood and red
wine to meat. Plastic in a machine makes about as much sense
as a foam-rubber cunt.

PLAYBOY: The "technological society" more directly affects
— and you would say, oppresses — the middle and upper
classes. Is that the reason you've written that the lower classes
enjoy a more satisfactory sex life?

MAILER: I think the lower classes probably have more sexual
vitality than the upper classes. They have fewer outlets in life.
Another reason: They tend to work more with their bodies
than with their minds.

PLAYBOY: But according to Kinsey, the lower economic
groups suffer from more sexual rigidity and engage in less
sexual experimentation than the upper and middle classes.

MAILER: All such statistics show is that attitude to which
people are ready to confess. I don't know how valid such findings are. What we're talking about here is old-fashioned sexual perversion. Members of the upper classes and the more
prosperous middle classes tend to be fond of their own
pet perversion; they look upon it as an entertainment, an
adornment, an enrichment; the lower class, on the other hand,
looks upon sexual perversion as weakness; they see it in its
other aspect. Perversion has two aspects: it is an adornment; it
it also a need, and so they see it as a weakness and they despise
it. To the lower classes, need is weakness.

PLAYBOY: What do you mean by "perversion"?

MAILER: Whatever it might be — fellatio, cunnilingus, you
name it. Lower-class people see it as a weakness in themselves
if they desire it. Envision a strong guy who wants to go down
on his girl. He thinks he's weak. Of course he's weak. Giving
head to your woman is weakness; it's also a good way to get rid

of some of your weakness. It's also dangerous because it gives the Devil introduction into the vagina.

PLAYBOY: The Devil? How so?

MAILER: Oh, the mind's a devil. Didn't you know? And the mind, after all, is connected to the tongue.

PLAYBOY: You've said that D. H. Lawrence was the first novelist who gave you the idea "that sex could have beauty." Do you continue to admire Lawrence?

MAILER: My objection to Lawrence is that he's sentimental about sex. Sex is not only a divine and beautiful activity; it's also a murderous activity. People kill each other in bed. Some of the greatest crimes ever committed have been committed in bed. And no weapons were used.

PLAYBOY: About the art of fiction in general, do you agree with critics such as Norman Podhoretz who claim that the novel as an imaginative art is dead because of the recent incorporation of reportage techniques into fiction?

MAILER: Obviously, I don't agree with them. I believe the novel has its own particular resource, which is almost magical. If you write purely and your style's good enough, you can establish a communion between yourself and the reader that can be found in no other art. And this communion can continue for hours, weeks, years. When the novel is dead, then the technological society will probably be totally upon us. You'll need a score card to be able to tell the Communists from the Texans.

PLAYBOY: Many critics have said that of all the writers of your generation, you seem best equipped to write the fabled Great American Novel. How do you feel about that?

MAILER: Let's assume they're right.

PLAYBOY: What would it be about?

MAILER: That's something I want to keep to myself.

PLAYBOY: Several times you've compared your generation of writers with the generation of the 1920's — Hemingway, Fitzgerald, Faulkner, and the rest — and you've argued that the older writers were far superior. Do you still believe this?

MAILER: They're doubtless greater; and they're certainly more fascinating as men.

PLAYBOY: You said that if Hemingway had been a pimply-faced kid instead of the man he was, his books wouldn't have had the audience they commanded. Some critics claim about you that if you were a middle-class, conservative man who wrote novels rather than a brawling, pugnacious, hard-drinking hipster, your books would never have sold as well as they have. What do you feel about your relation to your public image?

MAILER: Hemingway had a clear image, if you will: the work and the man bore a certain resemblance to each other. But my relation to my public personality is more surrealistic than that. People are in an incredible state of confusion about me. So my public personality probably hurts my sales, because Americans like answers, not enigmas. It's precisely the middle-class conservative authors who sell in huge quantities: Herman Wouk, Louis Auchincloss, James Michener. Make your own list.

PLAYBOY: How do you want to be remembered?

MAILER: The surest way not to be remembered is to talk about the way you want to be.

PLAYBOY: Do you feel good about the future of American fiction?

MAILER: I don't want to predict. I can't even predict my own work.

PLAYBOY: You've said about your latest book, *Why Are We in Vietnam?*, that it sometimes displeases you; but at other times, you decide it's one of the ten funniest books written since *Huckleberry Finn*. To which of your previous works do you feel closest?

MAILER: Probably *The Deer Park* and *An American Dream*. And one day a month, I really like *Barbary Shore*. Whenever I'm depressed, I'm always pleased *The Naked and the Dead* is around.

PLAYBOY: Why do you write?

MAILER: Why do I write? You can't beat the hours.

PLAYBOY: Do you think you'll continue to write political and cultural essays? Some of your critics complain that in *An American Dream*, for instance, you rehash ideas already expressed in your essays and book reviews and columns. What are your feelings?

MAILER: Everything I write is a card out of the same deck. You can reshuffle them; but in a way, I've been working on one book most of my writing life. Probably since I started with *Barbary Shore*, certainly with and since *The Deer Park*, I've been working on one book.

PLAYBOY: Including the books of essays — *Advertisements for Myself*, *The Presidental Papers*, and *Cannibals and Christians*?

MAILER: Yes.

PLAYBOY: What's the book about?

MAILER: Existentialism. That is to say, the feel of our human condition, which, by the logic of existentialism, is the truth of the human condition. Of course, it takes no mean artistry to get the feel.

PLAYBOY: At the beginning of our talk, you said you like interviews because they sometimes serve as a psychic house-cleaning for your current ideas. Do you feel you've accomplished that here?

MAILER: I hope we haven't had a curettage.

PLAYBOY: Is there any final statement you'd like to make?

MAILER: Yes.

> Up the Irish
> Down the Feds
> Say we sad Irish
> Anarchists and Reds.

Not bad doggerel, when you realize I learned my Hebrew in Brooklyn. Cheers to the brogue. Let's get a drink.

# A Biographical Chronology

1923    January 31. Born to Isaac Barnett Mailer and Fanny Schneider Mailer in Long Branch, New Jersey.

1939    Graduates from Boys' High, Brooklyn, New York. Elects Harvard over M.I.T. for the study of engineering.

1941    Publishes first short story, "The Greatest Thing in the World," in the *Harvard Advocate*. Submitted to *Story* magazine's annual college contest, it wins first prize, is published in *Story*, and draws some attention from representatives of New York publishers.

1943    Graduates from Harvard (B.S. with honors), having written, among a wide variety of shorter fiction, two unpublished novels—"No Percentage" and "A Transit to Narcissus."

1944    Marries Beatrice Silverman.
       March. Enters the U.S. Army and serves with the 112th Cavalry at Leyte, Luzon, and Japan.

1946    April. Discharged from the army.

1947    September. Completes the manuscript of *The Naked and the Dead* and departs for Europe, where he studies on the GI bill at the Sorbonne.

1948    May 8. Publication of *The Naked and the Dead*.

July. Returns from Europe and in the fall is active in Henry Wallace's campaign for the Presidency.

1949 He works for some months at scriptwriting in Hollywood. August 26. Birth of his first daughter, Susan.

1952 Divorced from Beatrice Silverman.

1954 Marries Adele Morales.

1957 March 16. Birth of his second daughter, Danielle.

1959 September 28. Birth of his third daughter, Elizabeth Anne.

1962 Divorced from Adele Morales.
Marries Lady Jeanne Campbell.
August 18. Birth of his fourth daughter, Kate.

1963 Divorced from Lady Jeanne Campbell.
Marries Beverly Bentley.

1964 March 17. Birth of his first son, Michael Burks.

1966 March 10. Birth of his second son, Stephen McLeod.

1967 January 31. Premiere performance of *The Deer Park* at the Theatre de Lys, New York City. (A run of 127 performances in all.)
Filming of his first movie, *Wild 90.*
Filming of his second movie, *Beyond the Law.*
Elected to the National Institute of Arts and Letters.
Participates in the march on the Pentagon.

1968 Filming of his third movie, *Maidstone.*

1969 Wins both the National Book Award and the Pulitzer Prize for *The Armies of the Night.*
Awarded the honorary degree of Doctor of Letters by Rutgers University.
Runs unsuccessfully for mayor of New York City.

# A Checklist of Mailer's Published Work

1941   "The Greatest Thing in the World." *Harvard Advocate,* No. 5 (April 1941), pp. 3–6, 24–28. Story.\* (Reprinted in *Story,* Nov.–Dec. 1941, pp. 17–26.)

1942   "Right Shoe on Left Foot." *Harvard Advocate,* No. 5 (May 1942), pp. 12–18, 30–33. Story.

      "Maybe Next Year." *Harvard Advocate,* No. 6 (May 1942), pp. 25–27. Story.\*

1944   "A Calculus at Heaven." *Cross Section: A Collection of American Writing.* Ed. by Edwin Seaver. New York: 1944. pp. 60–81. Novella.\*

1948   "Do Professors Have Rights?" *New York Post,* 8 Oct. 1948, pp. 5, 34. Article.

      *The Naked and the Dead.* New York: Rinehart, 1948. Novel.

1951   "Talk with Norman Mailer." Int. Harvey Breit. *New York Times,* 3 June 1951, Sec. 7, p. 3. Interview.

      "The Defense of the Compass." *The Western Defences.* Ed. by Sir John George Smyth. London: Allan Wingate, 1951. Essay.

      *Barbary Shore.* New York: Rinehart, 1951. Novel.

1952   "Our Country and Our Culture," in "America and the Intellectuals," *Partisan Review,* Summer 1952, pp. 298–301. Symposium contribution.\*

      "The Paper House." *New World Writing II.* New York: New American Library, 1952. Pp. 58–59. Story.\*

\* Included in *Advertisements for Myself* (1959).
† Included in *The Presidential Papers* (1963).
‡ Included in *Cannibals and Christians* (1966).
§ Included in *Deaths for the Ladies (and other disasters)* (1962).

"The Dead Gook." *Discovery* #*1*. Ed. by John W. Aldridge and Vance Bourjaily. New York: Pocket Books, 1952. Pp. 56–76. Story.*

1953 "The Notebook." *The Cornhill*, 1953, pp. 166, 481–484. Story.* Reprinted in *The Berkeley Book of Modern Writing No. III*. Ed. by William Phillips and Philip Rahv. New York: Berkeley, 1956. Pp. 106–109.

"The Language of Men," *Esquire*, Apr. 1953, pp. 61, 115–117. Story.*

1954 "The Meaning of Western Defense." *Dissent*, Spring 1954, pp. 157–165. Essay.*

"David Riesman Reconsidered." *Dissent*, Autumn 1954, pp. 349–359. Essay.*

1955 "The Homosexual Villain." *One: The Homosexual Magazine*, Jan. 1955, pp. 8–12. Essay.*

"What I Think of Artistic Freedom." *Dissent*, Spring 1955, pp. 98, 192–193. Essay.

"An Intimate Interview with Norman Mailer." Int. Lyle Stuart. *Exposé*, Dec. 1955, pp. 1, 4. Interview.* Reprinted in *Advertisements for Myself* under the title "Sixty-Nine Questions and Answers."

*The Deer Park*. New York: Putnam's, 1955. Novel.

1956 "Quickly." *The Village Voice*. 11 Jan.–2 May. Weekly column.

| | |
|---|---|
| 11 Jan., p. 5* | 7 Mar., p. 5 |
| 18 Jan., pp. 5, 11* | 14 Mar., pp. 5, 9 |
| 25 Jan., p. 5* | 21 Mar., pp. 5, 11 |
| 1 Feb., p. 5 (see also | 28 Mar., pp. 5, 11 |
| letter, p. 11) | 4 Apr., p. 5 |
| 8 Feb., p. 5 | 11 Apr., p. 5 |
| 15 Feb., pp. 5, 10 | 18 Apr., p. 5 |
| 22 Feb., pp. 5, 14 (see | 25 Apr., p. 5 |
| also letter, p. 4) | 2 May, p. 5* |
| 29 Feb., pp. 5, 9 | |

"A Public Notice by Norman Mailer." *The Village Voice*, 9 May 1956, p. 12. Paid advertisement, reviewing Samuel Beckett's *Waiting for Godot*.*

"The Tragedy of Parris Island. *Dissent*, Fall 1956, p. 435. Essay.

"The Notebook." *The Berkeley Book of Modern Writing No. III.* Ed. by William Phillips and Philip Rahv. New York: Berkeley, 1956. Pp. 106–109. (Reprinted from *The Cornhill*; see 1953 entries.) *

"The Man Who Studied Yoga." *New Short Novels II.* New York: Ballantine, 1956. Pp. 1–29. Novella.*

1957 "The White Negro, Superficial Reflections on the Hipster." *Dissent*, Summer 1957, pp. 276–293. Essay.*

1958 "Reflections on Hip[sterism]." *Dissent*, Winter 1958, pp. 73–81. Essay. (Brackets indicate portion of title added by editors.)*

"Advertisements for Myself on the Way Out." *Partisan Review*, Fall 1958, pp. 519–540. Story.* Reprinted in *Advertisements for Myself* with subtitle: "Prologue to a long novel."

"Norman Mailer." Int. Mike Wallace. *Mike Wallace Asks.* Ed. by Charles Preston and Edward A. Hamilton. New York: Simon and Schuster, 1958. Pp. 26–27. Television interview, edited.

1959 "Comment." *Dissent*, Winter 1959, pp. 9–10. Commentary on Irving Howe's "A New Political Atmosphere in America."*

"Hip, Hell, and the Navigator." Int. Richard G. Stern. *Western Review*, No. 23 (1959), pp. 101–109. Interview.*

"From Surplus Value to Mass Media." *Dissent*, Summer 1959, pp. 254–257. Essay.*

"Scenes from *The Deer Park*." *Partisan Review*, Fall 1959, pp. 527–537. Play.*

"The Mind of an Outlaw." *Esquire*, Nov. 1959, pp. 87–94. Essay.*

"An Eye on Picasso." *Provincetown Annual*, 1959, pp. 27–28. Essay.*

*Advertisements for Myself.* New York: Putnam's, 1959. Miscellany.

1960    "The Shiny Enemies." *The Nation,* 30 Jan. 1960, inside cover. Letter regarding a Gore Vidal review.

"A Program for the Nation." *Dissent,* Winter 1960, pp. 67–70. Essay.†

"She Thought the Russians Was Coming." *Esquire,* June 1960, pp. 129–134. Essay. † Reprinted in *Dissent,* Summer 1961, pp. 408–412.

"Superman Comes to the Supermart." *Esquire,* Nov. 1960, pp. 119–129. Essay.† Reprinted in *The Presidential Papers* (1963) with title "Superman Comes to the Supermarket."

1961    Letter to the Editor. *Esquire,* Jan. 1961, p. 15. Letter complaining of editorial treatment.

"An Interview with Norman Mailer." Int. Eve Auchincloss and Nancy Lynch. *Madmoiselle,* Feb. 1961, pp. 76, 160–163. Interview.

"An Open Letter to JFK and Fidel Castro." *The Village Voice,* 27 Apr. 1961, pp. 1, 14–15. Letters.†

"Angry Young Rebel with a Cause." Int. Bruce Cook, *Rogue,* Apr. 1961, pp. 16–18, 76. Interview.

"The Blacks." *The Village Voice.* Part I: 11 May 1961, pp. 11, 14. Part II: 18 May 1961, pp. 11, 14–15. Essay.†

"Mailer to Hansberry." *The Village Voice,* 8 June 1961, pp. 11–12. Reply to her *Voice* letter of June 1, 1961, responding to "The Blacks" essay.

"Sex and Censorship in Literature and the Arts." *Playboy,* July 1961, pp. 27–28, 72, 74, 76, 88, 92, 95–99. Editorial discussion by Mailer and others.‡ Partially reprinted in *Cannibals and Christians* (1966) as part of "Petty Notes on Some Sex in America."

"She Thought the Russians Was Coming." *Dissent,* Summer 1961, pp. 408–412. Essay.† Reprinted from *Esquire,* June 1960, pp. 129–134.

"The First Day's Interview." *Paris Review,* Summer-Fall 1961, pp. 140–153. Platonic dialogue.‡

*302*

"Gourmandise." *The New Yorker,* 16 Sept. 1961, p. 107. Poem.§

"Eternities." *The New Yorker,* 11 Nov. 1961, p. 200. Poem.§

"Open Poem to John Fitzgerald Kennedy." *The Village Voice,* 23 Nov. 1961, p. 4. Poem.† Reprinted in *Dissent,* Winter 1962, pp. 33-34.

"TV Violence? It's a Sedative." Int. David Griffiths. *TV Times,* Nov. 1961, p. 18. Interview in London television guide.

"Foreword" to *Views of a Nearsighted Cannoneer* by Seymour Krim. New York: Excelsior, 1961. p. [6]. One-paragraph essay.

1962   "Poems." *Atlantic Monthly,* Jan. 1962, p. 62. Poems.§

"A Glass of Milk." *The Village Voice,* 1 Feb. 1962, p. 4. Poem.†

"Poem to the Book Review at *Time.*" *Time,* 6 Apr. 1962, p. 12. Letter in the form of a poem, rebutting *Time's* poem-review of *Deaths for the Ladies.*†

"The Womanization of America." *Playboy,* June 1962, pp. 43-50, 133-134, 136, 139-144. Discussion by Mailer and others.‡ Partially reprinted in *Cannibals and Christians* (1966) as part of "Petty Notes on Some Sex in America."

"An Evening with Jackie Kennedy." *Esquire,* July 1962, pp. 56-61. Essay.†

"Truth and Being: Nothing and Time." *Evergreen Review,* Sept.–Oct. 1962, pp. 68-74. Story.† Reprinted in *The Presidential Papers* (1963) with the subtitle: "A Broken Fragment from a Long Novel."

"The Big Bite." *Esquire,* Nov. 1962, p. 134; Dec. 1962, p. 168. Monthly column.† (Continued throughout 1963, q.v.)

"Responses and Reactions I." *Commentary,* Dec. 1962, pp. 504-506. Column.† The first of a series of six (see entries for 1963).

"Open Letter to JFK." *The Village Voice,* 20 Dec. 1962, p. 7. Letter.

"Sing the Ballad of the Sad Saint." *Esquire,* Dec. 1962, p. 169. Poem.† Reprinted in *Cannibals and Christians* (1966) as "The Ride of the Sad Saint."

"Open Poem to JFK." *Dissent*, Winter 1962, pp. 33–34. Poem.† Reprinted from *The Village Voice*, Nov. 23, 1961.

"An Impolite Interview." Int. Paul Krassner. *The Realist*, Dec. 1962, pp. 1, 13–16, 18–23, 10. Interview.† Abridged when reprinted in *Presidential Papers* (1963).

*Deaths for the Ladies (and other disasters)*. New York: Putnam's, 1962. Poems.

1963  "Punching Papa." *The New York Review of Books*, Special Issue, Winter 1963, p. 13. Review of Morley Callaghan's *That Summer in Paris*.‡

"The Big Bite." *Esquire*. Monthly column. (The first two pieces in the series appeared in Nov. and Dec. 1962.)

| | |
|---|---|
| Jan., p. 65† | July. pp. 63–69, 105 (under title |
| Feb., pp. 109–121 | "Some Children of the |
| (under title "Ten | Goddess") ‡ |
| Thousand Words a | Aug. pp. 16–24† |
| Minute") † | Sept., pp. 16–20†‡ |
| Mar., pp. 98, 138† | Oct., pp. 50–52† |
| Apr., p. 74† | Nov., pp. 26–32 |
| May, pp. 37, 40† | Dec., pp. 22–26 |
| June, pp. 23, 24, 28, 32‡ | |

"The Real Meaning of the Right Wing in America." *Playboy*, Jan. 1963, pp. 111–112, 165, 167–170, 172–174. Essay.† (Subtitled by *Playboy*: "Opposing Statements on the Role of the Right Wing in America Today: A Liberal's View." See next entry.)

Letter to the Editor. *Playboy*, Feb. 1963, p. 15. Letter protesting being called a "liberal" in *Playboy*'s subtitle to his Jan. 1963 essay.

"The Role of the Right Wing." *Playboy*, Feb. 1963, pp. 115–116, 119–22. Transcript of a debate with William F. Buckley, Jr.

"Ten Thousand Words a Minute." Expansion of column

"The Big Bite." See above. Subtitled "Death."

"Responses and Reactions." *Commentary*. Column. (The first of the six pieces appeared in Dec. 1962, q.v.)

II: Feb., pp. 146–148†     V: Aug., pp. 164–165‡
III: Apr., pp. 335–337†    VI: Oct., pp. 320–321
IV: June, pp. 517–518†

"Classes." *The New Statesman*, 8 Feb. 1963, p. 207. Poem.†

"The First Presidential Paper." *Dissent*, Summer 1963, pp. 249–254. Essay.†

"Jean Genet and 'The Blacks'—An Impulse to Destroy." *Panorama* (Chicago *Daily News*), 13 July 1963, p. 3. Essay.

"Some Children of the Goddess." Expansion of column "The Big Bite." See above.

"The Leading Man." *Book Week*, 29 Sept. 1963, pp. 16–17. Review of Victor Lasky's *JFK: Man and Myth*.‡

"The Mary McCarthy Case." *The New York Review of Books*, 17 Oct. 1963, pp. 1–3. Review of *The Group*.‡ Reprinted in *Cannibals and Christians* (1966) under the title "The Case Against McCarthy."

"The Fate of the Union: Kennedy and After." *The New York Review of Books*, 26 Dec. 1963, p. 6. Discussion by Mailer and others; foreshadows the "Special Preface" to the Bantam edition of *The Presidential Papers*, 1964.

"The Last Night." *Esquire*, Dec. 1963, pp. 151, 274–280. Story.‡

*The Presidential Papers*. New York: Putnam's, 1963. Miscellany.

1964   "The Art of Fiction." Int. Steve Marcus. *Paris Review*, Winter–Spring 1964, pp. 29–58. Interview.‡

"Mailer vs. Scully." *Architectural Forum*, Apr. 1964, pp. 96–97. Condensation of two "Big Bite" columns, with an afterword.‡

"The Killer." *Evergreen Review*, Apr.–May 1964, p. 26 ff. Story.‡

"Architects: Blindness Is the Fruit of Your Design." *The Village Voice*, 18 June 1964, p. 5. Essay.

*An American Dream*. Novel appearing in monthly installments in *Esquire*. Jan.–Aug. (Published in book form in
1965, q.v.)

| | |
|---|---|
| Jan.: "The Harbors of the Moon" | May: "A Caternary of Manners" |
| Feb.: " Messenger from the Casino" | June: "A Vision in the Desert" |
| Mar.: "A Messenger from the Maniac" | July: "A Votive is Prepared" |
| Apr.: "Green Circles of Exhaustion" | Aug.: "At the Lion and the Serpent" |

"The Executioner's Song." *Fuck You, Magazine of the Arts*,
Sept. 1964, pp. [23–25]. Poem.‡..

"A Vote for Bobby K. — Possibility of a Hero." *The Village
Voice*, 29 Oct. 1964, pp. 4, 10. Essay.‡

"*My Hope for America:* A Review of a Book by Lyndon B.
Johnson." *Book Week*, 1 Nov. 1964, pp. 1, 7–8. Essay.‡

"In the Red Light: A History of the Republican Convention
of 1964." *Esquire*, Nov. 1964, pp. 83–89, 167. Essay.‡

1965    "Talking of Violence." Int. W. J. Weatherby. *Twentieth Century*, Winter 1964–1965, pp. 109–114. Interview.

"Cities Higher than Mountains." *New York Times Magazine*,
30 Jan. 1965, pp. 16–17. Essay.‡

"Norman Mailer on LBJ." *The Realist*, June 1965, pp. 1,
10–15. Essay.‡ Reprinted in *Cannibals and Christians* (1966)
with title "A Speech at Berkeley on Vietnam Day."

"On Vietnam." *Partisan Review*, Fall 1965, pp. 638–639, 641–
643, 645–646. Essay.‡ Response to "Statement on Vietnam
and the Dominican Republic" in the Summer 1965 *Partisan
Review*.

"Norman Mailer on Lindsay and the City." *The Village
Voice*, 28 Oct. 1965, p. 1. Essay.‡

*An American Dream*. New York: Dial, 1965. Novel.

1966    "3 — Poems." *East Side Review*, Jan.–Feb. 1966, p. 43.
Poems.‡

"Modes and Mutations: Comments on the Modern American Novel." *Commentary*, Mar. 1966, pp. 37–40. Essay.‡

Letter to the Editor. *The New York Review of Books*, 28 Apr. 1966, pp. 26–27. Letter concerning Richard G. Stern's account of Mailer at the 1965 MLA.

"On Cannibals and Christians." *Dissent*, May–June 1966, pp. 304–306. Essay.‡ Reprinted in *Canibals and Christians* with title "On Introducing Our Argument."

"*Rush to Judgment*." *The Village Voice*, 1 Sept. 1966, pp. 1, 24–27. Review of the Mark Lane book. (Also Published in *Book Week*, 28 Aug. 1966, pp. 1, 11–13, as "The Great American Mystery.")

"Henry Miller." In *Double Exposure* by Roddy McDowell. New York: Delacorte, 1966. Pp. 168–169. Biographical sketch. *Cannibals and Christians*. New York: Dial, 1966. Miscellany.

1967  "A Requiem for the Rube." *The Village Voice*, 5 Jan. 1967, pp. 4, 16. Essay.

"A Statement of Aims." *The Village Voice*, 5 Jan. 1967, p. 16. On *The Deer Park* play.

"In Clay's Corner." *Partisan Review*, Summer 1967, p. 461. One of six statements on the draft status of Cassius Clay.

"Mr. Mailer Interviews Himself." *New York Times Book Review*, 17 Sept. 1967, pp. 4–5, 40. Platonic dialogue.

"The Crazy One." *Playboy*, Oct. 1967, pp. 91–92, 112, 211–214. Essay. (Substantially the same as "Footnote to *Death in the Afternoon*" below.)

"Footnote to *Death in the Afternoon*." In *The Bullfight, a Photographic Narrative with Text by Norman Mailer*. CBS Legacy Book Collection Book. New York: Macmillan, 1967. Essay, with photo text and record album.

García Lorca, Federico. "Lament for Ignatio Sánchez Mejías." Trans. by Susan and Norman Mailer. In *The Poetry Bag*. Ed. by R. P. Dickey et al. Columbia, Mo.: 1967. Pp. 5–10. Printed version of the translation spoken by Mailer on the phonograph record that accompanies *The Bullfight* (see entry above) .

*The Deer Park, a Play.* New York: Dial, 1967. Play with introduction.

*The Short Fiction of Norman Mailer.* New York: Dell, 1967. Paperback collection of previously printed fiction, with new introduction.

*Why Are We in Vietnam?* New York: Putnam's, 1967. Novel.

1968 *"Playboy* Interview: Norman Mailer." Int. Paul Carroll. *Playboy,* Jan. 1968, pp. 66–72, 74, 76, 78, 80, 82–84. Interview.

"The Steps of the Pentagon." *Harper's Magazine,* Apr. 1968, pp. 47–142. Narrative; long excerpt from *The Armies of the Night.*

"The Battle of the Pentagon." *Commentary,* Apr. 1968, pp. 33–37. Narrative; excerpt from *The Armies of the Night.*

"Up the Family Tree." *Partisan Review,* Spring 1968, pp. 235–252. Essay-review of Norman Podhoretz's *Making It.*

"Black Power: A Discussion." *Partisan Review,* Spring 1968, pp. 218–221. Symposium contribution.

[untitled]. *Partisan Review,* Summer 1968, p. 490. Reply to a letter from Irving Howe, critical of Mailer's "Black Power" remarks.

[untitled]. *Partisan Review,* Fall 1968, pp. 649–650. A second exchange with Irving Howe.

"When Irish Eyes Are Smiling, It's Norman Mailer." Int. Vincent Canby. *New York Times,* 27 Oct. 1968, Sec. 2, p. 1. Interview.

"Miami Beach and Chicago." *Harper's Magazine,* Nov. 1968, pp. 41–52, 55–56, 69–84, 89–104, 107–130. Narrative; text of *Miami and the Siege of Chicago.*

"Open Letter to Richard Nixon." *Newsweek,* 9 Dec. 1968, p. 85. Letter.

*The Idol and the Octopus: Political Writings by Norman Mailer on the Kennedy and Johnson Administrations.* New York: Dell, 1968. Paperback collection of previously printed essays, with new introduction.

*The Armies of the Night.* New York: New American Library, 1968. Narrative.

*Miami and the Siege of Chicago.* New York: New American Library, 1968. Narrative.

1969  "Looking for the Meat and Potatoes: Thoughts on Black Power." *Look,* 7 Jan. 1969, pp. 57–60. Essay.

"Twentieth National Book Awards." *Publishers' Weekly,* 24 Mar. 1969, pp. 26–27. Text of National Book Award acceptance speech.

"Who Is to Declare That the Minority Do Not Deserve to Determine the Schools' History?" *New York Times Magazine,* 4 May 1969, pp. 35 plus. Essay.

"On Accepting the Pulitzer Prize." *The Village Voice,* 6 May, 1969, p. 5. Acceptance speech. Reprinted in *Running Against the Machine.*

"Why Are We in New York?" *New York Times Magazine,* 18 May 1969, pp. 30–31 plus. Essay. (Titled by Mailer "An Instrument for the City.") Reprinted in *Running Against the Machine.*

"The Norman Conquest." Int. by Betsy Dirnberger. *Other Voices* (magazine of Elmira College), June 1969, pp. 36–43. Interview.

"A Candid Talk with Norman Mailer." Int. Joe Walker. *Muhammad Speaks,* 20 June 1969, pp. 11–12. Interview.

"Shoot for the Moon Mailer." Int. Leticia Kent. *Vogue,* 15 Aug. 1969, pp. 86, 88–90, 139. Interview.

"A Fire on the Moon." *Life,* 29 Aug. 1969, pp. 24–41. Narrative; excerpt from *Of a Fire on the Moon.*

"The Psychology of Astronauts." *Life,* 14 Nov. 1969, pp. 50–63. Narrative; excerpt from *Of a Fire on the Moon.*

"Interview with Norman Mailer." Int. Oriana Fallaci. *Writer's Digest,* Dec. 1969, pp. 40–47, 81. Interview.

"Foreword" to *The End of Obscenity* by Charles Rembar. London: Andre Deutsch, 1969. Pp. [viii]–xi. Essay.

Dedication in *Running Against the Machine*. Ed. by Peter Manso. New York: Doubleday, 1969. P. [v]. One-paragraph dedication dated July 22, 1969.

"Speech at the John Jay College of Criminal Justice." In *Running Against the Machine*, pp. 38–49. Text of May 6, 1969, speech.

"At the Village Gate." In *Running Against the Machine*, pp. 59–64. Text of May 7, 1969, speech.

"Mayoral Candidates Debate, Norman Mailer and others." In *Running Against the Machine,* pp. 81–105. Text of May 15, 1969, television debate.

"A Speech to the *Time-Life Staff*." In *Running Against the Machine*, pp. 81–105. Text of May 15, 1969, television debate.

"Be My Guest, Norman Mailer." In *Running Against the Machine,* pp. 138–140. Mailer's guest column. (Originally printed in the *New York Post*, 1 July 1969.)

1970 "A Dream of the Future's Face." *Life*, 9 Jan. 1970, pp. 56–74. Narrative; excerpt from *Of a Fire on the Moon*.

*Of a Fire on the Moon*. Boston: Little, Brown, 1970. Narrative.